Rapt in the Name

SUNY series in Hindu Studies
Wendy Doniger, Editor

Rapt in the Name

The Ramnamis, *Ramnam*, and Untouchable Religion in Central India

Ramdas Lamb

State University of New York Press

Published by
State University of New York Press, Albany

Printed in the United States of America

For information, address State University of New York Press,
90 State Street, Suite 700, Albany, NY 12207

Production by Judith Block
Marketing by Anne Valentine

Library of Congress Cataloging-in-Publication Data

Lamb, Ramdas.
Rapt in the name : the Ramnamis, Ramnam, and untouchable religion in Central India / Ramdas Lamb.
p. cm. — (SUNY series in Hindu studies)
Includes bibliographical references and index.
ISBN 0-7914-5385-5 (alk. paper) — ISBN 0-7914-5386-3 (pbk. : alk. paper)
1. Ramnami-samaj. 2. Rāma (Hindu deity)—Cult. 3. Dalits—Central India—Religion. I. Title II. Series.
BL1295.R36L36 2002
294.5'5—dc21 2002070695

10 9 8 7 6 5 4 3 2 1

For
Susan, Sachi, Ravi
Meena Bahin, Leelaji
and all the Ramnamis

राम

Contents

This sect member's *mukut* (hat) shows the physical diversity with which Ramnamis can express themselves.

Preface

It has been nearly three decades since I first became aware of the Ramnami Samaj, an Untouchable religious movement in Central India, and nearly two-and-a-half decades since I began my relationship with the group. I was a Hindu monk at the time I first met them and my interest was strictly personal. I was initially attracted by their striking visual appearance, then by their theological, philosophical, and social views. Later, after returning to America and beginning my academic career, my interest in the *samaj* expanded to include a variety of scholastic curiosities and concerns as well. This book, then, is a result of both my personal and professional relationship with the Ramnamis.

I first visited India as a tourist for three weeks in 1968. Intrigued by my experiences there, I returned in the spring of 1969 and resided there until 1977. Since then, I have returned more than a dozen times to the subcontinent to continue my research on and relationship with the land and its people. Although I have continually sought to expand my horizons and understanding of India over the last several decades, the magnitude and multivalence of the country is such that it is extremely difficult for any one individual to do more than scratch the surface and comprehend all that is there. However, with each contact, I have been fortunate to broaden my understanding of, and experiences with, the Ramnamis. I hope this presentation will pay tribute to their uniqueness, sincerity, and genuineness.

The purpose of the present study is twofold: (1) to examine the evolution and elaboration of the Ram *bhakti* tradition in India, with specific reference to the roles of the *Rāmcaritānas* and the practice of *Ramnam* therein; and (2) to provide a detailed exposition on a present-day manifestation of Ram *bhakti* in the form of the Ramnami Samaj. While the Ramnamis exist on their own as a unique illustration of contemporary antinomian Hindu devotionalism, the sect is also a vibrant example of what has been an integral part of the ever-changing Ram tradition in India, from its inception to the present: the involvement and influence of those on the social and religious periphery in the growth of Ram *bhakti*.

Among the corollary South Asian issues addressed in these pages are the concepts of self-identity formation and the role of brahmanical scholars and scriptures in the construction of Hinduism and Indian history. With respect to the former, this work examines the varying approaches to, and notions of, caste and identity, for these have had pivotal influences on path, practice and practitioner throughout Indian religious history. With respect to the creation and construction of South Asian history, it considers broadly the influences of both priests and scholars in configuring their writings to preconceived notions and ideologies, both Indian and non-Indian.

Before proceeding any further, it is important for me to acknowledge the patience, love, and many contributions of my wife Susan, and also to credit the editing assistance of my sister, Prof. Meena Sachdeva, whose tireless help and guidance were fundamental in bringing this project to fruition.

Notes on Transliteration

The spelling used for the transliteration of all individual Indian language terms herein reflects the standard contemporary Hindi pronunciation, since this most closely approximates the way these terms are spoken today by most of the people of northern and central India, the geographic focus of this study. All proper names (of individuals, places, etc.) are presented without italics or diacritics. Also, following more recent scholarly trends in transliteration, such terms are presented in italics but with no diacritics. Readers interested in the scholarly diacriticalized transliteration are directed to the glossary, where each term is presented with diacritics (in parentheses) preceding its definition. However, transliteration of text names, textual verses, and specific mantras is given with diacritics and follows the standard method adopted by most Indologists.

Abbreviation of Text Titles

AdhR	*Adhyātma Rāmāyaṇa*
NptUp	*Nṛsiha-pūrva-tāpanīya Upaniṣad*
NutUp	*Nṛsiha-uttara-tāpanīya Upaniṣad*
RC	*Rāmcaritmānas*
RptUp	*Rāma-pūrva-tāpinīya Upaniṣad*
RrUp	*Rāma-rahasya Upaniṣad*
RutUp	*Rāma-uttara-tāpinīya Upaniṣad*
Vāl	Valmiki *Rāmāyaṇa*

The Ramnam *kambha* from the 1989 Bhajan Mela.

Introduction

Hinduism has long been a mixture of popular and orthodox religious beliefs and practices. Much of the focus of the academic study of Hinduism has been on Sanskrit texts and the evolution of brahmanical (priestly) and brahmanized thought. Sanskrit texts have been used to circumscribe what has come to be considered the normative tradition and have thus been the foundation upon which most assumptions, in India and abroad, about the history and practice of Indian religion have been based. However, the brahmanical scriptures are limiting for two fundamental reasons: the narrow perspective their authors present, and the texts' inability to encompass the vast and diverse oral tradition that has long thrived in India.

The orthodox religious scriptures are valuable in that they reveal those beliefs and practices that were, and are, sanctioned within the orthodox tradition. At the same time, however, they tell us little or nothing directly about the religious life of those on the periphery of brahmanical society—the low castes, tribals, Untouchables, and others. Instead, this body of literature either downplays or omits the existence, evolution, and popularity of the various dimensions of the religious life of the peripheral populace. As a consequence, many Indians have felt disenfranchised from the religious traditions presented in the orthodox literature as the "real" Hinduism.

Mark Juergensmeyer relates a conversation he had with a group of Untouchable sweepers in Delhi. In discussing religious affiliation, one said to him, "Hinduism is not ours. It is the religion of the rich people and the upper castes."[1] If we conceive of Hinduism solely in brahmanical terms and categories, a religion bound in the Vedic tradition and the socioreligious stratification expressed in the *varnashrama-dharma* system, then we would have to say that the majority of Indians are, in fact, not Hindu. If, on the other hand, we think of Hinduism as the religion of India's masses, with its vastly differing customs, values, beliefs, and practices, then we must reject the brahmanical model as the norm. While the latter's nomenclature and certain of its dimensions function as a veneer to make India's religious and cultural diversity appear unified, this covering obscures many of the divisions and gaps that give popular Hinduism its broadly diverse shape and character. Thus, speculating on the contents of these gaps is an important part of the study of the Ram *bhakti* tradition.

The Ram tradition, while a major part of the religious life of India, has not been given the kind of attention in Western scholarship that it arguably deserves. Instead, the vast majority of academic research on, and knowledge of, Hindu devotionalism has focused on Krishna worship. This, I believe, is due to several factors, including: (1) the popularity of the *Bhāgavad Gītā* and other Krishna-related texts among Western Sanskritists; (2) the prevalence of Krishna *bhakti* in Bengal, from where the vast majority of early Indian academics came; (3) the earlier and more complete appropriation of Krishna *bhakti* tradition over Ram *bhakti* by the religious elite; and (4) the visual and sometimes controversial presence of ISKCON and other Krishna-related groups in the West. Consequently, Western and scholarly awareness and understanding of Ram *bhakti* in India has been relatively limited.[2] It is with a desire to counter this confined view that I will attempt to place the Ram tradition in perspective in India, both past and present.

Romila Thapar, in commenting on the various written versions of the Ram story, provides an approach to reading and interpreting Indian history that can be equally valuable when seeking to comprehend Hinduism as a whole.

> The cultural centrality of a narrative may be stated through recourse to variant versions, suggestive of a debate, where each version attempts to authenticate its own perspective on the past. This requires that the historian be both familiar with the variants and cautious in ascribing the narrative invariably to the particular variant regarded as dominant.[3]

Once we move beyond a reliance on the dominant variant, that is, brahmanical thought and practice, we can begin to search for clues to understand what was taking place in the life of the non-elite, nonliterate masses. One way to detect indications of popular influence on the evolving religious orthodoxy is by juxtaposing the early Vedic brahmanical tradition with its changing manifestations over the ages. In doing so, we can then see the vast array of non-Vedic elements that have subsequently entered the orthodox religious tradition and its system of beliefs, values, and practices. Much of this absorption of non-Vedic components came about through the sanskritization and brahmanization of indigenous folk traditions and low caste and peripheral religious movements.[4] It is to these sources that we must look in order to understand better the growth of the Ram tradition.

Just as the *brahman* authors wrote little that was positive about the beliefs and practices of heterodox sects, such as Buddhism and Jainism, so they had little positive to say about the religious life of the low castes and others outside the brahmanical value system, no matter how prevalent or popular such beliefs and practices might have been. Thus, if we wish to discern the popular religion, we must not only utilize the textual history of Hinduism for what it can suggest as well as provide, but we must also search for clues and indications of what might underlie or lie beyond it. For example, J. N. Farquhar suggests that by looking at the earliest parts of Valmiki's *Rāmāyaṇa,* one gets a "reflection of some aspects of the popular faith. And we do well to look at it carefully."[5] Indeed, the writings of heterodox groups intimate and perhaps reveal elements of the periphery and popular religious life that brahmanical texts have overlooked. What we can get from the latter is primarily a brahmanized reformulation of what has been appropriated or adapted from indigenous and peripheral sources.

In addition to looking beyond the Sanskrit scriptures, we must also venture beyond writings in general, for Hinduism is essentially an oral tradition in its existence and transmission. To confine our understanding of the Hindu tradition to only those elements that are available in written texts is to reinforce the limited perspective they present. As scholars, we need to be aware of what William A. Graham refers to as the "relentless dominance of textuality in the scholarly mind," for this often causes us to

> uncritically affirm and strengthen the valuation of the sacred document as the primary source and most reliable index of what is normative in a given tradition.[6]

Concepts and Terms

Center and Periphery: Mechanisms of Appropriation and Accommodation

Persons and groups existing on the Hindu periphery have long used a variety of mechanisms in interacting with and attempting to alter their status vis-à-vis the brahmanical social and religious authorities and their value systems. Edward Shils presents a conceptual framework for viewing the value system of a society and the interaction between its various components. His ideas are not culture-specific and are indeed useful for looking at the Hindu system of values, beliefs, and practices and the various forms of interaction between its center and periphery.

Shils speaks of the center of a society as the realm of "ultimate and irreducible . . . values and beliefs that govern that society." [7] He refers to this set of values, which are espoused by those in authority, as the "central value system" of the society, since it is connected with that which the society holds to be sacred. The connection between this "sacred" and its espousers is vital, for they define and support each other:

> By their very possession of authority, [the elite] attribute to themselves an essential affinity with the sacred elements of their society, of which

they regard themselves as the custodians, since they are connected with that which the society holds to be sacred.[8]

Looking at the Hindu social and religious tradition, the central value system is contained in what is often called "Brahmanical Hinduism." Here, the "irreducible" central values have traditionally focused on adherence to *dharma* (truth, right action, etc.), which is manifested in (a) the sacrificial and domestic rites of the *karmakanda* sections of the Vedas, as expounded in the various brahmanical texts, including the Vedic Samhitas, Brahmanas, and Sutras; and (b) the social and religious system of duties laid out in the priestly law books and known as the *"varnashrama dharma"* system.

Shils also says that in every society there is "an ideal order" that transcends authority and legitimates the central value system.[9] For the Hindu orthodox, *dharma* is both a part of the central value system and the ideal order that transcends and legitimates it. Thus, fulfillment of one's ritual and social duties is viewed as necessary for the maintenance of the social and cosmic orders.

Over the ages, the orthodox value system has been both influenced and challenged by the presence of several competing brahmanical value systems. The more ancient Veda-dominated brahmanical value system commanded central religious authority until the rise and competition of the various sectarian movements. Many of these movements had been either established by high-caste Hindus or appropriated by them, and each evolved its own sectarian theology. Eventually, they sought to modify the existing value system in order to reflect the superior status of their own sectarian values, deities, beliefs, and so forth.

Because many of these sectarian movements resulted from the solidification and/or brahmanization (see definition below) of localized sects and traditions, their value systems took on a regional *ethos* and flavor. Thus, for example, the orthodox value system of Bengal has a uniquely Bengali character, many of the beliefs, values, ritual techniques, and deities, being uniquely Bengali. The same process of localization occurred in many other regions as well. By the end of the first millennium C.E., the older central value system, based solely on Vedic and Shastric thought and values, ceased to be the dominating value system of the upper caste, replaced instead by multiple sectarian or regional value systems. Eventually, these alternate sets of values have come to be viewed, rightly or wrongly, as regional expressions of an elusive pan-Hindu central value system.

Shils contrasts this "center" with its "periphery." The latter refers to that part of the society that, by choice or coercion, does not share in the power and values of the elite center. For our purposes here, the term "periphery" is used to refer to all the low caste, tribal, and heterodox groups that do not actively partake in, or give deference to, brahmanically defined values and power structures. This periphery has long included the vast majority of Indians, since the followers of the central value system are but a small percentage of the Hindu elite.

Brahmanization. Ever since the Vedic religion first encountered the non-Brahmanical beliefs of the Jains and the Buddhists, the brahmanical religious elite, the "custodians" of the Vedic value system, have long sought to spread the umbrella of their authority over values, beliefs, practices, and texts existing in the social and religious periphery. In the process, the religious elite would modify these to better reflect and support their own set of values. This strategy of incorporation and modification by the orthodox has been called "brahmanization."[10] This process can be clearly discerned in the alteration and interpolation of texts such as the Valmiki *Rāmāyaṇa,* the *Mahābhārata,* the Puranas, and even Tulsidas's *Rāmcaritmānas*. The *brahmans* who make such modifications may either be a part of the traditional orthodox hierarchy or may be affiliated with a peripheral sect, wishing to raise its status in relation to the central value system in the eyes of the orthodox. The process of brahmanization has two goals: to align the brahmanized element more closely to the orthodox value system, and to reshape and prepare it for inclusion into the system. This latter process is referred to as "vedacization," as discussed below.

The brahmanization of regional and sectarian texts assured that they supported, if not promoted, much of the central value system and assisted in maintaining a certain degree of pan-Indian commonality among the various regional value systems. At the same time, however, in the brahmanization and elevation of vernacular texts to positions of primary importance in the everyday religious life of the commoner, non-central values expressed in these texts also gained a certain degree of legitimacy. This process inevitably led to regional variations in the expression of the central value system, as well as in the values themselves.

Sanskritization. The concept of Sanskritization was first introduced by M. N. Srinivas in his *Religion and Society Among the Coorgs of South India* (1952). Over the next decade, a variety of South Asianists used, criticized, or modified Srinivas's concept. After several attempts to refine his theory, Srinivas ultimately arrived at the definition below, which is the one used herein.

> Sanskritization is the process by which a "low" Hindu caste, or tribal or other group, changes its customs, ritual, ideology, and way of life in the direction of a high, and, frequently, "twice born" caste. Generally, such changes are followed by a claim of higher position in the caste hierarchy than that traditionally conceded to the claimant caste by the local community.[11]

I use this term in the broad sense of modifying one's own beliefs, rituals, dress, food, habits, and so forth, in order to pattern them more closely after those of the dominant religious, social, or cultural groups of one's region. As observed by Srinivas, those in the position of dominance need not be *brahman* and often are not. The difference between "brahmanization" and "sanskritization," then, is that the former refers to a practice of *brahman* elite, while the latter process is undertaken by those wishing to emulate the elite.

Vedacization. Vedacization refers to an attitudinal, as opposed to material, change with respect to a practice or text by members of the brahmanical orthodoxy. It involves the incorporation of nonorthodox elements by the religious elite into their central value system. The process of vedacization generally occurs after practice or text has been modified through brahmanization by members of the orthodox community and/or elevated through sanskritization by those within a sectarian movement. It generally occurs when the followers of a text or practice have become sufficiently influential in a region so as to compel the brahmanical orthodox religious system to accommodate them through the vedacization of element/s of their sect. Through this process a text, for example, is accepted by the religious orthodox as *smriti,* or even *shruti.*[12]

All three of the above mechanisms have recurred throughout the religious history of India. While the processes of brahmanization and vedacization deal primarily with religious rituals, doctrines, and texts, and are controlled for the most part by *brahmans*, sanskritization is undertaken by peripheral groups, has a much broader arena, and can be found in many aspects of life.

A Note on Caste and Caste Terminology

As a social/religious paradigm, the caste system permeates Hindu life. While Western cultures did not develop the same kind of religious hierarchical structure, most did, and continue to have, hierarchies: racial, ethnic, political, economic, and so forth. Although these hierarchies have gone through a variety of changes during the last millennium, and distances and relationships between the various elements in the hierarchies have changed, the basic structures have not altered significantly. In most areas of the world, lighter-skinned, economically advantaged, urban groups have generally dominated and have had far more influence on the social and political agendas than have darker-skinned, poorer, rural peoples.

The same can be said of India. Distances and strategies between various caste and subcaste groups have changed, but the basic structure itself has tended to remain: lighter-skinned, wealthier, high-caste groups generally dominate over darker-skinned, poorer, low-caste groups. Skin tone, caste, and economic status still have the tendency to go hand in hand in many areas.

There is no absolute consensus on what constitutes caste in India. While the term *"varna,"* which is translated herein as "caste," is often used in classical Sanskrit texts and by contemporary scholars, it is seldom a part of the indigenous vocabulary. Instead, *jati,* or "subcaste," that is more commonly used and has great social importance. It is one's subcaste that determines the parameters of social and religious interactions, abilities, and limitations. It is one's subcaste that forms the basic support group and community. In rural Chhattisgarh, however, the term *"samaj"* (literally, community) is actually more commonly used to refer to one's "subcaste" than is *"jati."*

Untouchable. This is a literal translation of *antaj,* the traditional Sanskrit term used to label those who have long been viewed by the brahmanical elite as too polluted even to be touched, because of their occupations or family background. Moreover, they have historically been vilified, despised, feared, and oppressed. Since ancient times, they have been refused access to most aspects of brahmanical Hinduism, as well as participation in much of the social, political, and economic life of India. In the early part of the twentieth century, Mahatma Gandhi began referring to them as *"harijan,"* or "children of God." He viewed the removal of the stigma of untouchability as one of his primary goals for India and Hinduism, and he hoped that a change in name would aid in that process. Although untouchability was officially outlawed shortly after India's independence, the mark has not disappeared. For this text, I use both *"harijan"* and "Untouchable" as caste group labels because both are widely understood, and the latter helps to remind the reader of the stigma that such persons have had to bear throughout their lives.

Over the last decade or two, there has been a growing political awareness and empowerment among many Indian Untouchables, some of whom have adopted the term "Dalit" over the more common "Untouchable" or *"harijan"* for self-identity. Moreover, many Dalits now consider these more common terms to be derogatory. Indologists who have been drawn to this political movement have tended to depict Dalits and their political ideologies as representative of contemporary Untouchables as a whole, and many have begun to employ this new terminology. However, my own experience among *harijans* in the states of Himachal Pradesh, Uttar Pradesh, and Madhya Pradesh suggests that most of them do not feel the same way. In Chhattisgarh, where the vast majority of Ramnamis reside, and which has a high percentage of Untouchables, "*harijan*" is the most common term used for caste identity. Moreover, I have heard in the region "Dalit" used for self-identity by a villager only once. Thus, I will include the terms "Untouchable" and *"harijan,"* but not "Dalit," in referring to the caste background of such individuals in this study, both because of its lack of use in the area and also because it carries with it a definite political connotation with which few, if any, Ramnamis find affinity.

Caste Hindu. This refers to members of all four of the "touchable" castes: *brahman, kshatriya, vaishya,* and *shudra.*[13] For many contemporary Indians, the religious and social lines between these castes have lost much of their previous relevance and adherence, except for marriage alliances. The chasm between caste Hindus and Untouchables, however, is a much more difficult one to bridge for many in the former category. It is into this abyss that many attempts at social reform in India have fallen. It has also been a primary reason for many of the conversions throughout the last millennium to Islam, Christianity, and Buddhism.

Low Caste. In this category are included both *shudra* and *harijan*. As non-Aryans and nonparticipants in the brahmanical religion were incorporated into early Vedic society, they were assigned the rank of *shudra* by the brahman hierarchy. Even though Untouchables have emerged as a functionally separate caste, during much of the history of India a close association between *shudras*, tribals, and Untouchables has existed in the minds of most members of the upper castes.

Upper Caste. Also known as "twice-born" *(dvij),* this includes members of all three upper castes, *brahman, kshatriya,* and *vaishya*. In contemporary India, these castes tend to be economically dominant, but are seldom, if ever, looked upon by others as religiously significant categories. The distinctions today are primarily social, and they seem to only possess any real significance for most of their members in the domain of marriage alliances.

High Caste. This refers only to *brahman* and *kshatriya*. This particular category has virtually no religious relevance in India today, except to some of the more conservative members of these castes.

Overview of This Work

Chapter 1 provides the context for understanding the geographic environment in which the Ramnami Samaj has developed, as well as my own relationship with India, the Ram *bhakti* tradition, and the *samaj*. The latter is important in order to provide the reader with an understanding of the context in which the research presented herein has taken shape.

Chapter 2 looks at the origins and development of the Ram tradition, as revealed in the Valmiki *Rāmāyaṇa,* the Ram-related Vaishnav Upanishads, and the *Adhyātma Rāmāyaṇa*.[14] I have chosen to focus on these works because of their influence on the development of North Indian Ram *bhakti* and the practice of *Ramnam*.[15] While Valmiki's work presents Ram primarily as a human with divine qualities, the latter works identify Ram with Brahman, the unqualified absolute, and elaborate on the uses of his name. Where relevant, I also examine the contributions of non-Brahmanical and low-caste movements to the growth and enrichment of Ram *bhakti.*

Chapter 3 focuses on Ram *bhakti* as found in various writings in Hindi and its dialects, especially in Northern India, with specific focus on the writings of Kabir and of Tulsidas.

Chapter 4 provides an historical overview of the rise of various low-caste sectarian religious movements in Central India, exploring in particular the conditions and factors that led to the formation and development of the Ramnami Samaj.[16] The last portion of this chapter explores the origin and development of the Ramnami movement and its maturation during the last hundred years.

Chapter 5 examines the present-day forms and structure of the sect, including a discussion of the distinctive modes of ritual dress and practice that characterize it. Because the functioning of the sect's annual festival, or Bhajan Mela, is so intimately tied in with its organizational makeup, this chapter concludes with a section devoted to the *mela* and its pivotal role in the evolution of the *samaj*.

Chapter 6 focuses on the Ramnamis' appropriation and adaptation of the Ram story and *Ramnam* in their ritual practices. Since both the story and the practice have been incorporated into the orthodox religion, their use by low castes, such as the Ramnamis, provides both an alternative approach to the orthodox form as well as a challenge to the religious hierarchy seeking to be the primary mediators and guardians of these practices.

Chapter 7 contains biographical sketches of six of the Ramnamis I have come to know well over the past several decades. The lives of each of these individuals help reveal the diversity and freedom of self-expression that characterizes much of the membership of the *samaj*.

Chapter 8 reflects upon the role of contemporary value systems among the low caste in Chhattisgarh. It explores how the various groups in the region have sought to relate to the caste Hindu social and religious value systems and the ways in which the Ramnamis approach and use the various sets of values with which they live.

Appendix I begins with a review of the evolving concepts of scripture, then looks at the historical development of the Ram story and the practice of *Ramnam* in various textual genre outside of the texts discussed in chapters 2 and 3. This material is presented for those interested in tracing these developments from non-Ramayana sources.

Appendix II gives a summary of the Shambuka incident as presented in the last book of the Valmiki *Rāmāyaṇa,* in which Ram kills a *shudra* ascetic because he had angered the heavens by practicing austerities. The incident is clearly a brahmanical addition to the text meant to warn the low caste from attempting to advance themselves religiously through the rejection of orthodox prohibitions against their doing so.

Devotees performing an *arti* ritual to a copy of the *Rāmcaritmānas* during a night-long chanting session.

An innovative sect member printing a Ramnam shawl with a hand-carved woodblock.

Chapter 1

Providing the Context

Field Research and the Field

As with the ethnographic portion of most research on India, the present study is heavily dependent upon fieldwork. Whenever I read a study or watch a documentary about people, especially in a culture foreign to the researchers, I cannot help but speculate as to the kind of personal relationships that exist or existed between researcher and subject. As a student of fieldwork who has been involved in observing India and its people for over thirty years, it has become quite apparent that the type of association and familiarity field-workers have with their subjects and the biases and preferences of both researcher and subject combine to have a powerful influence on the results of the studies done. Yet, such biases are not supposed to affect academic research and are rarely discussed or disclosed. In performing and presenting their field studies, researchers are assumed to use scholarly objectivity and detached subjectivity. Those of us who do anthropological field research are generally expected to communicate effectively the feeling of having, in Clifford Geertz's words, truly "been there," but without actually allowing the experiences to compromise our ability to maintain distanced objectivity. Such an approach places a great deal of expectation on the researcher, and is not necessarily realistic or beneficial. As humans studying and seeking to understand other humans, it is natural to be influenced, and to influence others, by our interactions and experiences. Rather than deny this, it seems more realistic and appropriate to recognize and acknowledge the influences and take them into consideration as we attempt an objective orientation to the endeavor. In this way, we allow for individuality, personal experience, and scholarship all to be used as tools in crafting our work. It is with this approach in mind that I include in this chapter not only a background survey of the area of this study, but also my own relationship to India, to the Ram *bhakti* tradition, and to the Ramnami Samaj.

The primary geographic focus of the field research portion of this study is Chhattisgarh, an ethnographically designated region in Central India. Formerly comprising the eastern portion of Madhya Pradesh, it became its own state on

November 1, 2000.[1] Chhattisgarh consists of approximately twenty thousand villages and has a variety of cultural traditions unique to the area. Although there has been a great deal of road work over the last few decades, a large portion of the rural population still lives in small hamlets accessible only by foot, oxcart, or two-wheeled vehicles. There are large forested areas in the state, yet much of the land used in farming is arid and relatively infertile, depleted by centuries of farming practices that have increasingly deprived the land of nutrients with little reintroduction of organic matter in the process. In some sections of the state, even though the soil remains fertile, a lack of irrigation water prevents large-scale production. The result is low crop output and a relatively impoverished rural population.

Chhattisgarh is home to nearly two-thirds of the "Scheduled Castes"[2] and a large majority of the tribals of the former Madhya Pradesh. In addition, *shudras* dominate the ranks of caste Hindus in the state, and in many villages *harijans* are actually the dominant caste. Therefore, relative to India as a whole, the region has a high percentage of non-upper-caste Hindus, especially in the rural areas. The state then provides a unique setting in which to study those in the social and religious periphery. An observer or researcher is afforded ample opportunity to see low caste and Untouchable life more or less in its own context, separated from the direct daily subjugating influence of high castes upon them. In the introduction to his valuable and insightful study of the *chamars* of Lucknow, Ravindra Khare writes of the Untouchable:

> Whatever he is reflects on the larger society and its values. Although he is now more studied and talked about, he himself remains a social enigma. This is so because he is too readily stereotyped by others while he himself often remains remote and silent. . . . Once we prepare ourselves to consider the Untouchable on his own terms, after penetrating certain stereotypes, his arguments for alternative self-evaluation begin to surface.[3]

In rural Chhattisgarh, the voice of the Untouchable is much louder than what can be heard in much of India, because it is not muted by the caste Hindu society that dominates urban areas. In the villages of the region, *harijans* have more opportunity for self-expression, and this gives us an excellent opportunity to see them more "on their own terms." Writing on Chhattisgarh in his early-twentieth-century study of the Central Provinces, R.V. Russell observes,

> Here the Chamārs have to some extent emancipated themselves from their servile status and have become cultivators, and occasionally even *mālguzārs* or landed proprietors.[4]

Prior to the 1930s, the name of the dominant *harijan* subcaste in the region was *"chamar,"* which is also the largest of the Untouchable subcastes in India. The large number of poor and illiterate Chhattisgarhi *harijans* has long reinforced the common preconception and stereotypes of the area held by many Indians, that it is a place bereft of culture and religion. A closer look at the place and its people, however, proves this to be far from the case.

The early history of Chhattisgarh is obscure, although mention of it can be found as early as the fourth century C.E., when it was considered a part of the southern portion of the kingdom of Kosala. Since that time it has been subsumed in various kingdoms, sometimes divided among several. The boundaries, as they exist today, are roughly the same as they were under the Haihaya dynasty, which ruled the region from the tenth century until the 1740s.[5] The Maratha conquest of Chhattisgarh was complete in 1758, and some historians have suggested that during the next hundred years the Marathas stripped the region of anything and everything of value, leaving it in the condition of extreme economic poverty that persists even in the present.[6]

During their respective reigns, both the Haihayas and the Maratha conquerors brought in their own *brahman* priests, whose languages and cultures differed from the local population. These immigrants from the north and the west remained primarily in the urban areas, as did most of the upper-caste immigrants to the region, especially during the last few centuries. Consequently, a greater variety of languages and more members of upper castes are found in the cities of Chhattisgarh than in the rural areas, where local dialects and the low caste tend to dominate. Chhattisgarh has also been a refuge for, and seat of, nonestablishment movements and activities in the social, religious, and political arenas. Expatriots from many other regions of India have settled there, adding to the diversity of its cultural and religious dimensions. From the latter part of the nineteenth century and until Indian independence, the Central Provinces served as an important center of anti-British activity and agitation, much of which took place in Chhattisgarh. Thus, on religious, social, and political levels, the region has long been the home for nonorthodox Indian life.

The multifaceted culture of the area is still alive with various forms of traditional music, singing, and dancing. When asked to identify themselves, most of the residents, young and old, refer to themselves first as "Chhattisgarhi" rather than Indian or Hindu. Until recently, modernization, Westernization, and secularization have not had the same degree of influence in the region that they have exerted in many other parts of North India. More dominant influences have included sanskritization, urbanization, and nonorthodox religions.[7] However, during the last decade, a sharp rise in modernization and Westernization can be seen in all the urban areas, with inroads into the rural areas as well.

Rather than concentrating on a particular Chhattisgarhi village, my research examines the religion of the region, focusing primarily on the Ramnami

Samaj, who reside, for the most part, in the central and northern portions of Chhattisgarh. Over the centuries, the region has given birth to a variety of low-caste religious movements, and the Ramnami sect is fairly new by Indian standards, having existed for barely a hundred years. In that short time, however, the *samaj* has had a significant influence on the religious and social life of the region. Since over 95 percent of the sect members live in rural areas and over 99 percent are *harijan,* a study of the sect requires focus on *harijan* religion and life in Chhattisgarh. This study does not dwell on contemporary caste Hindu religious beliefs and practices of the region, except as points of reference, for they have relatively little direct impact on the religious life of contemporary Ramnamis.

In India, it is difficult to understand a single village without looking at its connections with surrounding villages and cultures. Nevertheless, it must be realized that, depending upon the area of focus, the sphere of influence can be large or small. A village in one of the more populous states like Uttar Pradesh, for example, is more strongly influenced not only by its surrounding villages but also by the state and the nation. This is due to the central role such states tend to play in national politics, the infrastructure of the state (i.e., roads, railway, bus system, electricity, etc.), the prevalence of government schools (from elementary to college level), and so forth. Such is not the case in much of rural Chhattisgarh. Lacking roads, transportation, and electricity, Chhattisgarhi villages are not nearly as connected to the outside world, physically, economically, or culturally. They have close relations with the other nearby villages but often have little direct contact with the country beyond that. In addition, the lower caste status of so many of the area's residents has traditionally restricted their involvement in the brahmanical religious culture and society that tended to connect the urban centers of Madhya Pradesh with urban centers to the north and west.

Personal Background and Research Experience

> In formal settings anthropologists are supposed to be dispassionate analysts; because our confrontations with the extraordinary are unscientific, we are not supposed to include them in our discourse. It is simply not appropriate to expose to our colleagues the texture of our heart or the uncertainties of our "gaze."[8]

I first visited India in early 1968. It was only a three-week excursion, but it instilled in me a strong desire to return. That opportunity came during the spring of the following year. A few months after returning to India on my second trip, I became acquainted with a Ramanandi Vaishnav *sadhu,*[9] or monk, and this connection led to my initiation in the Ramanandi order in January of 1970. Having been raised in a devotional Italian Catholic family, I found it both familiar and comfortable to be surrounded by, and immersed in, the sensuous ritualism and emotional personalism of contemporary Hindu India. During my years as a *sadhu,* my time was divided between living essentially alone in a lower Himalayan valley, spending time and studying with my ascetic teachers and other *sadhus*, and wandering through villages, generally but not exclusively in the northern plains and in the Himalayas. At first, the fact that I was a foreigner was a strong influence in what and how I experienced India. Later, as I became more familiar with the religious culture and with various dialects of Hindi (the dominant language in the North), my not being Indian seemed to have less and less direct influence on my daily life. Since more than four hundred million Indians speak at least some dialect of Hindi, either as their first or second language, it is the indigenous language of greatest access. As my knowledge of various dialects increased, so did the opportunities for direct personal relationships with Indians in the areas I frequented.[10]

Generally speaking, rural Indians tend to have quite a provincial geographic view of their world, and thus tend to see all those from a different cultural and linguistic region as outsiders, be they Kashmiri, Keralan, or Kenyan. Obviously, those who share aspects of the broader pan-Indian cultural traditions are seen as less distant than those who do not. Most villagers are quite friendly and tend to be curious when meeting any outsiders. Often, when a villager discovered that I understood or could converse in his or her dialect, I would immediately be asked questions about my village, such as what people do there, what the cows are like, how much milk do they give, or why I became a *sadhu*. Being a Vaishnav monk actually opened many doors for me, since most rural Hindus, regardless of their caste background, like to talk with wandering *sadhus* who have knowledge from and experiences in the outside world. Additionally, the scriptural frame of reference most common to North Indian villagers is Tulsidas's *Rāmcaritmānas,* the primary text of my monastic order. Many villagers look to *sadhus* for advice concerning family, emotional, or financial problems. Others seek talismans or *mantras* to help them fulfill any of a number of wishes, both material and nonmaterial. Still others solicit charity or like to associate with monks out of a desire to vicariously experience the freedom they perceive wandering mendicants to have. Finally, some simply hope to partake in the various smokable intoxicants *sadhus* are often believed to possess.[11]

As a whole, the Ramanandi order has become extremely sanskritized, although on the individual level a great many nonorthodox beliefs and practices are prevalent in its ranks. The more I lived and traveled with Ramanandis, the more I was made aware of various value systems that exist in India, independent of the central value system of the orthodox *brahman*. For the most part, Ramanandi *sadhus* have learned to adapt to the idiosyncrasies and values of each ethno-cultural group with which they come in contact, and many become quite proficient at doing so. The older monks with whom I spent time impressed upon me the importance of doing the same, making it quite clear to me that they did not see the movement back and forth between various value systems as necessarily negative. To them, it is simply a means to adopt and to encompass various cultural forms, thereby enhancing a *sadhu*'s ability to communicate with a broader section of the populace.

During the mid-1970s, I spent several years traveling in and out of India with a Vaishnav teacher. Frequently acting as translator and interpreter for English-speaking foreigners, Bengalis, or South Indians who visited him, I began to see an even greater diversity of religious and cultural value systems and expressions. It became apparent that many Hindus have adopted and adapted orthodox religious lexicon to identify vastly divergent concepts and practices. It seems that the sanskritization of religious language, more than actions, has helped to foster the misconception that there exists an overarching adherence by Hindus to orthodox beliefs and values.

The Indians with whom I had the most frequent interaction as a *sadhu* were high caste.[12] These included religious teachers and philosophers, temple priests and patrons, astrologers and politicians, landlords and businessmen. Also, since there were so few Westerners living as Hindu monks in those days, many Indians regarded a *videshi* (foreigner) *sadhu* as an object of interest. This somewhat unique status helped provide me with an introduction and access to a relatively diverse cross section of the population. I mention this because my relationships with many of the people who have subsequently become important sources for the data and information used in this book started as personal friendships, some more than thirty years ago. Moreover, even though my academic research has focused on the beliefs and practices of some of them, my relationship with most of them continues to be primarily personal, rather than one of researcher and subject. This situation has both advantages and disadvantages. On the one hand, I have been able to learn and experience aspects of their lives and beliefs that an "outsider" could not, however, at the same time, I have found myself hesitant to delve into or question certain things about them that an outsider could more easily do.[13]

When I first ventured to India, I had no academic training in fieldwork or in the study of culture or religion. I also had no intention of staying more than a few months. With neither academic goals nor typical tourist interests to guide me, I was forced to find my own niche in my new religious and cultural environment. Looking for nothing in particular, I was fortunate to find a great deal. My early understanding of India and Hinduism developed primarily from personal experiences and the interpretations of *sadhus* and villagers. My learning was guided by indigenous elements and approaches rather than academic theoretical constructs as tools for discernment.

The greater a researcher's ability to cognize and perceive a belief system through indigenous understanding, the more successfully he or she can juxtapose it with academic perceptions in attempting to gain a broader viewpoint from which to observe the particular field of study. Many of the nuances and subtleties of a culture reveal deeper meanings to the people involved, but these are not always translated by informants, nor do they necessarily fit preconceived academic theories and methodological frameworks. Not having had previous exposure to such theories and frameworks at the time, I was naturally compelled to be open to indigenous understanding and categories in evolving concepts with which to absorb and interpret my observations and experiences. Later, this both helped and hindered me in my academic approach to my area of research, for the parameters of every methodology of learning have a tendency not only to reveal certain techniques of thinking and viewing, but also to obstruct, or at least downplay, alternate perspectives.

Seeing Differences, Seeing Prejudices

Most of the literature about the caste system in India has been written by either high-caste Indians or by foreigners whose primary sources have been high-caste Indians. This pattern began in the mid-1800s when British officials and Bengali *brahmans* dominated as authors of English-language literature on caste and society in India. In more than a century, the indigenous writing on caste has continued to be dominated by high-caste authors. Even the majority of Indian contributors to the popular and scholarly *Subaltern Studies* series, dealing with various issues of oppression in South Asia are from the *brahman* caste. Due to the nature of the caste system and its inherent social restrictions, *brahmans*, as a group, are probably the least likely of Indians to be able to have the kind of relationship with *harijans* that would facilitate comprehensive, objective studies of the latter. Although many high-caste scholars have been able to overcome such obstacles, many have not.

The fact that many researchers' informants are also high-caste can exacerbate the situation. In her first experience of fieldwork, Chie Nakane, author of the seminal *Japanese Society,* studied upper-caste village Bengali women. In her work, she came to realize most of them did not even know where the Untouchable women in their own village lived. Orthodox Hindu doctrine prohibits caste Hindus from having anything but the most distant and superficial contact and relationship with Untouchables. As a result, most caste-Hindu understanding of *harijans* and *harijan* life is fraught with inaccuracies and misconceptions. Yet, most caste Hindus do not perceive their limitation this way. An example of this can be found in *The Remembered Village,* by M. N. Srinivas, the well-respected Indian anthropologist. Referring to the beliefs in the village where he was doing research, and where he admittedly had next to no interaction with the *harijans* there,

> I must reiterate that what I have written so far about the basic religious ideas of the villagers is drawn from my experience of the "touchable" Hindu castes. But I think that it is true of the Harijans also.[14]

This is a revealing statement, reflecting the assumption held by many upper-caste Hindus and scholars that they can know Untouchables—what they think, how they live—or even write extensively about them, without actually getting to know any of them.

As with so many non-Indians, my initial introduction to and understanding of the caste system was almost entirely provided me by high-caste acquaintances and friends. As the ones who benefit the most from this ancient cumbersome system of social and religious hierarchy, most high-caste Hindus consciously and unconsciously justify its existence, presenting biased, incorrect explanations and defenses for it. I was occasionally warned to avoid anything more than superficial contact with *harijans*, for, I was told, they are dirty, ignorant, immoral, untrustworthy, and/or unevolved beings whose religious beliefs and practices have little if any relationship to "true" Hinduism. I was also cautioned by many of my high-caste Hindu friends that it was not "proper" or "karmically" prudent for a *sadhu* to have a personal association with *harijans*. Hearing such viewpoints so often, I regrettably made little effort during my first years in India to associate with anyone I knew to be Untouchable.

Monks and ascetics tend to observe caste with more distance. With the exception of the acutely caste-conscious Shaivite *sannyasis*, who are predominantly from the *brahman* caste, most Hindu ascetics traditionally do not discuss their own caste background with anyone; it was and still is considered by many a taboo question for *sadhus*.[15] Thus, many *sadhus* ignore the discussion of caste in their conversations with each other, and seldom bring up the issue of caste in their conversations with devotees and followers, unless specifically asked for advice, such as in the case of marriage alliances. Ramanandi *sadhus* like to see themselves as beyond the limitations of caste, it is one of the things they have renounced. For many of them, the renunciant/householder dichotomy is the socioreligious differentiation that tends to hold greater significance. In line with this, *sadhus* often adhere to this distinction in keeping a certain distance, either physical or social, between themselves and all householders, with the exception of those specifically initiated into their denomination. Such renunciants see close association with any householder as potentially polluting, since householders typically are much more lax in their adherence to purity/pollution rules and practices.

Over the years, my interest in spending time with lay villagers in various regions of North and Central India increased, and I sought to learn more about their life-styles and beliefs. As I began to develop friendships with various Untouchables and their families, it became exceedingly apparent that so much of what high-caste Hindus had told me about *harijans* was erroneous and pejorative.

As I mentioned earlier, most caste Hindus actually know very little about Untouchables, limited in the type of interaction they might have by strict social and religious prohibitions. This was, and still is, especially the case for most caste Hindus who adhere to orthodox brahmanical rules. Little did I know at the time that one of the primary vehicles for my further understanding of India and contemporary Hinduism would be Untouchables.

Meeting the Ramnamis

As a Ramanandi *sadhu,* two of the practices that became an integral part of my daily life were the chanting of the name of Ram and the study of the Ram story, especially its Hindi telling in the form of the *Rāmcaritmānas* of Tulsidas. For Ramanandis, this is the most sacred of scriptures, and many members devote their scriptural reading exclusively to the *Mānas,* as the *Rāmcaritmānas* is generally known. The chanting of the name of Ram is something a Ramanandi is expected to perform throughout the day, be it silently in meditation, as a chant, or in conjunction with one's other daily activities. Thus, the name and the story garnered a great deal of my focus and attention.

My first awareness of the Ramnami Samaj came in early 1972, when my father sent me a copy of the October 1971 issue of *National Geographic Magazine.* On the cover was a striking photograph of a woman whose face was covered with name "Ram" tattooed repeatedly in *devanagari* script.[16] Because of this woman's obvious devotion to Ram, I was intrigued and felt compelled to find her and the group with which she was affiliated.[17] At a religious festival in Haridwar in 1974, I had a brief encounter with a few Ramnamis but was not able to establish contact with the sect until January 1977, at the Kumbha Mela festival in Prayag (Allahabad). I spent the next several months with nearly two hundred members of the *samaj* and have been involved with the Ramnamis, on various levels, ever since.

My study of the Ramnamis is based on information gathered in ongoing research since 1977. I have made more than fifteen visits to Chhattisgarh, some lasting for only a few weeks, others for several months. In addition, I have spent months at a time with sect members traveling to and staying at a variety of pilgrimage and festival sites in North India. During my stays in Chhattisgarh, I have attended more than ten of the sect's annual festivals and numerous smaller ones. Over the years, I have stayed in or visited more than forty Chhattisgarhi villages, nearly all of which had at least a few resident Ramnami families. The population of several of these villages was over 95 percent *satnami* and nearly 80 percent Ramnami.[18] In the early years, my primary modes of transportation in the region were oxcart, bicycle, and foot. Increasingly, however, dirt roads are being widened to permit the use of buses in the region, but such transportation is still relatively scant and predictably unreliable.

Each time I returned to Chhattisgarh, during the first decade after meeting the Ramnamis, I was struck by how little things appeared to change. Then, in 1986, the Madhya Pradesh government completed a vast hydroelectric project, and large areas of Chhattisgarh started to become electrified. It was only after their demise that I realized how many aspects of the culture and life-style there had persisted because of the lack of electricity. Lights opened up the night to increased activity, which, in turn, influenced the activities of the daytime. The life-styles of those who could afford electricity became increasingly disengaged from those who could not. Something as rudimentary as an electric flour mill in a village significantly altered the way food was prepared, the way it was eaten, the control women had over its production and storage, and even, to some extent, the balance of power between various members of a family. Further, electrification and industrialization, at least in the short run, have tended to diminish further the status of manual labor and thus of low castes, who usually perform such work. Because my current research has focused on marginalized groups of people, the negative effect of modernization on their lives is clearly more striking than the obvious short-term benefits for those who can afford to partake in them.

Much of my understanding of the Ramnamis has come from living with them in their villages and participating in their festivals. My initial relationship with most of my friends, acquaintances, and informants in Chhattisgarh was as a *sadhu,* and many have chosen to hold onto the parameters of that relationship in our continued friendship and interactions. Now that I am a householder and parent, however, I have been able to forge many new relationships, as well as add new dimensions to old ones. Obviously, my involvement with the Ramnamis has drastically altered my view of *harijans* and of the caste system in general. The more time I spend with Untouchables in North and Central India and the more I read caste studies written by high-caste Indians, the more it has become apparent to me that the views of *harijans* commonly held by most people, Indians and non-Indians alike, tend to be distorted and extremely limited. One can only suspect the degree to which political, economic, and racial considerations are the underlying bases for the continued promotion of stereotypic views of the low caste. Each caste, and even subcaste, is traditionally endogamous; each has traditionally tended to limit its association with members of other castes. The restrictions on socialization and interaction have resulted in the development of distinct ethnic and cultural groups, each with little actual knowledge of the others. While prejudice is diminishing in urban India, the conservative social environment prevalent in many rural areas and among the religious high caste make eliminating caste discrimination difficult. In many ways, the situation is similar to the impediments encountered in attempting to eliminate racial and ethnic prejudice in the United States.

In gathering information on the Ramnamis, the primary language I have used is Uttar Pradeshi Hindi. Although the Chhattisgarhi dialect is quite distinct and I have developed a fairly good understanding of it, most Chhattisgarhi villagers today find ease in conversing in standardized Hindi. Moreover, it is the dialect taught in the region's schools and is slowly replacing Chhattisgarhi as the primary dialect of the non-tribal residents of the state. While the majority of the elderly village women still speak only the local dialect, many of their children and grandchildren increasingly speak only standardized Hindi. During the first several years of my relationship with the *samaj,* I had no intention of making them a part of any formal academic study. Nevertheless, my curiosity motivated me to ask various members a myriad of questions about their lives, longings, beliefs, practices, and so forth. I recorded many of the answers, along with my personal observations and reflections in the journals I have kept regularly while in India.[19]

Fortunately, I have been able to maintain regular contact with numerous Ramnami friends and informants during the last twenty-five years, and I have had an opportunity to ask many of the same questions over again. I have occasionally received variant and contradictory answers, sometimes coming from the same people. Some of the differences have obviously resulted from an increased understanding on my part of the Ramnamis' way of thinking, as well as from my informants' willingness to share with me aspects of their beliefs and themselves. Many of my adult informants were either mere children or not yet born when I first began studying the Ramnamis, so there has also been a generational change in my pool of sources and their ways of thinking.

Over the years, I have sought a variety of local individuals and groups to use as my primary contacts and sources for gaining information and understanding of Untouchable life and belief in Chhattisgarh. A few deserve specific mentioning here. Ramtaram Ramnami was one of my first Ramnami acquaintances.[20] He is an elder member of a *harijan* family and was a Ramnami leader *(sadasya)* for many years. His home has been one of my main residences during any lengthy stay in Chhattisgarh. He arranged my initial contacts with the sect and helped facilitate my access to the *sadasya*s and their council meetings. He has also been a primary informant on many of the sect's dimensions, generally providing a seasoned perspective on them and on the culture of the region. An elementary school teacher in his village served as my initial introduction to another important group of informants. Now numbering approximately two dozen, these teachers, both Untouchable and touchable from half a dozen different villages in the area, have provided me with local educators' views, the changing dynamics of caste interaction, and the increasing influence of secularization and Westernization on their region.

In 1980, I met a young *vaishya* engineer from Raipur at a Ramnami festival. He is from a well-to-do urban family and has long had an interest in rural India, frequently spending time in villages, attending a variety of religious and cultural activities. His family members are strong devotees of Ram, and they have even invited Ramnamis to their home to perform their chanting rituals for them and their friends. In the process, they have shown sect members a great deal of kindness and respect and have openly ignored caste rules that restrict Hindus' relationships with Untouchables. The family members find justification for their actions in devotional teachings that explicitly disregard caste and class barriers for the true devotee. This family has also been my means of meeting a large number of upper-caste urban Hindus who eagerly participate in religious activities, yet openly criticize and ignore caste restrictions. The willingness of upper-caste Hindus and their families to interact with *harijans*, while still rare in rural areas, is increasing; it suggests a trend that is becoming more prevalent in urban India. Urbanization and secularization have reduced fears of retribution by one's own caste community for infringement of caste rules, such as those governing contact and commensality. Increasingly, urban Hindus ignore or even reject the rigid casteism found in most village areas. Urbanites are becoming more open to a Western, secular, social value system, in which caste rules play a diminished role. This is not to suggest that urban Hindus actively reject all caste boundaries; however, many now do question them and even ignore them. The only caste restrictions that seem to have remained largely intact in urban areas are those involving marriage, yet even these are no longer completely sacrosanct.

In looking at the Ramnamis and at contemporary low-caste religion, I have employed the work of a variety of early and contemporary Western Indologists, ethnographers, and anthropologists. Among these Edward Shils, McKim Marriott, Clifford Geertz, and Victor Turner have been especially helpful. However, using prevailing academic concepts, theories, and methodologies in interpreting and presenting my understanding of the Ramnamis has often proved frustrating for, while these tools inspire a great deal of insight, they can also mislead. It is necessary to consider the criticism directed at Western anthropology and the scholastic approach by indigenous scholars from cultures subjected to Western-style critique. Hussein Fahim asks,

> Is anthropological instruction and training in the West actually producing scientific observers, or is it inadvertently transforming students with diverse cultural perspectives into practitioners of a standard Western anthropology of culture-bound models?[21]

Fahim presents a fascinating challenge: to interpret the ways of other peoples in a manner that is both scholastically rigorous and yet conducive to indigenous self-understanding. This can clearly be a daunting task. When one looks at the work of indigenous scholars, especially in India, it becomes clear that some of them suffer from the same kinds of socially and politically motivated ideological myopia that has distorted the work of some Western scholars and historians of

India. The social sciences provide unique tools with which to work; however, the way in which we choose to use them determines the outcome of our efforts. At times, none of the tools are right for the job, and we have to simply work bare-handed, without any pattern to follow. Hopefully, the background material presented above will help the reader better understand the context of, and conceptions that motivated this study.

Chapter 2

Historical Development of the Ram Tradition

Both prayer and story are ways in which human beings use language to domesticate the enormity of the cosmos, bringing it into scale with the human dimension, and both are fundamentally personalistic.
—Harvey Alper, *Mantra*

Devotion is the focus and goal of the practices of the Ramnami Samaj, and the primary vehicles to achieve this are chanting and recitation of the Ram story. Whether it is sitting together in a group at one of their frequent gatherings or just waiting for a bus, they often fill any idle time with these. Their chanting consists primarily of verses extracted from any of several versions of the Ram story, and amidst their chanting, they will also break into impromptu storytelling sessions. Both of these practices are means by which they pray to and communicate with Ram. At the same time, they are also the vehicles for communicating with each other, as we will see later. In chanting the name and story of Ram, they are affirming their own special common bond to him, as well as to the goal they have chosen in life. This they do while living in a social and religious environment that frequently tells them they have no bond with Ram and their only goal in life is to serve the caste-Hindu society, and then from a distance.

The Ramnamis are representative of a consistent paradigm of religious development in India for at least the last millennium, that is, the formation of non-Brahmanical and even anti-brahmanical devotional movements from the ranks of the low caste and Untouchable. These have taken various forms, but a common feature found to most of them has been the challenging and reinterpreting of the orthodox characterization of Hinduism. As mentioned earlier, both the orthodox tradition (the center) and the folk traditions throughout the subcontinent (the periphery) have borrowed and modified elements of the other, the former to gain following, the latter to gain legitimacy. This process is apparent in the various low-caste religious movements in Central India as well. The Ramnamis, while unique in their own right, are nonetheless part of a long tradition of both low-caste Ram *bhaktas* and *nirgun nam bhaktas*. This chapter briefly examines some of the textual sources of the tradition, especially those that have most influenced its contemporary manifestations such as the Ramnami Samaj. In looking at these developments with respect to the Ram tradition, this analysis focuses especially on the two major dimensions of Ram *bhakti: Ramkatha* and *Ramnam*.[1] The former refers both to the Ram story as well as to the reading, recitation, and/or chanting of it, while the latter refers to the practice of repeating or chanting the name of Ram.

The role that the *Ramkatha,* or Ram story, has played in the lives of the peoples of South and Southeast Asia is immeasurable. From its origins more than twenty-five hundred years ago, up through the present day, it has been pivotal in shaping the religious, artistic, and literary history of cultures throughout much of the area and well beyond the borders of India. Since the earliest known elaboration of the Ram story attributed to Valmiki, this epic tale has inspired over three hundred renderings in at least twenty-five Asian languages.[2] Its history and growth in many ways parallel the evolution and maturation of the Hindu tradition itself.

The Ram Story in the *Valmiki Rāmāyaṇa*

There has been an enormous development in the theological conceptualization of Ram as well as the social, philosophical, and ritual uses of the Ram story, or *Ramkatha* since Valmiki sought to put it into written form at least two and a half millennia ago. While little incontrovertible evidence exists regarding the story's origin, there is a great deal of information with which to speculate. Three tellings of the Ram story have the greatest significance in the context of the present study: the Valmiki *Rāmāyaṇa,* the *Adhyātma Rāmāyaṇa,* and Tulsidas's *Rāmcaritmānas*. Taken together, they provide a useful framework with which to view the evolution of the *Ramkatha* and the system of beliefs and practices that it has inspired.

We know from occasional mention in the *Ṛg Veda* that the non-Aryans had their own rites and religious life, although whatever is told about them is sparse and generally negative. Since most of the popular folklore and beliefs were, like those of the early Aryan elite, sustained and nourished through oral tradition, we are forced to look for possible indications of their influence on the central value system as one of the few ways we have to learn something of their character and qualities.

At the same time the Vedas were evolving as sacred truth for the brahmanical orthodoxy in northwestern India, the remainder of the populace had its own beliefs, legends, and myths, which provided the people with their own sense of history and continuity. While the *brahman* priest memorized his *mantras* and chanted them to communicate with the gods, the commoner's bard memorized the stories in his repertoire to communicate with the people. Storytellers have always had a central role in the religions and cultures of nonliterate peoples. In India, the tradition of storytellers is ancient and may even predate the rise of the Aryan culture in the northwest. In most traditional cultures, bards have functioned both as entertainers and as disseminators and perpetuators of the stories, myths, and legends that help circumscribe cultural beliefs. As is still the case in present-day India, storytellers have historically "individualized" their narratives to accommodate changing cultural values and social realities, as well as their own personalities, beliefs, and styles. The history and diversity of the Ram story suggests that it has frequently undergone this process. Rather than requiring a literal exactness, it has readily adopted regional values and cultural themes. This may be one of the reasons why it gained popularity with storytellers and garnered interest among it listeners. Most likely, it is from the repertoire of these early bards and storytellers that the tales subsequently combined into what we now know as the Ram story. Thus, these same expounders of the story have likely been intimately involved in its development as well. In his *Das Ramayana,* Hermann Jacobi maintains that both before and after Valmiki's rendering of the Ram story, its primary vehicles of dissemination were wandering bards.[3] The plethora of diverse Ram story renderings found throughout South and Southeast Asia shows that its reciters have continued to modify the tale to meet the changing needs and values of various cultures, time periods, and sectarian belief systems.

All we can know of the early bards and their stories comes from whatever remnants became part of the mainstream of religious literature or survived in some form within existing folk traditions. Early Indian sources make clear that two dominant figures emerged as focal points of the subcontinent's oral myths and legends: Ram and Krishna. Because both are described as dark in color, in contrast to the relatively light-skinned Aryans, and neither is mentioned in the earliest of the Vedic hymns, it seems safe to posit a non-Vedic origin for both figures. The legends and tales of Ram, the prince of Ayodhya, and of Krishna, the central figure of the mythology of a variety of early northwestern clans, must have enjoyed a great degree of popularity, for they continued to expand and eventually became brahmanized and consolidated into the Valmiki *Rāmāyaṇa* and the *Mahābhārata,* respectively. The *Ramkatha* appears to have had its origin among the peoples of the northern and central regions of eastern India.

While it is impossible to say precisely when the Ram story arose, or even when it first gained popularity, it is generally believed that Valmiki authored a "core" *Rāmāyaṇa,* comprising most of what is now Books II through VI, and that over the ages subsequent additions and interpolations were made. In his *Righteous Rama,* J. L. Brockington provides evidence to suggest there are multiple discernible stages in the development of Valmiki's *Rāmāyaṇa* from its original to its final form. Over a period beginning in the mid-first millennium B.C.E. and extending as late as the tenth century C.E., a gradual metamorphosis of content and concepts took place.[4] According to Brockington, each succeeding stage incorporated additional brahmanical elements into the narrative, which served to make the story more consistent with orthodox beliefs and practices and developing brahmanical doctrines. This also aided the process of attempting to establish the *brahman* priest as the primary, if not sole, mediator of devotion to Ram.[5] Unlike the situation with Krishna *bhakti,* however, this last goal has yet to be fully realized, although the movement in that direction continues.

The picture that begins to emerge of the origins of the *Ramkatha,* then, suggests its initial formation took place in an area outside of strong brahmanical influence, in the repertoires of storytellers peripheral to Vedic orthodoxy. As propagators of the story, these peoples had the greatest input in the tenor and scope of its development. As I shall attempt to show below, their influence has continued up into contemporary times.

The Valmiki *Rāmāyaṇa* tells the story that has been long considered by most Hindus to be the "original" version, and direct or indirect reference and deference to it exist in most subsequent tellings of the story. In Valmiki's work, the depiction of Ram is predominantly as a hero, with certain suggestions of divinity. Later renditions, however, have all tended to expand on the greatness and divine stature of Ram. The subsequent Sanskrit works that are most responsible for this alteration include the Vaishnav Upanishads and the *Adhyātma Rāmāyaṇa.*[6]

The Ram Story in the *Adhyātma Rāmāyaṇa*

The *Adhyātma Rāmāyaṇa*[7] is a medieval rendering of the Ram story, and for many North Indian Ram *bhakta*s it is the only Sanskrit version that presents Ram in the "proper" theological light. As a result, it has far greater importance among Ramanandi *sadhus* and many other Ram devotees than does the brahmanized Valmiki *Rāmāyaṇa.*[8] The *Adhyātma Rāmāyaṇa* is generally said to be a part of the *Brahmāṇḍa Purāṇa,*[9] although it does not appear in several currently available versions of that Purana. The date generally assigned to the *Adhyātma Rāmāyaṇa* is between the fourteenth and fifteenth centuries. Brockington suggests that it was either written or popularized during the time of Ramananda, the fifteenth-century founder of the Ramananda Sampraday. The text makes reference to a community of Ram *bhakta*s who may have been the followers of Ramananda, and for whom this work likely became the central scripture.[10]

Its extant form is modeled after the brahmanized Valmiki *Rāmāyaṇa,* containing seven books that bear the same titles and basic story line as the earlier epic. In the introduction to his translation, Swami Tapasyananda explains that he omitted Book VII *(Uttarakāṇḍa)* from his translation of the *Adhyātma Rāmāyaṇa* because of its apparently extraneous relationship to the first six books.[11] My own study of the text leads to a similar conclusion, as discussed below. Thus, I will refer to the first six books as "core" and Book VII as *"Uttarakāṇḍa."*[12]

The story is presented in the form of a dialogue between Shiva and Parvati, following the pattern found in many of the Tantric texts. In his extensive study of classical India literature, Maurice Winternitz sees a great deal of other Tantric influences as well in the text, referring to it as "only an epic in its external form—in reality it is a manual of devotion, Tantric in character."[13] The *Adhyātma Rāmāyaṇa* stands apart from the Valmiki *Rāmāyaṇa* in two fundamental respects: (1) its theological presentation and elevation of Ram, and (2) its philosophical view of life and its goal, both of which suggest the influence of the ascetic, tantric, and devotional traditions absent in the Valmiki *Rāmāyaṇa*. It is from the *Adhyātma Rāmāyaṇa* that Tulsidas drew his greatest inspiration in telling the Ram story.

Throughout the Valmiki *Rāmāyaṇa,* the primary depiction of Ram is as a human. Although some later interpolations assign him the status of *avatar,* or incarnation, the general tenor of the story does not support this. The *Adhyātma Rāmāyaṇa* revises this view. In its very name and its opening verses, the *Adhyātma Rāmāyaṇa* announces that its approach to and theology of Ram is very much in the context of devotional spirituality:

> He—the Light of Consciousness, the Undecaying One. . . . He who is the sole cause of the origin, the sustentation and dissolution of the world-systems; who is the support of the manifesting power known as Maya but is at the same time free from all its effects; whose form transcends all mental conceptions; who is a condensation of Bliss and Pure Consciousness—Him, the Lord of Sita and the knower of Truth, I adore.[14]

The Ram of the Valmiki *Rāmāyaṇa* is practically absent in the *Adhyātma Rāmāyaṇa*. In his place is Ram, the supreme Brahman, eternal, untouched, and perfect. Since the text is written from this viewpoint, Ram's divinity is its focus and goal. The narrative, then, becomes little more than a vehicle for the exposition of Ram *bhakti*. While Valmiki *Rāmāyaṇa* does include occasional reference to Ram as *avatar,* or divine incarnation, the *Adhyātma Rāmāyaṇa* clearly presents him as Maha Vishnu, Supreme Brahman, who from time to time manifests himself in the various incarnations, except that of Krishna. Frank Whaling suggests that the exclusion of Krishna from Ram's *avatars* may have been to prevent any antagonism with that branch of Krishna devotees for whom Krishna alone is a full *avatar*. At the same time, however, the text refers to Ram with epithets that remind one of Krishna, such as "Madhava" and "Murari."[15]

In the Valmiki *Rāmāyaṇa,* the goal of life is focused primarily on maintaining *dharma,* necessary for the smooth functioning of the universe. It is this world that is important. The path advanced in the *Adhyātma Rāmāyaṇa* is clearly one of liberation to which all actions in the world are to be directed. The philosophical approach combines both Advaita Vedanta and Ram *bhakti,* the form of the latter being similar to the Krishna *bhakti* of the *Bhāgavad Gītā.* In this fusion of Vedantic philosophy with devotional conceptions, Ram is depicted as both *sagun* and *nirgun,* personal and impersonal.

Several key additions to the core text set it even more clearly apart from the Valmiki *Rāmāyaṇa.* Besides the absolute status of Ram as Paramatman, the Highest Being, his spouse Sita is also unquestionably divine. In a speech to Hanuman near the beginning of Book I, she reveals both her and Ram's true natures:

> He is Pure Existence devoid of all adjuncts, whom the senses cannot perceive as their object. . . . Know me to be the Primeval Prakriti, the material and instrumental cause of the creation, sustentation, and dissolution of the universe. In the mere presence of Rama the Supreme Brahman, I, His Prakriti (Power), create the universe unwearied.[16]

Sita then summarizes the entire Ram story in nine verses, explaining everything that transpires in creation as nothing other than Ram's divine *leela.* She concludes,

> As He is the substratum of Maya . . . He underlies all these transformations of the constituents of Maya . . . for those who cannot distinguish the substratum from the changeful constituents of Maya, He seems to get transformed.[17]

In this way, Sita and Ram are equated, respectively, with the "Purusha" and "Prakriti" (spirit and nature) of Samkhya philosophy and the "Brahman" and "Maya" (absolute and creation) of Advaita Vedanta philosophy. A disclaimer is offered for any events in the story that might cast doubt on Ram's absolute divinity. Because of Sita's status, it would not be proper for her to be kidnapped by Ravana, as occurs in the Valmiki *Rāmāyaṇa.* Instead, just prior to the abduction, Ram tells her to hide herself in the fire in an invisible form and produce an illusory Sita, who is then taken by the fooled demon.[18] This, then, provides the excuse for Ram to demand that she endure the test of fire after the killing of Ravana. It is at that time that the real Sita can return from the fire to be reunited with Ram.

Throughout the text, nearly everyone who encounters Ram realizes his divinity, even the demons. When first hearing about Ram, Ravana reflects to himself that Ram may be God, then assures himself with the thought, "If I am killed by the Supreme Self, I shall reign in the Supreme Realm of Vaikuntha."[19] When Ravana approaches the demon Maricha,[20] seeking his help to kidnap Sita, Maricha relates his first encounter with Ram in battle years before and says that out of fear he has been able to think of nothing else. He warns Ravana to stay away from Ram, whom he identifies as Narayana, the Great Vishnu, in human form.[21]

Another significant aspect of the *Adhyātma Rāmāyaṇa* is that it lacks the caste emphasis and praise of *brahmans* that typifies Valmiki's work. As a consequence, there is only infrequent mention of caste and caste relations in the core *Adhyātma Rāmāyaṇa*. In *Ayodhyakāṇḍa,* for example, Ram travels to Chitrakut after his exile and encounters Valmiki along the way. The sage then relates his early life and the saving grace of *Ramnam*. He says he was a *dvij* (twice-born) by birth alone but married a *shudra* woman and became a thief.[22] While attempting to rob seven sages in a deep forest, he was made to see the error of his ways, and he begged them to save him. Believing his wickedness made him unsuitable to repeat *Ramnam* correctly, the sages taught him to repeat it backwards, *"ma-ra."* His devotion, coupled with the power of the name, resulted in his liberation.[23]

A few points are worth noting here. First and foremost, the greatness of *Ramnam* is clearly stressed. It is shown to have such power that even when recited backwards it can grant salvation. The caste message is more ambiguous. While the low castes are obviously belittled, there are no statements asserting the inherently venerable status of *brahmans*, so often found in brahmanized texts. Later in the episode, the sages comment that a *dvij* who has evil ways should be shunned by all, for "this is the law."[24] This is a clear contrast to brahmanizing statements in other texts that suggest that even ignoble *brahmans* should be worshipped.[25]

As in the core Valmiki, here too Guha, the Untouchable *nishad* chieftain, and Shabari, the low-caste woman ascetic, are present. Although the degraded status of the *nishad* had long been established by this time in brahmanical society, Guha is again said to be the friend and devotee of Ram and referred to in respectful terms. On their meeting at the Ganges, Guha falls at Ram's feet, but the latter immediately helps him up and embraces him.[26] It is essentially the same relationship as described in the earlier epic.

The Shabari episode, as well, is the same basic story as that found in Valmiki, with some embellishment. She is shown to be a great yogini, *gyani* (wise one), and devotee of Ram. When she tells Ram of her low-caste status, he responds by expounding his doctrine of devotion, in which *bhakti* is the only criterion determining both one's relationship with him and suitability for liberation:

> If a man has no devotion to me, neither sacrifice nor charities, neither Tapas nor the study of the Vedas and performance of rituals can help one to see Me. By Bhakti alone am I attained.[27]

Ram continues to elaborate on the elements of devotion to him. These include many of the ingredients found in Tulsidas's later presentation of Ram *bhakti.* He emphasizes the repetition of *Ramnam,* which Shiva "imparts with joy" to all beings who die in Kashi "for their spiritual redemption."[28] The entire core text is filled with hymns to Ram, sung by various divinities and sages. These praises "establish the doctrine that non-duality is the Supreme Truth but the way to its realization is through devotion and divine grace."[29] Such devotional sentiment is similar to that of Krishna worship found in the *Bhāgavata Purāṇa.* The two differ in that the Purana is filled with brahmanizing elements: interwoven with the praise of Krishna is Krishna's praise of *brahmans.* This element is lacking in the *Adhyātma Rāmāyaṇa,* that is, until the final book.

The *Uttarakāṇḍa* of the *Adhyātma Rāmāyaṇa* has an entirely different tenor. In the previous books of this work, the principal motives of recounting the Ram story are to proclaim Ram's absolute divinity and to show that all situations in which he appears to have human failings are just parts of his *leela,* or divine play. In the last book, however, Ram is once again the Ram of the brahmanized Valmiki *Rāmāyaṇa.* Gone are the frequent reminders of his infinite power and compassion and the recurrent references to him as Paramatman. In their place are reminders of brahmanical importance and superiority. Ram is still divine but firmly under the constraints of orthodox religious values.

Those major events in Valmiki's last book that help assure Ram's position as the upholder of orthodox *dharma* are also found in this final section of the *Adhyātma Rāmāyaṇa.* Moreover, several of its episodes are nearly identical to the last book in Valmiki in their language as well as in their message. Ram worships *brahmans* with great devotion and refers to them as his gods.[30] He rules according to brahmanical injunctions, since he is a "knower of duty," and he performs many horse and other large sacrifices "consisting of costly gifts to Brahmanas."[31] As in Valmiki's *Uttarakāṇḍa,* Ram kills a *shudra* ascetic for the sake of a *brahman* boy.[32] Sita is once again sent into exile—although here it is part of a plan with which she complies.[33] The episode in the Valmiki *Rāmāyaṇa* in which Lakshman is banished because of a threatened curse by the *brahman* sage Agastya appears in an abbreviated form in the *Adhyātma Rāmāyaṇa,* as does the story of Ram's final departure from Earth.[34]

The earlier books of the *Adhyātma Rāmāyaṇa* elaborate on a theme found in the *Bhāgavata Purāṇa* with respect to Krishna, and the motif is later picked up by Tulsidas: Ram is he whom the Vedic scriptures praise as Absolute Brahman. He transcends all duality and is influenced only by the love of his devotees. In *Uttarakāṇḍa,* however, Ram appears, as he does in the Valmiki *Rāmāyaṇa,* as subordinate to the Vedas and under the jurisdiction of the brahmanical value system: Ram is great, but brahmanically constructed *dharma* is greater.

The *Adhyātma Rāmāyaṇa* is the first known version of the Ram story to develop the perspective of Ram as the Absolute Brahman. It replaced Valmiki's as the Sanskrit version of the story that could be more easily appropriated by

Ram *bhakti* movements in the process of sanskritization. With the exception of the last book, the *Adhyātma Rāmāyaṇa* provided Ram devotees with a specific theology on which to base their traditions. Further, it provided the platform from which Tulsidas could launch his own rendering of the story, expressing and elaborating a similar devotional theology in a vernacular tongue.

Ramnamis chanting before a copy of the *Rāmcaritmānas*.

Chapter 3

Ramnam and the Ram Story in Hindi

Since the time of its control by the Haihaya dynasty, the overwhelming religious *ethos* among the non-tribal peoples of Chhattisgarh has been Ram *bhakti*. Although until recently no sacred texts had been written in the Chhattisgarhi dialect of Hindi, many of region's people have long found relatively easy linguistic access to devotional writings on Ramnam and the Ram story through Hindi authors using other, but related, dialects. The two primary composers of such works are Kabir and Tulsidas. In addition to these, a nineteenth-century Ram devotee named Raghunathdas penned the *Vishrām Sāgar,* and this text has become another important writing used by Ram *bhakta*s of the region. Taken together, these authors have set the tenor for Chhattisgarhi devotion to Ram and are the subject of this section.

Ramnam in Kabir

Probably the greatest medieval impetus in the development of a *nam*-centered devotionalism in North India came in the form of the Sant tradition,[1] said to have begun with Kabir.[2] The term *"sant"* has come to be associated historically with two groups of medieval poet-mystics who sang the glories of a personal, formless God. One group, collectively referred to as the Varkari sect, is from Maharashtra and includes Gyanadev (1275–96), Namdev (1270–1350), Eknath (1548–1600), and Tukaram (1598–1649). The focus of their devotion was Vithoba, a form of Krishna enshrined in the main temple at Pandharpur, Maharasthra. The other group of *sant*s is from Hindi-speaking North India and includes Kabir and a number of his followers, such as Nanak (1469–1539) and Dadu Dayal (1544–1603).[3] It is in the writings of Kabir and others from this era that the practice of *nirgun* (formless) *bhakti* emerges, or at least becomes apparent, as a powerful force in the popular religion, particularly in the North Indian Ram tradition. The two dominant characteristics all *sant*s are said to have in common are a *nirgun* theology and devotion, coupled with a rejection of caste as having any ultimate religious significance.[4] Although *Ramnam bhakti* had already become an important part of the religion of the north, it was the *sant*s who first expressed it in vernacular devotional writings. Many of the above-mentioned *sants* have inspired sectarian movements, such as the Kabirpanthis, the Dadupanthis, the Satnamis, and the Sikhs.

The greatest known exclusively *nirgun* exponent of *Ramnam* is clearly Kabir. His words and poetry reveal a variety of religious and philosophical influences, especially Indian Sufis, the existing Ram *bhakti* tradition, and the followers of Gorakhnath. There is some indication that the latter practiced *Ramnam,* even though they were considered to be Shaivite.[5] Coupled with his praises of *nirgun* Ram, Kabir exhibits a contempt for scriptural authority comparable to that found among Tantric groups, Buddhist Sahajiyas, and Gorakhnath Yogis.[6] He rejects completely the brahmanical value system and the religion promoted by it, in a straightforward and often acerbic voice:

> Saints, the Brahman is a slicked-down butcher.
> He slaughters a goat and rushes for a buffalo
> without a twinge of pain in his heart.[7]

Kabir's devotional presentation of Ram combines both Advaita Vedanta philosophy and *madhurya bhakti,* devotion to God as lover to beloved. On various occasions he stresses that his devotion is not to any incarnated Ram but to the supreme Brahman, whom he usually addresses as "Ram." Throughout his poetry, Kabir rejects caste and ritualism, underscores the necessity of religious tolerance, and stresses the practice of *Ramnam* and the need for a guru. For him, only knowledge of and devotion to the One lead to salvation, and the greatest vehicle for gaining both is *Ramnam.* Praise of the practice permeates the writings attributed to Kabir:

> Kabīr, this body is a fragile vessel
> made of fragile stuff;
> To make it durable, invoke Rāma,
> otherwise, you are lost.[8]
> He who, taking Rama's name, lays hold upon the raft will safely float to shore across the world.
> Sakhi: The name of Rama is exceedingly precious; I have no concern for others.[9]
>
> Repeat the name of Rama, the name of Rama: awake and look within your mind. . . .
> Kabir says, Without meditation upon Rama all wisdom is sunk in the deep.[10]

While Kabir extols the immense value of repeating the name, nevertheless he emphasizes his conviction that thoughtless repetition of *Ramnam* is worthless:

> O pandit, all your talking is a lie.
> If by repeating Rama's name the world is saved, then by repeating "sugar" the mouth is sweetened . . .[11]

Although Kabir was raised as a Muslim, he made caustic attacks on orthodox Muslim practices as well as on orthodox Hinduism and idol-centered ritualism. In the process, he gained a large following and several of his devotees established their own *nirgun bhakti* movements in North India. Among those founded by his direct disciples include the Mulpanthis, the Dadupanthis of Rajputana, the Shiv Narayanis of Ghazipur, and the Mulukdasis of Kara Manikpur. However, the most profound influence of Kabir's teachings can be seen in the works of Guru Nanak and of Tulsidas. The latter took Kabir's theology of Ram and combined it with the other streams of the Ram tradition, discussed above, to bring forth his famous telling of the Ram story, changing forever the texture of Ram *bhakti* and elevating it like none before.

The Ram Story and Ramnam in Tulsidas's *Rāmcaritmānas*

> Westerners used to say that Tulsidas' work was the bible of India, but the comparison is inadequate now, for Tulsidas' book is probably better known today in North India than the Bible is in any country of the West.[12]

Among the most important and widely revered of vernacular scriptures in North India is the *Rāmcaritmānas,*[13] a Hindi rendering of the Ram story by the poet Tulsidas (1543–1623). Sir George A. Grierson, a nineteenth-century Indologist, called him "the greatest of Indian authors of modern times."[14] Over the past four hundred years no Hindu text has generated as large and as active a following as Tulsidas's *Mānas*. Even as a non-Sanskritic text, it has been elevated to the status of *shruti* (Veda-like) in North India, in the eyes not only of Ram *bhakta*s but also of the general populace.[15] More than any other text, it has been reinterpreted, recreated, and imitated in a large variety of literary, ritual, and performative genres such as commentaries, oral recitations *(kathas),* dramas *(leelas),* and devotional chanting *(bhajans)*. As Philip Lutgendorf points out in his valuable study, in North India the *Mānas* has become "the text of choice for filling any vacuum in popular religious practice."[16] This section will begin with a brief sketch of Tulsidas's life, then investigate his telling of the Ram story and the unique contributions its theology has made to the development and practice of Ram *bhakti*.

Little is known about the details of Tulsidas's life. He makes brief mention of certain events in several of his writings, but such references are rare and are primarily intended to show his impoverished, sinful condition and his dependence on Ram's grace. For example, in his *Vinay Patrikā,* Tulsidas writes that he was abandoned by his parents at birth due to an inauspicious astrological configuration ordained by Brahma, the Creator. He further states that he begged from door to door and was in such a sorry condition that he even caused pain to pain itself.[17] In the opening lines of the *Mānas,* Tulsidas mentions the name of Narhari in what appears to be a reference to his spiritual (and possibly adopted) father.[18]

Most of the information on the life of the poet comes from a variety of sources dating back to the seventeenth and eighteenth centuries.[19] The earliest of these texts, the *Bhaktamāl* (1624) of Nabhadas, contains only a six-line stanza on Tulsidas, in which he is said to be an incarnation of Valmiki who was reborn in Kali Yug, the age of darkness, to retell the story of Ram, to proclaim the power of *Ramnam,* and thus to aid in the salvation of countless souls.[20] That Nabhadas wrote these lines when he supported a commonly held theory that the *Mānas* had become a popular, as well as controversial text even before Tulsidas died. Nearly a century later, Priyadas wrote a commentary on much of the *Bhaktamāl.* Its forty-four verses on events in the life of Tulsidas contain many of the episodes in the currently popular hagiography of Tulsidas, including several miracles, one of which shows the superior power of *Ramnam* vis-à-vis the brahmanical religion.[21] Both the *Bhaktamāl* and Priyadas's commentary are popular among Ram devotees in North India; they are held to be true accounts.

The *Gautam Candrikā,* purportedly written in 1624 by Krishnadatta Miśra, a contemporary of Tulsidas, gives 1543 as the year of the poet's birth. The author claims to have met Tulsidas in Kashi (Varanasi) and tells of a group of devotees closely associated with him. Tulsidas's following was composed primarily of low castes, outcastes, and even "Mir, the Muslim minstrel."[22] The *Gautam Candrikā* gives 1623 as the year of Tulsidas's death and cremation on the banks of the Ganges river in Kashi.[23]

It is difficult to know exactly how much Tulsidas actually wrote, since his popularity seems to have resulted in writings by other authors being attributed to him. Grierson was the first Western scholar who attempted to distinguish the authentic writings of Tulsidas from among the various works attributed to him. These efforts were continued by W. D. P. Hill and F. R. Allchin, resulting in a list of writings generally attributed to the poet.[24] The most commonly accepted chronology and dating of these works is listed below:

Gyān Dīpakā	1564
Rāmāgyā Praśnāvalī	1564 (1598)
Rāmlalā Nahachū	(no date)
Vairāgya Sandīpinī	(no date)
Jānakī Mangal	(no date)
Rāmcaritmānas	1574 (date given by text itself)
Pārvatī Mangal	1586 (date given by text itself)

Gītāvalī	(no date)
Vinay Patrikā	post-1616
Kavitāvalī	post-1616

Hill and Allchin[25] add four other works to this list, the authorship of which is more frequently questioned by scholars:

Rām Satsaī	1585
Kṛṣṇa Gītāvalī	pre-1605
Hanumān Bāhuk	post-1616
Dohāvalī	post-1616

There is a story commonly repeated by North Indian Ram devotees regarding the life of Tulsidas and the spiritual power of the *Mānas*. The incident was originally recorded by Benimadhavdas, a disciple of Tulsidas, in his *Mūl Gosāīṅ Caritra,* and it supports Tulsidas' own claim, found throughout his writings, that the *Mānas* was of sacred origin.

According to the legend, after Tulsidas wrote his work the *brahman* priests of Kashi were furious that the story of Ram had been written in a vernacular language instead of Sanskrit. They criticized his work as a debasement of the holy scriptures.[26] Subsequently, Tulsidas took the *Mānas* to the main Shiva temple in Varanasi where a test of its validity was devised by a respected Sanskrit scholar of the temple. That night the book was placed before the main image in the temple. On top of it were placed the Shastras, eighteen Puranas, Upanishads, and, lastly, the four Vedic Samhitas. The temple was then locked for the night, and when it was re-opened in the morning, the *Mānas* was found on top of the pile. Immediately, Tulsidas was hailed by all present and recognized for his work.

Consistent with the *Ramkatha* tradition, the *Mānas* is an original work that constitutes a unique retelling of the Ram story. By the time Tulsidas wrote his famous epic, a Ram *bhakti* movement had become established throughout much of North India, and there were numerous versions of the Ram story from which to draw inspiration and ideas. In addition, Tulsidas's work shows a knowledge of assorted Puranas, Upanishads, and various philosophical treatises. Of all these texts, however, the *Adhyātma Rāmāyaṇa* seems to have had the greatest influence on Tulsidas's work. Much of the theology that he incorporated into his presentation of the Ram story can be traced to this earlier text. Both versions are presented as a dialogue between Shiva and Parvati, but Tulsidas greatly expands the role of Shiva, to whom he also reveals a strong devotion.

There has long been a controversy among scholars, Ram devotees, and other North Indians concerning the social views of Tulsidas. Several currents appear to flow within the text. On the one hand, the text contains numerous statements emphasizing the supremacy of *bhakti* over brahmanical *dharma* and the limited value of social duty in the face of devotion. The text's praise of low-caste individuals such as Guha and Shabari, its denunciations of caste as a factor in Ram *bhakti,* and the omission of most of the events supporting the orthodox value system that are found in the *Uttarakāṇḍa* sections of both Valmiki *Rāmāyaṇa* and the *Adhyātma Rāmāyaṇa* all suggest that Tulsidas cared little for the rigid regulations of *varnashrama-dharma.* In addition, none of the other writings attributed to him contain pro-*brahman* or pro-caste statements. Finally, his hagiography portrays him in close association with the low castes.

On the other hand, the *Mānas* contains frequent references to the importance of *brahmans*. Ram is called the "protector of Vedic boundaries" who is busy maintaining them.[27] His devotees "endure suffering for the sake of *brahmans* and cows" and give *brahmans* food and numerous gifts.[28] Such statements have led many people to speak against Tulsidas and his *Mānas,* calling him a tool of the religious elite. The emotions generated have been intense. In the 1980s, a member of the Uttar Pradesh Legislature publicly tore pages out of the *Mānas* to protest a particular verse belittling women and *shudras*. However, several factors presently restrict our ability to evaluate Tulsidas's actual social teachings, some of which will be addressed at the end of this chapter.

Edmour J. Babineau isolates three religious currents that were present in Hindu India during the time of Tulsidas: (1) Vedic orthodoxy (2) antinomian theism, and (3) orthodox theism. The first stream encompasses the religious beliefs and practices that support the brahmanical value system. The second stream is that form of *bhakti* in which God takes precedence over everything else and is viewed as an end in itself. The traditional laws of *dharma* are seen as secondary and may at times be disregarded in the name of *bhakti*. The ideal of antinomian theism is said to be represented by Krishna's *gopis,* as depicted in the *Bhāgavata Purāṇa,* who dismiss the world of taboos and Vedic injunctions and forsake their familial and social duties for the sake of devotion to Krishna. The medieval Sant movement, and especially Kabir, advanced this stream of devotion and brought it close to Tulsidas, both temporally and geographically.[29]

The third stream, orthodox theism, provides a middle ground between Vedic orthodoxy and antinomian theism. The exponents of orthodox theism uphold the value of brahmanical concepts of *dharma* while giving a central place to *bhakti* as the supreme path to salvation. This perspective is best represented by the *Bhāgavad Gītā* and also the Valmiki *Rāmāyaṇa,* both of which seek to reconcile the claims of *dharma* and *bhakti* by emphasizing the importance of fulfilling one's duty in accordance with the orthodox values, while surrendering the fruits of one's actions in devotion to the Lord.[30]

From the opening verses of the *Mānas,* it is apparent that the text seeks to give itself Vedic authority. It begins with propitiation of the major Hindu deities, followed by a verse in which Tulsidas aligns his work with various Puranas, the Vedas, and the Tantra Shastras, as well as Valmiki *Rāmāyaṇa* and other writings.[31] Many post-Vedic writings adopt a similar pattern. Friedhelm Hardy suggests that when such works seek to legitimize themselves in the context of the brahmanical tradition, thereby showing acceptance of the Vedas as authoritative, it is usually done in a purely formal sense for the purpose of social cohesion and has little to do with the text's own ideology.[32] This is especially the case with vernacular devotional writings whose goals have little in common with those of the Vedas.

The *Mānas* clearly recognizes Vedic affiliation when it is beneficial. In several places the Vedas are invoked to validate the beliefs advanced. At the same time, Tulsidas shows a willingness to challenge these beliefs, both in the *Mānas* as well as in his other writings. In the *Vinay Patrikā,* for example, he rejects any existing value in the Vedic tradition, saying that in Kali Yug all religious practices, such as non-attachment, Vedic sacrifices, yog, austerities, and renunciation are worthless. Only *Ramnam* works. He then adds,

> *Ramnam* is the wish-fulfilling tree that grants the four fruits of life,
> So say the Purāṇas, Vedas, pundits, and Śiva.[33]

In the *Mānas,* Tulsidas implies that his text has the power of Vedic *mantras.* He ends sections dealing with important events, as well as each chapter, with a *phalashruti,* which claims that repetition of the preceding verse will grant blessings and even liberation. This is a common practice in various Puranas and subsequent works. Typical is the *doha* verse at the end of the *Mānas* book entitled *Sundarkāṇḍ:*

> Recitation of the virtues of Raghunayak [Ram] grants all blessings. He who reverently listens to them crosses the ocean of worldly existence (gains liberation) without the need for a boat.[34]

Among the greatest contributions that Tulsidas has made to the development of Ram *bhakti* are found in his treatment of the *nirgun/sagun* dichotomy with respect to his portrayal of Ram and in his depiction of the name of Ram and its supreme power. Tulsidas directly addresses the problem of the impersonal versus personal aspects of Ram's nature by bringing them together under the rubric of the *nirgun* and *sagun* aspects of Brahman. For Tulsidas, Ram's status as an *avatar* is clearly subordinate to his status as Brahman, the formless absolute, which is actually believed to transcend both form and formlessness. At various times Tulsidas shows a preference for one aspect over the other, as in the following verse, in which Indra praises Ram's *sagun* nature:

> Some meditate on *nirgun* Brahman,
> whom the Vedas call unmanifest.
> My heart is drawn to *sagun* Ram,
> In the form of Kosal's king.[35]

In other verses, Tulsidas emphasizes the superiority of the *nirgun* dimension, which transcends all duality and all conception. Tulsidas ultimately seeks to show that Ram has multiple realities, all of which are tied together in a complex theological paradigm. The following verse is commonly repeated by members of the Ramananda order in North India today. While it is not attributed to Tulsidas, it nevertheless succinctly delineates the levels of his multivalent theology:

> One Ram is Dasarath's son.
> One Ram ever resides within.
> One Ram is the object of devotion.
> One Ram lies beyond all comprehension.[36]

On the first level, Ram is an *avatar* of Vishnu. On the next level, he is the indwelling spirit, the *atma* that resides in the heart of each individual. On the third level, Ram is identified as *ishvar,* the personal God who is the object of devotion. Here he may be viewed as Vishnu, who incarnates in various forms, or as *sagun* Brahman, the source of Brahma, Vishnu, and Shiva. On the final level, he is *nirgun* Brahman, transcending all distinctions and dualities. In *Uttarakāṇḍ* of the *Mānas,* Kakbhusundi, the crow, describes Ram's greatness in a dialogue in which all of the above aspects of his nature are mentioned:

> Ram is existence, consciousness and bliss,
> Unborn, wisdom incarnate, abode of all strength.
> Pervading and pervaded, infinite and eternal,
> Whole and perfect Lord of unfailing power.
> Formless, spotless, immortal, imperceptible,
> All-seeing, flawless, and invincible. . . .
> Untouched by matter but lives in every heart,
> Desireless Brahman, dispassionate and endless.[37]

Tulsidas presents one of the most innovative aspects of his philosophy with reference to *Ramnam.* He no doubt received great inspiration from various texts as well as from Kabir in developing his views of the name, but he goes beyond those earlier views. Moreover, several of Kabir's statements on the nature of human birth and the importance of *bhakti* are reiterated by Tulsidas, sometimes in almost the same words.[38] Differences become apparent in looking at the view each expresses regarding *Ramnam.* While Kabir sees real value in *Ramnam* only if it is practiced with devotion, Tulsidas rejects this view, seeing immense power in the name regardless of how or why it is repeated.

In nearly fifty verses following the opening invocations in *Bālkāṇḍ,* Tulsidas expounds on the greatness and power of *Ramnam.* He often juxtaposes it with the incarnate form of Ram, saying that the name is superior. For example, he gives the names of two women whom the incarnate Ram liberated and then asserts that the name, in contrast, has destroyed the sins of millions of devotees.

The incarnate Ram gave immortality to a few devoted servants, while his name has saved countless beings. It is by means of *Ramnam* that Shiva liberates souls who die at Kashi.[39]

In much of this section of the *Mānas,* the name is given the status of *sagun* Brahman. It is "the essence of Brahma, Vishnu, and Shiva," the "sustainer of the universe," and the protector of humanity. It is the object of "supreme affection" and it "grants liberation." The name is said to dispel the ignorance of all those who have faith in it.[40] On the other hand, Tulsidas describes the name as *nirgun,* calling it "beginning less," "eternal," "unqualified and unequal," and "indescribable."[41] Ultimately, he reveals his belief that the name is even superior to *nirgun* Ram:

> *Nirgun* and *sagun* are two forms of Brahman,
> unspoken, unknown, without end or comparison.
> I believe the Name is greater than the two,
> By its strength it has subdued them both.[42]

Tulsidas ends this section of praise of the name by asserting that the power of *Ramnam* is not based on the intentions of the reciter. Reciting the name transcends any such limitations. Whether repeated for good or evil, or even while yawning, it spreads auspiciousness in all directions.[43]

In his later writings, Tulsidas continues to express his devotion to *Ramnam,* and it becomes the major focus of much of his later poetry. His praise and use of the name have helped to elevate it to one of the primary forms of religious practice for the masses of North India. "Ram" is one of the most frequent names given to young boys, in one form or another. *"Ram Ram"* is a common greeting throughout village North India, even in Braj, the land of Krishna *bhakti*. It is a common chant in most Vaishnav temples and many Shaivite ones as well. The last thing heard as dead bodies are carried to the funeral pyre is *"Rāmnām satya hai"* (The name of Ram is truth). Mahatma Gandhi used to prescribe the chanting of *Ramnam* as a part of the remedies he would give to those who were ill and said that if everyone would chant *Ramnam* the riots of his time would end. He called it the essence of all prayers, superior even to Sanskrit *shlokas*.[44] The name of Ram was such an integral part of his thoughts that his last words after being shot were, *"He Rām, he Rām."*[45]

Lutgendorf argues that the *Mānas* has undergone a process of vedacization over the last century in North India and that this process may ultimately diminish the vitality of the text and place it in the category of the Vedas, "in the world beyond change and aspiration."[46] The focus of his field research has been urban North India, especially Varanasi, where the brahmanical orthodoxy has, to a large extent, appropriated the public ritual recitation of the *Mānas,* and, in that social and religious environment, his observations seem quite accurate. In rural India, on the other hand, the situation is vastly different from that of the cities.

People of all castes view the *Mānas* as their own religious text. It is read, memorized, and chanted by *brahman* and *bhangi* (sweeper) alike. Moreover, as will be shown in the following chapters, in the life of groups such as the Ramnamis, the *Mānas* is itself being transformed in the process, continuing the tradition of change that has been integral in the evolution of the story.

Raghunathdas and the *Vishrām Sāgar*

During the middle part of the nineteenth century, a somewhat antinomian caste Hindu Ram *bhakti* movement arose in the north; its followers were known as the Ramsnehis (lovers of Ram). They were initially centered in the Gangetic plain and eventually spread into Central India. Small in numbers but still in existence, the Ramsnehis adhere to a *nirgun* Ram *bhakti* philosophy similar to that of Kabir. Among the early teachers of the sect was an poet/ascetic named Raghunathdas, and his *Vishrām Sāgar* is one of the only surviving texts of the group from that time period. However, its use by the Ramnamis gives it relevance here.

The *Vishrām Sāgar* has three major sections, entitled "*Itihāsāyan,*" *"Rāmāyaṇ," and "Kṛṣṇāyan."* The first section contains nearly fifteen pages in praise of *Ramnam*. Its style and sentiment reflect that which is found in the early pages of the *Mānas* where the exclusive focus is on praise of the name. The "*Rāmāyaṇ"* section is divided up into seven chapters with the same titles as those of the *Mānas* and following the same basic story lines, but with significant divergences in the narrative. Here, Raghunathdas uses his creativity to present Ram and Ram *bhakti* from the viewpoint of the Ramsnehis. The main difference between this text and the *Mānas* is that the former tends to follow more strictly the *nirgun* approach to Ram. The last section, *"Kṛṣṇāyan,"* uses expresses the same devotional sentiment to Krishna. Here *sagun bhakti* is the dominant theology found, as is nearly always the case with respect to Krishna.

Over the years, the text has found a limited following with Ram devotees other than the Ramsnehis, primarily in the north and central regions of India. As Ram *bhakti* has increased in popularity over the last several generations, so has almost any text that contains devotional writings to Ram. Thus, although the *Vishrām Sāgar*'s greatest audience remains the Ramsnehis, an increasing number of Chhattisgarhi Ram devotees have included it as a regular part of their study and reading. For the Ramnamis, it has become a vehicle to provide them with another dimension in their broadening conceptualization of the Ram story.

Chapter 4

Religion and the Low Caste in Central India

The Brahman is the guru of the world,
but he is not the guru of the devotees—
He got entangled in his four Vedas,
and there he died.
—Kabīr Granthāvalī, *The Sants*

In looking for those movements that had found fertile ground in the relatively barren and economically depressed region of Central India prior to the formation of the Ramnamis, traces of and reference to many can be ascertained. Some arose only to die away within a few generations, while others were able to survive and thrive beyond the initial stimulus and nurturing of their charismatic founders. Two of the continuing groups whose early presence in Chhattisgarh show their indelible imprint on the growth of the Ramnami movement are the Kabirpanth and Satnami sects. A brief discussion of these is meant to help provide the reader with the contextual tools for viewing the emergence, direction, and success of the Ramnami Samaj.

The Kabirpanth in Chhattisgarh

The discussion in the last chapter of Kabir and his theological interpretation of Ram and use of *Ramnam* shows the impact he and others in the Sant tradition have had in the popularization of *nirgun nam bhakti* in North India. The beliefs and teachings of Kabir also had a more direct effect on the Untouchables of Central India in the form of the Chhattisgarh *sakha,* or branch, of the Kabirpanth. Although tradition names Dharamdas, a close disciple of Kabir, as its founder, it is Kabir who is actually credited with establishing the Central Indian branch for his followers in the region.

According to his hagiography, Dharamdas (originally named Judawan) was born to a *vaishya* family in the village of Bandogarh, Jabalpur District, M.P. He first met Kabir while on a visit to Banaras, then again in Brindaban. He did not become a disciple, however, until Kabir visited his home and convinced him

A respected elder, this Ramnami is one of the relative few women who choose to wear a *mukut*.

This picture was taken in 1982 of a Ramnami family. The boy was one of the last of the Ramnami children to be tatooed at the age of two.

of the futility of pilgrimages and image worship. Dharamdas's first son, Narayandas, refused to accept Kabir as his guru, but his second son, Churaman, became a disciple and was eventually named head of the Chhattisgarh branch by Kabir himself. Churaman, then, is considered to be the first head of this *sakha,* although it is named after his father, Dharamdas. It is said that Kabir instituted the rule that only Dharamdas's descendants should have the right to give the initiation *mantra* and to be *mahant*s (heads) of the order.[1] Unbroken adherence to this rule is observed up to present day.

Over the centuries, the Dharamdas branch of the Kabirpanth attracted such a large following that by the beginning of the twentieth century, nearly 60 percent of the *panth* membership resided in the Central Provinces (now Madhya Pradesh and Chhattisgarh).[2] While this branch and the one in Kabir's birthplace, Banaras, are assuredly the main branches, David N. Lorenzen contends that the Kabirpanthi's own tradition recognizes four distinct branches of the sect, each following a main disciple of Kabir. Besides the two centers listed above, Lorenzen gives the names of two in Bihar, one at Bidupur in Muzaffarpur District and the other at Dhanauti in Chapra District.[3]

Currently, as in the past, the *panth* draws its following from two main groups: low-caste Hindus and tribal peoples. According to Lorenzen:

> In both cases membership in the *panth* embodies an element of social protest against the hierarchical structure of the Hindu socioreligious order at the same time that it represents a general acceptance of the hegemony of that same order.[4]

The Banaras and Chhattisgarh *sakha*s have each reinterpreted the teachings of Kabir in response to the specific Hindu environment in which they exist. Having evolved in different socioreligious milieu, they have developed along somewhat different philosophical and sociocultural lines as well. Banaras has long been known to be a center for orthodox brahmanical beliefs but has also given birth to its share of anti-brahmanical sentiments, such as those expressed by Kabir. The most prevalent value system there, however, has been and remains brahmanical. Thus, most peripheral religious movements that have arisen in Banaras have subsequently either died away or gradually become brahmanized, the latter being the case with the Banarsi Kabirpanthis.

In the Banaras branch of the sect, centered at the site said to be Kabir's home, adherence to caste restrictions slowly became an established part of its belief system. The order, although formally accepting all people, began restricting the active participation of *harijan*s. Recent research on the Kabirpanthis by Lorenzen shows that this trend has continued. Upper-caste sect members wear a sacred thread and *tulsi* beads, accoutrements suggestive both of upper-caste status and ritual purity within the broader Hindu tradition. At the same time, few *harijan*s are allowed to become initiated members of the sect and to live in the monastery. The upper-caste members who dominate the ruling positions in the *panth* like to emphasize their Vaishnav Hindu orientation and the "clean" caste makeup of their order. In 1939 the Kabir Press, a *panth*-owned press, published a version of the *Bījak* with a Sanskrit commentary, clearly aimed at high-caste Hindus and likely meant to help sanskritize and legitimize the sect in the eyes of the orthodox.

In the Banaras center, high-caste *panth* members will not eat with lower-caste members except on rare, special occasions, such as the anniversary of the birth of Kabir. However, this brief caste mixing seems to be more of a formality than a demonstrated adherence to Kabir's rejection of caste bias. The reasons traditionally attached to commensality restrictions in India have been the fear of vegetarians being polluted by eating with non-vegetarians. Yet, because all Kabirpanthis are said to be vegetarian and to follow its strict purity rules, this separation in the *panth* suggests little more than the perpetuation of the existing caste prejudices and a desire for high caste acknowledgment and acceptance. Intercaste marriages, even within the sect, are also strictly prohibited. Although ascetic groups in India tend to be more liberal in their interpretation of caste rules and restrictions, the Kabirpanth ascetic wing has been primarily responsible for the degree of sanskritization and caste discrimination that has taken place.

The Dharamdas *sakha* in Chhattisgarh, on the other hand, has resisted the adoption of caste rules to the degree found in Banaras. Moreover, since its genesis it has had a large percentage of *harijan*s as members.[5] It has therefore been more accepting of the low castes and their culture in the region. This fact appears to be one of the fundamental causes of the strain in relations between these two dominant branches of the sect, resulting in very little actual association. In Chhattisgarh, there is also much more interaction between the monastic and lay groups of the sect than is the case in Banaras. The central Indian *panth* has two rival factions, centered at the *panth*'s Damakheda and Kawardha monasteries. Each site claims to be the valid seat of authority for the region. Currently, the former tends to attract more caste Hindus than the latter. It also contends that most of its early initiates were of the *kshatriya* caste, and many of its current members claim the same caste status. The majority of *panthi*s attached to the Damakheda monastery actually come from various *low*-caste groups. The heads of the Kawardha monastery, on the other hand, claim to be direct descendants of Dharamdas.[6] There are close to a dozen smaller monasteries located throughout the region, and these tend to attract primarily *harijan* followers. H. L. Shukla claims that all the members of the Chhattisgarhi village watchman subcaste, the *panka,* belong to the sect, as do many members of other low-caste groups, such as *ganda*s, *taili*s, *marar*s, and *kunbi*.[7]

Sect members in Chhattisgarh are referred to as "*Kabirpanthi*" in Hindi, but as *"Kabirha"* in the local dialect. They are spread throughout the region, although their membership is found in the greatest numbers in the northwestern portions.

The sect has had and continues to have a great deal of influence on the *satnamis* there. Between the different caste groups represented in the membership, caste restrictions on marriage and commensality are strictly observed.

In accordance with the rules of the Chhattisgarh *sakha,* each *mahant,* or sect head, lives with his wife as a householder until the birth of a son. At that time his wife is to become a celibate member of the sect, and the *mahant* is to remain in office for twenty-five years and twenty days, after which time he is succeeded by his son.[8] The celibate teachers in the sect, called "*bairagis*," can be drawn from any caste and many of them are *satnami.* In Banaras, women play a minimal role in the functioning of the order; in Chhattisgarh, however, they can take a somewhat more active role, and there are an increasing number of female Kabirpanthi gurus in the region, mostly attached to the smaller monasteries. Unlike the male teachers, their female counterparts are nearly all single, either having been widowed or never having been married.

Despite the degree of sanskritization the Dharamdas *sakha* has undergone, it stands for many in the region as a symbol of the rejection of brahmanical values and authority. Because of the participation by many different castes in the *panth,* most Chhattisgarhi low castes view the sect as providing a vehicle for religious involvement that crosses the immense chasm between touchable and Untouchable. It was the first surviving religious movement in the area to openly court low-caste Hindus and offer them the possibility of a religious life with Hindu devotional trappings but without intense brahmanical restrictions. Even though the sect has moved closer to the orthodox value system, it has still left its door open for *harijan* participation. Lorenzen proposes that instead of leaving its element of social protest, the *panth* has simply "modified and institutionalized" it to better serve the changing needs of its members.[9]

The primary scripture for the *panthi*'s in Central India is the *Bījak*. It is generally highly revered by all factions, and some even worship its physical presence, much the way the *Ādi Granth* is venerated by the Sikhs. There are also several more recent works, including the *Kabir Manśūr, Kabir Sāgar, Gyān Prakāś,* and the *Anurāg Sāgar,* that have become popular with literate members. Most of these are of unknown origin, although it has become common to attribute them to Kabir. The *Anurāg Sāgar* is written in the form of a dialogue between Kabir and Dharamdas and legitimizes the Chhattisgarhi *sakha* in the eyes of its followers.

The sect's present relationship with *nirgun bhakti,* with the Ram story, and with *Ramnam* is a complex one. While Kabir rejects completely the *sagun* form of *bhakti* and sees *Ramnam* as the most powerful means of union with *nirgun* Brahman, both beliefs have gone through adjustments in the evolution of the *panth.* In the main temple of the Banaras *sakha,* the *puja* (religious rituals) that are performed twice daily closely resembles brahmanical Hindu temple worship. A pair of *kharaun* (wooden sandals), representing the feet of Kabir, is the focus of much devotion there. During the daily *puja,* the *kharaun* are washed and the water is then used as sacred water, given out to the devotees who are present.[10] Because of its strong adoption of caste ideology and many of the ritual trappings of orthodox Hindu devotionalism, in many ways the Banaras *panth* has simply become another Vaishnav sect. The Chhattisgarh *sakha* also has a *math* (religious center) in Banaras. As in the main *sakha*'s temple there, an image of Kabir is the object of worship, and the rituals performed parallel those done in most Hindu temples.[11] In Chhattisgarh itself, however, there is a general rejection of *sagun bhakti* among the followers, although the heads of both factions are revered almost to the point of worship.

In the Banaras branch, the more learned *mahant*s study a variety of Hindu texts, including the *Mānas* and the *Gītā*. In the discourses given at the *math,* references are made to the *Mānas* and occasionally its verses are quoted. *Ramnam* is practiced by some members, although chanting Kabir *bhajan*s is given more emphasis. In Chhattisgarh, the situation is quite different. Rarely is the *Mānas* mentioned, the overwhelming focus being on the *Bījak* and the *Anurāg Sāgar.* The practice of *Ramnam* is conspicuous by its absence. Even G. H. Westcott, who studied the Kabirpanthis in the early 1900s, writes nothing of the practice of *Ramnam* by the sect. The only *mantra* used by the Chhattisgarhi *panthi*s to which he refers is the *satnam mantra (Satyanam)*.[12] Even in R. V. Russell's study of the Central Provinces, done a decade later, there is no mention of the practice. Instead, Russell writes that the *panthi*s of the region occasionally chant *"Sat Sahib"* (lit. True Master) as a short morning prayer.[13]

While no one has yet pointed to any evidence explaining the apparently early rejection of the practice of *Ramnam* by the Chhattisgarhi *sakha,* in contemporary times, it seems to be the desire on the part of the *panth* to distance itself from the practice or people with whom *Ramnam* is most identified in the region, namely, the Ramnamis. Morover, the Ramnami Samaj has become so associated with the chanting of *Ramnam* that throughout the region people tend to connect the chanting of *Ramnam* with the Ramnamis. This clearly frustrates many Kabirpanthis who, in the process of sanskritizing themselves, have tried to place as much social and religious distance as possible between their sect and the Ramnamis. This is because the *panthi*s see the Ramnami's refusal to sanskritize and adopt caste-Hindu practices as harmful to Kabirpanthi attempts to alter the status of the *harijan*s of the region. In discussing the teachings of Kabir with me, and the lack of *Ramnam* chanting by her sect, one of the more popular Kabirpanthi teachers in Bilaspur District, a *satnami* by caste, lamented in quite a frustrated tone, "The Ramnamis do not use *Ramnam,* they ruin it!"[14]

The Satnamis

Kabir not only inspired the movement that carries his name, the Kabirpanth, but through his disciples and his teachings he indirectly inspired a variety of other *nirgun bhakti* movements in North India. A common feature of these, at least in their early years, was a rejection of key aspects of the brahmanical value system, especially its attitude toward the low castes. The Chhattisgarhi Satnami Samaj has its historical as well as ideological roots in several such groups.

Prior to the present-day Satnamis,[15] two previous movements of the same name existed, both centered in Uttar Pradesh. Historical accounts of the first are scant and contradictory. Ahmad Shah's contention that it was founded by a direct disciple of Kabir named Jivandas would likely put its genesis in the sixteenth century.[16] P. D. Barthwal claims it was begun in the seventeenth century by Jagjivandas, a disciple of Dadu Dayal (1544–1603), however, this may actually be a reference to the latter revival of the sect.[17] Saurabh Dube refers to another sect in the eighteenth and nineteenth centuries, named Sadh. This group's beliefs and practices, as well as their reference to the divine as "Satnam," suggest them as a likely precursor to the present-day Satnamis.[18] George W. Briggs sees the roots of the Chhattisgarhi Satnamis in the teachings of Kabir.[19] The name "Satnami" also has antecedents in the *nirgun bhakti* tradition. In several of his poems, Kabir refers to God's name as *"sat nam"* or *"satya nam,"* both of which can be translated as "true name." The term is also found in the important *mul mantra* of Guru Nanak's Sikh movement (*Ek onkār satnām . . .*).

Little is actually known of this first Satnami movement. Members apparently followed the path of *nirgun bhakti* and may have been involved in ascetic or tantric practices.[20] By the late seventeenth century, a large faction of the sect was made up of Hindu peasants in the Punjab, living under the growing social and religious oppression of Aurangzeb, the Mughal ruler of the time. His chroniclers indicate that Satnami membership included "gold smiths, carpenters, sweepers, tanners and other ignoble beings."[21] Apparently, as a result of the increasing tax burden placed upon them, the sect took a stand against Aurangzeb in 1672 and was subsequently obliterated in a violent confrontation with his vast army.

Two years before the massacre, another Jagjivandas (1669–1760) was born in Uttar Pradesh.[22] From an early age he was said to have had spiritual inclinations. Tradition assigns either Vishveshvar Puri from Banaras, or Yari Saheb, a North Indian Sufi, as his guru. Jagjivandas's first inspiration on the spiritual path is believed to have come from two disciples of Yari Saheb, Bulla and Govind. To commemorate his meeting with the two, his followers wore a black (or blue) and white thread *(andu)* on their wrists.[23] Although he was from an upper-caste family, he fought for the religious freedom of the oppressed classes, propagating his beliefs among the Untouchables of northeastern Uttar Pradesh.[24] It is said that while the majority of his followers were high-caste Hindus, he reportedly had Muslim, low caste, and Untouchable disciples, as well.[25] Possibly inspired by the earlier movement, he encouraged his followers to chant *"satya nam,"* and they also came to be called "Satnamis." The philosophy of the sect was an eclectic combination of Vedanta, Sufi mysticism, and *bhakti*. While sect adherents rejected the worship of idols, they practiced devotion to Ram and Hanuman.[26] According to N. N. Bhattacharya, both Jagjivandas and his guru, Yari Saheb, were part of a Sufi lineage started by Baori Saheb of Delhi. Bhattacharya also reports that the writings of Yari Saheb, in the Avadhi dialect of Hindi, equate Allah with Ram and Hari.[27] His works include the *Agh Binās, Gyān Prakāś, Mohāpralay,* and *Pratham Granth.*[28] One man who was either a part of the sect or at least inspired by this Satnami sect was Ghasidas, a Chhattisgarhi *chamar.*

In the 1820s, Ghasidas (1756–1850), an Untouchable from Girod, in Raipur District, founded the present-day Satnami movement, known locally as the Satnami Samaj or the Satnampanth. According to current hagiographic accounts, Ghasidas's birth took place on December 18, 1756, and from an early age, he reportedly had great yogic powers and divine insight. While still a child, he experienced both frustration and outrage at the apparent immobility inherent in the caste system. By the time Ghasidas was a teenager, he was already openly displaying his powers and wisdom. Episodes of miracles in which he saved friends from great calamities are recounted. Fearing the unusual behavior of their son, his parents arranged his marriage in hopes that married life would help make him "normal." It apparently worked for a short time. However, a permanent metamorphosis in his life was soon to begin.

There are several theories as to the primary sources of Ghasidas's inspiration and spiritual development. Reverend M. A. Sherring sees the teachings of Ravidas, an Untouchable disciple of Ramananda, as the major stimulus.[29] Others believe he was inspired by the social and religious teachings of Kabir, through the *panthi*s in Chhattisgarh. Most present-day Satnamis either deny or know nothing of a connection between Ghasidas and the previous Satnami movements in Uttar Pradesh. Instead, the current hagiography of Ghasidas says that when he was approximately eighteen years old, he and his brother set out on a pilgrimage to Jagannath in Puri, a temple in Orissa sacred to caste Hindus. He felt compelled to go there and express his defiance of orthodox restrictions by openly entering the temple. However, in Sarangarh, a town on the way, God appeared to him telling him not to waste his time traveling the distance to confront the ignorance and narrow-mindedness of those who worship inanimate temple idols while God's supreme reality is formless and active everywhere.[30] Ghasidas discontinued his journey and returned home, telling of his vision and praising the one God, whose name is Truth *(Sat).* He then retreated to the jungle near his village where he spent long periods of time in solitude and contemplation. He would visit the nearby villages and give talks, but few people listened to him in the early years. Some thought that he was possessed and an exorcism was attempted, without any effect. Villagers eventually began to visit him in the forest and hear his teachings, and thus his popularity grew. He would withdraw further into the woods for periods of seclusion, and after one such retreat he emerged with his teachings, saying that his direction, his goals, and the

Ultimate Truth had been revealed to him.[31] He proclaimed his revelation and began to preach that all men are created equal, regardless of their caste origins. Much of his original message was a reiteration of the teachings of many of the earlier Satnami movements mentioned above. This is especially true in the seven tenets to which both Jagjivandas and Ghasidas demanded their followers adhere.

Showing the influence of the Kabir and Sant tradition as well, Ghasidas's first and foremost rule was the worship of one true God, through the chanting of his name, "Satnam," and the abolition of any form of image worship. Because Untouchables were considered physically and spiritually unclean, they were prohibited from entering and praying in temples. Irrespective of its theological basis, this rejection of deity worship functioned to eliminate one of the major ritual situations in which untouchability and discrimination were strongest.

Second, Ghasidas demanded that all his Satnami followers abstain from eating flesh and consuming alcohol. Along with this was a prohibition against certain non-flesh foods that resemble flesh foods, such as eggplant (said to resemble the scrotum of a buffalo) and red foods, because of their blood-like color. Due to the influence of the Kabirpanthis and various Vaishnav movements in the region, such as the Ramsnehis and the Ramanandi *sadhus*, many of the low caste were probably already vegetarian. Nevertheless, most caste Hindus simply accept the often groundless assumption that all low castes are non-vegetarian. Thus, Ghasidas may have believed that the official alteration of his follower's dietary practices would help to serve notice of the pure diet of his followers to the caste Hindus in the region. Unfortunately, it does not seem to have influenced any substantial change in the negative view with which most caste Hindus of the region viewed them. Ironically, many high-caste Hindus, who consume both flesh and alcohol themselves, continue to use the Untouchable's supposed impure diet as one of the major rationales for discrimination against the latter.[32]

Third, Ghasidas made the use of brass utensils compulsory for his followers, many of whom no doubt had been using clay. For orthodox Hindus, only metal vessels are suitable for reuse in cooking and eating.[33] To them, clay pots, the only vessels many of the poor could afford in the days of Ghasidas, cannot be properly cleaned. Thus, their reuse pollutes the food cooked in and eaten from them. Once again, Ghasidas's rule was probably meant to help align Satnami practices with traditional Hindu views of purity.

Fourth, he asked his adherents to abstain from smoking or chewing tobacco. For centuries, tobacco use has been a pastime and addiction of the poor in general, not only Untouchables, and has long been considered a sign of a peasantry, unsophistication, and uncleanliness in the eyes of the upper caste, the urban, and the more affluent. The traditional form of smoking tobacco in the region is in a *chongi,* a type of pipe made from a large leaf, loosely rolled and bent upwards at the end. It is the traditional village equivalent to the *bidi,* the small hand-rolled cigarettes popular with the poor throughout the plains of India.

Fifth, Ghasidas beseeched his followers to cease working with leather and carcasses. The most widely used justification by caste Hindus for the Untouchable status of *chamars* has been the pollution of the latter's traditional, though seldom actual, profession. For centuries, the percentage of *chamars* who actually do such work has been extremely small; still all caste members have been looked down upon as equally polluted, irrespective of their actual occupation. For many generations in Chhattisgarh, it has been the *mahar* and the *ghasiya* castes, rather than the *chamars*, who generally work with carcasses and hides.

Sixth, Ghasidas forbade the use of cows for ploughing. Most poor farmers, who do not have oxen and often cannot afford to rent them, must use cows if they have any for ploughing and tilling the land. Because cows are accorded such a high status in Hindu culture, using them as beasts of burden is condemned. The practice of using cows in farming was not confined to the Untouchables but practiced by most poor farmers who had only cows and no oxen.

Seventh, Ghasidas told his followers to wear a necklace of beads made from *tulsi,* like those worn by Vaishnavs and Kabirpanthis. Wearing some form of necklace, called *"kanthi,"* is common in nearly every major Hindu sect. The Shaivite *kanthi* is made of *rudraksha* seeds, sacred to Shiva. The Vaishnavites wear *tulsi,* and goddess worshippers usually wear either lotus seed or red sandalwood necklaces. Only strict vegetarians are supposed to wear *tulsi kanthi,* so besides his closeness to Kabir, Ghasidas may have adopted the practice so that a Satnami's *tulsi kanthi* would help to proclaim his claim to purity.

In addition, Ghasidas encouraged his followers to use "Satnami" not only as their sect name but their caste affiliation as well (given herein as *satnami*). The negative connotations associated with the name *"chamar"* long ago turned it into a term of profanity used by many caste Hindus, much like the term "nigger" has been used by many non-black Americans. By officially separating his followers from a degraded livelihood, and by further attempting to disengage them from the pejorative connotations of *"chamar,"* Ghasidas again hoped to address and remove a major vehicle used by the caste-Hindu society for his caste community's social and religious ostracism and their status of untouchability.[34] In looking at India's history, one uncovers many low-caste and outcaste groups using the process of caste name change as a part of the process of attempting to elevate themselves in the social and religious hierarchy. Such a practice has seldom had much effect. Often, the results have been similar to what has happened in Madhya Pradesh and Chhattisgarh: most residents there simply see *"satnami"* as an alternate name for *"chamar."* It does seem to have some positive effect when *satnamis* move to a state or region unfamiliar with the connection of the two names. Then, such individuals have more of an opportunity to provide their own interpretation of the relative place of their caste in the hierarchy.

To imply that Ghasidas's only motive for these rules was social and religious acceptance by caste Hindus would be an unfair and improbable simplification of the man and his philosophy. Several of the above-mentioned rules resonate with the teachings attributed to many of the *nirgun bhakti* Sants. Further, Ghasidas must have had a strong belief in their validity and benefits on a personal level as well, since he must have realized that in the short run such outer changes would neither eliminate the stigma of untouchability nor raise the *chamars'* status in the eyes of orthodox Hindus. However, in the context of the Hindu social and religious traditions, the rules clearly indicate the direction Ghasidas sought for his movement. By sanskritizing it in the above manner, he strove to remove from his followers' lives many of the possible causes, enhancements, or justifications for caste prejudices and no doubt to effectuate some degree of acceptability for them in the conservative social environment of Chhattisgarhi villages.

Besides these dicta, little record exists of Ghasidas's teachings. He neither delved into philosophical controversies nor confronted classical religious questions. He did not even expand his particular theological concept of monotheism, for it seems his was more a rejection of deity worship than a developed theology. During the last two decades, however, some Satnamis have begun to record hagiographic accounts of the life of Ghasidas. Included in these are some philosophical elaborations as well.

While most caste Hindus ignored Ghasidas and his philosophy, Untouchables gradually became attracted by his teachings, his physical presence, and his powers. Stories abound of his miraculous healing abilities, including the resurrection of a devotee's just deceased family member. As an Untouchable, Ghasidas directed his teachings specifically to his own community, and he sought to elevate the status of those whom he felt caste Hinduism had spurned and abandoned. He stood firm against the injustice and discrimination that permeated the lives of the Untouchables but argued that the attitudes and life-styles of the low castes provided excuses for, and perpetuated prejudice against, them. In attempting to get out from under the socioreligious oppression of brahmanical Hinduism, many of Ghasidas's caste community had either come under their influence of the Christian missionaries who were active in Chhattisgarh at the time, or had converted to Islam. Seeking to stem such conversions, Ghasidas wanted to provide the low caste of the region with an alternative form of Hinduism, which he saw his movement to be.

Like Kabir, Ghasidas is said to have rejected not only image worship but also rituals in general. However, the Satnamis also found room in their developing tradition for borrowing a variety of rituals from caste Hinduism. In addition, there are a few rituals that are said to have a direct connection to the life of Ghasidas. One is the use of a tall wooden pole, or *stambha,* to mark a holy spot or the place of a Satnami festival. Tradition attributes the practice to Ghasidas's early days in the forest. His followers set up a large wooden pole near his forest hut to help newcomers find the path to him more easily. It later came to represent a type of spiritual lightning rod, and it is currently believed that wherever one is put up, it draws divine energy from the skies to help bless the festival and its participants.[35] Once the festival is over, the *stambha* no longer has a role and is eventually removed.

Another practice that developed quite early is the creation of a renunciant order, following closely the life of Ghasidas. The Satnami *sadhus* wear all white, as Ghasidas is said to have done, and they have added a large white turban to their dress. They say Ghasidas wore white because it signifies Truth, uncolored by the things of the world. The Kabirpanthi *sadhus*, who also wear all white, say that it is because their founding teacher did so. Both renunciant groups perform a variety of ascetic practices found in the Vaishnav ascetic orders and have little or no relation to the lives of either Kabir or Ghasidas. The Satnamis and Kabirpanthis also share a similar style of chanting, but it appears that both have simply adopted the local style. The chanting of both groups becomes quite energetic, and they use a variety of instruments, including a harmonium and a large *mridanga,* a drum popular in nearby Bengal. As will be discussed below, the use of the *stambha,* the adoption of a distinctive style of dress, and the practice of chanting all become reinterpreted in unique ways by the Ramnamis.

Although the Satnami sect theoretically has no temples or public rituals, Briggs found evidence of these in the sect during the early part of this century, and they are still evinced today. He said members also practiced devotion to both Ram and Krishna.[36] Recently, several Satnamis have said that Ghasidas was also a devotee of the *Mānas,* as were many of the Chhattisgarhi Untouchables of the region during his time. Although many Satnamis still continue to read and use the *Mānas,* the fact that it has become such a dominant text for the Ramnamis, and thus associated with them, it is avoided by the sect as a whole, in much the same way that the public practice of *Ramnam* has been largely ignored by the Kabirpanthis.

During his lifetime, Ghasidas's popularity extended beyond his own caste community, and many *tailis* (oil-pressers), the largest *shudra* subcaste in Chhattisgarh, became his disciples. He stressed unity among the poor and low caste and spoke against confrontation with high-caste Hindus. His following increased steadily, and by the time of his death in 1850, the great majority of Chhattisgarh *chamars* and a large number of caste Hindus considered themselves Satnami, either in practice or in spirit.[37] It is obvious from the formation and early development of the Satnami movement that Ghasidas sought to sanskritize his followers. He did not, however, attempt to claim a higher status within the caste structure for the sect; nor did he seek to stand apart from other *chamars.* On the contrary, he is said to have stressed the need for unity among all the low caste.

By the time of his death, his following was estimated to be nearly a quarter million, all but a few hundred being from the *chamar* caste.[38] According to the commonly held tradition, Ghasidas followed the example of the Chhattisgarhi Kabirpanth and stipulated that the lineage of gurus for the Satnami sect should follow the male line in his family.[39] His eldest son, Balakdas, who inherited the seat, signaled a marked departure in style from his father. He sought active confrontation with and antagonized *brahmans* and other high-caste Hindus, veering far from the path of peaceful co-existence taught by Ghasidas. He openly defied many of the restrictions against Untouchables and often disputed with caste Hindus. An example of Balakdas's contentious style is the way he adopted the practice of wearing a Hindu sacred thread, commonly called "*janeu.*" Traditionally worn only by upper-caste males who have gone through the requisite initiation, the thread denotes one's purity and qualifies one to partake in a *yagya,* or Vedic fire ritual. Balakdas embraced the practice of wearing a silk sacred thread, rather than the traditional cotton one, and he wore it over his shirt, in full view of all, instead of underneath his shirt, as is traditionally done. He also encouraged other Satnamis to do likewise. In the process, he not only made many enemies, but also frightened away many low caste from the movement who feared reprisals for his actions.

After several years of such attitudes and actions, Balakdas was assassinated in 1860. His son had a short reign but was without offspring and, upon his death, a power struggle ensued. One of Ghasidas's three other sons took over as guru. During this time, the Satnamis first began to claim a higher status for themselves in the caste hierarchy. With their life-style in strict accordance with the teachings of Ghasidas, many began to discriminate between themselves and other *chamars,* and some even denied their *chamar* origin, claiming to be *rajput* like the early Kabirpanthis of the region.

By the late 1800s a two-tiered organizational structure developed. At top sat the high priest, or guru, and below him a large number of village level priests, or minsters. These priests performed marriages, mediated disputes, meted out penance as well as acted as intermediaries in the organization. Since no unique or disparate religious ideology existed for the Satnamis, they became like a separate Hindu sect, functionally parallel to mainline Hinduism. Like the Kabirpanth, the sect adopted many caste-Hindu beliefs, rituals, and practices. To these they added their own set of Satnami priests, sacred places, rituals, and festivals. In his study of the popular religion of Central India, Lawrence Babb refers to the sect as "the rural variant of Hinduism practiced by most Chhattisgarhi villagers."[40] Although this is somewhat of an overstatement of the sect's present-day influence, it does accurately express the Satnamis' current relationship with Hinduism. It is not uncommon to find images of various Hindu deities on home altars, and in urban areas many attend and perform rituals at Hindu temples. Moreover, most sect members see themselves entirely within the context of Hinduism, and there continues to be a vocal element in the sect that deny their Untouchable status.

Nevertheless, the orthodox hierarchy has, since their respective inceptions, rejected both Satnamis and Kabirpanthis, seeing them as affronts to Hinduism. In an 1869 report to the Madhya Pradesh State Government, J. F. K. Hewitt describes his understanding of the prevalent caste Hindu perception of these groups:

> Chhutteesgarh to orthodox Hindoos is not only hateful as the land of the "Dasyus" and witches, but as the headquarter of religious dissent, as it is to its secluded wilds, that all those who opposed the prevailing tenets fled to escape from the persecutors, and consequently Hindooism sits lightly on most of the people, while large numbers are avowed dissenters belonging to the Kubeerpuntee and Sutnamee sects.[41]

At the same time, however, many British did not necessarily share those perceptions. In 1879, Sherring provides a different perspective of the low caste in the region, suggesting,

> As a people they are far superior to the depressed of Northern India, although doubtless of the same race. They are principally found in field-work, in which they display considerable energy and skill. Having discarded Brahmanical influence they have a priesthood of their own. Many of them are rich, and most live in comfort, while as a people they have the character of being the best subjects which the British Government has in those parts.[42]

During the latter part of the nineteenth century, the Indian struggle for independence gained momentum. Many regional religious and social groups became involved in the movement. Since one of the principal motivations for the Satnami movement was a desire to separate the Chhattisgarhi *chamars* from those areas of social and religious life in which they were looked down upon, the move into the political arena seems a natural step. Here, in theory at least, caste discrimination is less prevalent, and there is, therefore, an increased opportunity for Satnamis to experience a more socially horizontal relationship with caste Hindus. For the most part, urban Satnamis and those who had been able to gain some degree of economic independence supported the sect's political involvement. They saw it as a necessary step on the road to social and economic elevation. The sect encouraged a movement of its member's occupations into those that were traditional to caste Hindus and away from all "defiling" occupations.

Alteration of subcaste position with the structural hierarchy of caste has been a sociopolitical reality in India for nearly two millenia. With power and influence, almost anything is possible. Thus, as the Satnamis grew in size and influence within the existing political hierarchy of the Central Provinces, they began the process of seeking caste-Hindu status in order to secure legitimacy and acceptance in the caste-Hindu society. While many argued for recognition as *kshatriya,* the main objective seems to have been the traversing of the touchable/Untouchable chasm. From the late 1800s, there was also a concerted effort directed to getting an official name change from *"chamar"* to *"satnami."* Since the time of Ghasidas, many of his followers had begun to use *"satnami"* as their caste designation. In various government documents in the early 1900s, one finds reference to both *"satnami"* and *"chamar,"* or sometimes *"satnami-chamar,"* suggesting the sect was having some success, at least, in its attempt to alter its caste name.[43] Although unofficial, nearly all the Satnamis had begun using their sect name as their caste name as much as possible. At the same time, a struggle for power and control continued between two male descendants of Ghasidas. As the Indian freedom movement gained impetus in the 1920s and 1930s, the two factions took different sides in the conflict with the British. A few members of the bloc that supported the Indian National Congress and its Quit India movement had become politicians. In 1928, one of them, Naindas, was instrumental in convincing the state government to pass a law forbidding the labeling of anyone who does not do leather work as *"chamar."* At the same time, the official name of the caste in Chhattisgarh was changed to *"satnami."*[44] This brought a new popularity to the sect and increased its membership. With it, however, came even more fighting and a deeper rift between the two factions.

Agamdas was the head of the group that actively supported the nationalist movement, which was composed primarily of upper-caste Hindus. Muktavandas, whose faction controlled the sect headquarters in the village of Bhandar, sided more with the British and the local pro-British population, most of whom were low caste. After independence, Agamdas had the support of the Congress Party and was thereby elected representative to Parliament. His victory gave his Satnami faction new power and political clout and established its role in the politics of Chhattisgarh.

In many ways, the results of these events have made the Satnamis more of a sociopolitical movement than a religious one. Since that time, their festivals have become highly politicized and always attract politicians, especially from the Congress Party. During the last decade or so, a small but powerful group within the sect now denies its existence as a religious sect at all, claiming instead that it is simply a "touchable" Hindu subcaste that has its own religious practices. They claim that any past association of *satnamis* with *chamars* was based on inaccuracy, for they are two separate groups, each on a different side of the caste/outcaste abyss. They are caste Hindus who worship just like other Hindus, and their priests are *brahmans*. Moreover, according to the Census Report of 1911, some members claimed their caste to be *brahman.*[45] Such claims have had little or no success with the caste Hindus they are meant to influence. Moreover, many caste Hindus openly resent Satnami attempts at sanskritization and claims of such high-caste status. Those members of the group who make such claims have generally been few in number, but currently they are composed of many of the more educated Satnamis. With the political power that this group now has in the state, it may eventually be able to realize some of its claims.

There are, nevertheless, many Satnamis who still see themselves as a religious sect and continue to adhere closely to the teachings of Ghasidas as they understand them. However, they cannot deny the reality of the increasing role of politics and its effect on the direction of the sect, especially in the close bond that has been forged between the Satnamis and the Congress Party. In America today, religious groups that become politically active tend to associate themselves with political factions or parties for their ideological agreement or similarities on particular issues. This has not been the case with the predominantly Untouchable Satnamis and the Madhya Pradesh Congress Party, whose post-Independent leaders have been predominately *brahmans*. The two groups share little ideologically, but their relationship is nurtured by the benefits and power each gives the other. Moreover, for many of the Satnami leaders, ideological commitments and beliefs have taken a back seat to political pragmatism as a means to gain status, power, and recognition. In the process, the voices of those who want the Satnamis to return to their earlier spiritual roots are increasingly muffled by the ever-escalating clamor of those who demand social and political status. More and more, low castes who seek a vehicle for their religious expression are looking elsewhere. One such outlet available to them is the Ramnami Samaj.

The Ramnami Samaj and Its Historical Development

Since the time of Ghasidas, many Chhattisgarhi Untouchables have been inspired to reevaluate their generally unquestioned acceptance of the low social and religious position assigned them by the Hindu orthodoxy. Large numbers have aligned themselves with the Satnami sect; others have become Kabirpanthi, while some have turned to Christianity. In post-Independence India, still others have been attracted by an Ambedkar-inspired Untouchable Buddhist movement that has gathered a following in the region. Dr. B. R. Ambedkar was a popular Untouchable educator, leader, and statesman in the 1900s. A contemporary with Mahatma Gandhi, he was also a sharp critic of brahmanical Hinduism and the caste system. He vowed not to die a Hindu, and shortly before his death in 1956, he led a mass conversion in which nearly one million Untouchables converted to Buddhism. In the last two decades, missionaries of his movement have become a regular sight at religious festivals throughout Chhattisgarh. Long before Ambedkar-inspired Buddhists were active in the region, however, a poor village *chamar,* named Parasuram, had a life-changing experience that would significantly alter the religious dynamic, aspirations, and possibilities of many of his caste community there.[46]

There are several variants in the current oral hagiography of Parasuram, the founder of the Ramnami movement, as related by his followers. Since no written account of his life exists, I will present a general overview as related to me by various Ramnami elders, a few of whom knew Parasuram as children. It is significant and important to point out that very few Ramnamis actually know much about Parasuram. Rather than following the more common pattern of raising its founder to the level of superhuman, saint, or even deity, the sect essentially looks at Parasuram as an Untouchable villager, like them, who was blessed to become the first Ramnami. Actually, most members seem to evince only minimal interest in him, saying he was no doubt great, but then all who repeat *Ramnam* with faith and devotion are great. As will be shown below, this attitude reveals a deep-seated opposition to any type of religious hierarchy. It also points to the attitude with which Ramnamis generally approach many of their social and religious beliefs and practices.

Some Ramnamis like to portray Parasuram as a great saint, whose life was filled with miracles, although the majority tend to describe instead a simple but dedicated man whose life was devoted to Ram and to promoting equality for, and confidence in, his people. Ramnami elders tend to downplay most of the miracle stories, except those few which have given rise to prevalent sect practices. Instead, they present Parasuram as a villager who was blessed because of his intense devotion and who led a life that can be emulated by all of them as well. As one Ramnami put it, "Parasuram was a poor Chhattisgarhi villager, similar in many ways to us; therefore, we all have the capability and opportunity to become as great a *Ramnam* devotee as he was."[47]

Born in the mid-nineteenth century in the village of Charpara in eastern Chhattisgarh, Parasuram was *chamar* by caste. His family were poor illiterate farmers, as the great majority of Indian villagers are. His father was an ardent devotee of the various stories and tales found in the *Mānas* and the Puranic literature, but since he was illiterate, he memorized many of them, along with countless verses from Tulsidas's epic.[48] The young Parasuram was always captivated by the tales his father and other village elders would tell. As he grew older, he somehow gained rudimentary reading skills and would spend hours trying to read and understand the many stories in the *Mānas*.

Since he was an only child, from an early age Parasuram was obliged to work with his father as an agricultural laborer and to care for the home with his mother. In order to acquire another hand to assist with all the chores, his parents arranged and completed their son's marriage earlier than usual. Adolescent betrothal is a common practice among Chhattisgarhi *chamars,* and it is acceptable for such arrangements to take place for a child, anytime from infancy to puberty for a female, and up to early adulthood for a male. However, actual cohabitation, when the bride goes to live with her husband's family, is not supposed to take place until after the girl has reached puberty. However, in the case of Parasuram, their poor economic status and small family size led to his parents deciding to bring his wife to their home when she was but ten and he twelve years of age.

The only memorable elements of his life during the next twenty years was his increasingly high level of literacy and his sharp business acumen. Both of these helped him to become relatively well-off economically, in comparison to others of his caste community. Because of his ability to read *devanagari* script and his interest in the *Mānas,* he devoted much of his spare time to reading and memorizing from it, even though he did not have a good comprehension of the dialect in which the *Mānas* was written. As a consequence of his study, he was often called upon by members of his caste community to recite the text for them. Some even began to refer to him as *"pandit ji,"* a title traditionally afforded one of high religious understanding or intelligence.[49]

In his mid-thirties, Parasuram contracted a disease suspected by many to be leprosy. Coming to know this, other villagers began avoiding him and he them. Torn by his love and attachment for family and village and his fear of infecting them, he finally decided to leave home, renounce family life, and become a forest dweller until he was cured or he died. The morning before he was to depart, he sat alone by a small lake just outside his village. Lost in his thoughts he failed to notice the approach of a Ramanandi *sadhu,* who quietly sat down nearby. Startled, Parasuram warned the monk of his caste status and affliction and begged him to keep his distance. The *sadhu,* who called himself "Ramdev," simply smiled and replied that the only true disease is ignorance. All others are but its manifestations.

Deeply moved by the holy man, the villager asked for his blessings and guidance. They spoke for some time, and before departing, Ramdev promised to visit Parasuram's home that afternoon. Just as the sun began disappearing over the horizon, the *sadhu* appeared at the doorway of the small dwelling. As is the custom in the region for welcoming an honored or special guest, Parasuram's wife washed the feet of the monk and performed an *arti* ritual to him, then sprinkled the water around the house in order to purify it.[50] After some friendly conversation, the monk asked Parasuram to bring the family copy of the *Mānas* and instructed him emphatically, "This is your *ishtadev,* it will fulfill all your needs."[51] Ramdev assured the villager that Lord Ram was pleased with his devotion, and if his faith was deep enough, *Ramnam* would appear on his chest (or in his heart) during the night.[52] The monk spoke to the family for a short time on the greatness of *Ramnam* and of the *Mānas,* and Parasuram was so enamored of the presence of the *sadhu* and his words that he begged Ramdev to remain. The monk gazed at him silently, blessed the couple, then quickly rose and walked out. Although Parasuram attempted to follow, the *sadhu*'s gait was rapid and the visitor soon disappeared into the night. Parasuram returned crying and retired into a corner of his house where he spent the night sitting with his *ishtadev,* the *Mānas,* in his lap, repeating *Ramnam* incessantly.

The following morning, Parasuram rose, and as he took off his shirt he saw *("RamRam")* permanently imprinted on his chest. Believing that a miracle had taken place, he began to sing aloud joyously, *"Rāmanāma bhaju mana dina rātī"* (O heart, chant *Ramnam* day and night). As his family members gathered around him, they noticed not only the writing on his chest but also that his disease had disappeared. They, too, joined in singing, *"Rāmanāma bhaju mana dina rātī."*

Word of the miracle spread through the village and in no time a crowd surrounded and filled Parasuram's home. Soon, villagers from miles around were drawn by the event and came to witness, to take part in the *bhajan,* and to honor the villager who had received such great blessings. Oblivious to it all, Parasuram continued to chant *Ramnam*. For several days he remained immersed in this state, without sleeping or eating.

Eventually Parasuram returned to a normal awareness and began to talk with those who came to see him. He spoke of his experience and transformation, impressing upon them the importance of chanting *Ramnam* and reading or listening to the *Mānas*. Villagers began making regular visits to his home, and Parasuram began giving talks on the teachings of the *Mānas,* primarily those that centered on *nām*. Almost nightly, villagers gathered at his home for *Ramnam* chanting. Four of the more frequent visitors began to call him guru, and they became his first followers. To symbolize their devotion to Ram, *Ramnam,* and their new teacher, all four had *Ramnam* tattooed on their foreheads. Tattooing has long been a form of bodily adornment in Chhattisgarh but only practiced by tribals and poorer village women. Traditionally, non-tribal males in the region rarely ever had tattoos, and there is no record of a deity's name ever being a part of tattoo designs in the region.[53]

For the first several years, Parasuram's following remained small. They would spend their days doing their chores and would gather at night to do *bhajan* with Parasuram and listen to his telling of the Ram story. At this point, their understanding of, and devotion to Ram was still very much within the context of *sagun bhakti*. Moreover, there was even talk of setting up their own image of Ram near to Parasuram's home. As is still the case, Ramanandi *sadhus* frequented the region, and so the villagers asked the advice of several ascetics who were staying near their village at the time. The monks cautioned them that setting up an image would only lead to conflict with the caste Hindus in the area, and that their wisest move would be to concentrate all their energy on the practice of *Ramnam* instead.

Several months after Parasuram's transformation, residents of three villages across the river from Charpara visited Parasuram and his followers. The visitors invited the new teacher to their village so that he may instruct their entire families in the practice of *Ramnam bhajan*. Parasuram agreed and his travels began. Whenever he left his village in this way, he would be gone for months at a time; wherever he halted for a few days, people from surrounding hamlets would plead with him to visit their homes as well. Gradually, his following came to be spread throughout many villages in his district.

The small band of Ramnamis, as they had come to be called, would walk through villages chanting *Ramnam* wherever they went. Whenever they heard of a wandering *sadhu* in the area, Parasuram and the others would make a point of visiting him, in hopes of hearing any teachings that might help them. While Parasuram looked to Ramanandi *sadhus* for guidance and inspiration, many villagers looked to Parasuram for the same. To them, he was guru, and under his guidance, they began to memorize verses from the *Mānas,* especially those focusing on *Ramnam* and *satsang* (gatherings to discuss religious topics). Parasuram proclaimed the power of *nām* to all those he met, praising it as the best means for them to gain liberation.

During that time, the worship of various spirits was prevalent in rural areas, especially among the tribals and low castes. These included Sheetala, the goddess of smallpox, and Bhudevi, a village goddess of the soil who is usually propitiated in connection with the planting and harvesting of crops.[54] Parasuram spoke against the worship of such deities and the various ritual practices connected with them. More and more he came to see his calling as showing his community, the *chamars,* that *nirgun bhakti* and *Ramnam* were all they needed in order to gain God's blessings. He would often remind his people that the greatest deity is God himself, and *Ramnam* is the easiest way to gain his grace.

People continued to visit Parasuram daily when he was at his home. Sometimes as many as two hundred would gather for *bhajan* and *satsang*. Both practices have been given a highly elevated place in devotional Hinduism and are the subjects of much praise in the *Mānas*.[55] At such gatherings, Parasuram scattered hay on the ground on which his visitors would sit in front of his home. He would set his copy of the *Mānas* before him as they chanted together. Amidst the singing of *Ramnam,* he introduced verses from the *Mānas* for all to memorize. Since Parasuram was one of the only literate members of his community at the time, these meetings were the only opportunity many of the early Ramnamis had to learn verses from the text.

These sessions usually lasted late into the night, and those assembled would often wrap themselves in cotton shawls and don a turban, so common in the village, to keep out the chill of the night. As they chanted, they would huddle close together, man and woman, parent and child, drawing no lines of separation between the sexes, between people. It was in these early *satsang* gatherings that the foundations of the movements' philosophy and unique style of *bhajan* developed.

The Ramnami movement started in the early 1890s and by the turn of the century the fame of Parasuram and his movement had spread throughout much of eastern Chhattisgarh. Parasuram and his four original followers were often on the road, going from village to village, exhorting the people to chant *Ramnam* and to become literate, at least enough to read the *Mānas*. For his followers he set down few rules, since as an Untouchable he had experienced firsthand how religious restrictions can easily get out of hand and result in division and oppression.

He was aware of the Kabirpanthis and Satnamis in the region and their protests against the restrictions of caste-Hindu society. Unlike these groups, however, Parasuram did not attempt to sanskritize his followers in order that they may be more acceptable to caste Hindus. He knew well the teachings and rules of Ghasidas, since so many in his community were following them, but he believed that the Satnami movement had failed to gain the respect of most caste Hindus. On the contrary, many of the orthodox vehemently resented Untouchables who tried to live and act like caste Hindus. The former saw it as an attempt at deception, because in their view, Untouchables can never be clean, irrespective of their life-style. However, Parasuram did strongly urge his followers to abstain from meat, alcohol, and other intoxicants, warning them that these substances tend to cloud the mind and thus inhibit one's struggle to achieve wisdom.

As word of Parasuram and the Ramnamis spread, some of the upper-caste Hindus were angered to hear that a village *chamar* was preaching on Ram *bhakti* to throngs of people who looked upon him as a holy man. Furthermore, many of his followers had *Ramnam* tattooed on their foreheads, which the orthodox Hindus in the area considered to be a defilement of the sacred name by the inherent "filth" of the *chamars*.

Antagonism led to confrontation. Several Ramnamis had written " राम " in large letters on their white shawls, which they called *"ordhni."*[56] In addition, they would place a peacock feather in their turbans, a common Vaishnav symbol for *bhakti*. Some of the more brazen of the offended caste Hindus would steal and burn the Ramnamis' *ordhni*s and feathers. Sect members tell stories of caste Hindus capturing Ramnamis and burning or attempting to cut off tattooed skin from their foreheads. However, Parasuram prohibited his followers from retaliating and admonished them to avoid confrontation if at all possible, believing it could only aggravate the situation. At the same time, he encouraged them not to be intimidated and to continue chanting *Ramnam* and immerse themselves in the belief that Ram would ultimately protect them.

Not all caste Hindus expressed hatred and animosity for sect members. Some openly voiced approval of the Ramnamis and their practices, especially those who had been influenced by the teachings of the Ramanandi *sadhus* who frequented Chhattisgarh. Some caste Hindus, mostly *shudras,* even joined the movement and became tattooed as well. Nonetheless, the general attitude among upper-caste Hindus remained extremely disparaging of the Ramnamis and their use of "Ram." Long before this time, the Ram story and *Ramnam* had become integral parts of the brahmanical religion, and thus continued use of "Ram" by Untouchables was actively discouraged and on occasion forcefully prevented. It was felt that since "Ram" is a sacred Hindu name of God, its indiscriminate use on the cloth, on the forehead, and on the lips of Untouchables is a form of disrespect, even blasphemy. Many *chamar* villagers who had been initially attracted by the Ramnami movement began to avoid taking an active part in it, because the growing incidence of caste Hindu violence against sect members made them fear reprisal.

In 1907, the situation came to a head. Dasarath Singh, a wealthy *khsatriya* landowner from Raigarh district, hired a band of local thugs to attack a group of Ramnamis while they chanted at a *chamar* home in his village. The attackers seriously injured all those taking part in the *bhajan* and burned any clothing on which *Ramnam* was written. Parasuram and the elders in the sect decided they must act. At first they sought justice and protection from the primarily caste-Hindu police but were threatened and assaulted there as well. At about the same time, it became known that one of the literate Ramnamis had begun to record the early history of the sect and its treatment by caste Hindus. He, too, was attacked by caste-Hindu members of his own village and severely beaten. His writings were burned and he was threatened with death if he continued to write. As a result, no Ramnami since that time has attempted to record their history.

For a while, a deep sense of frustration came over the entire group, and they were uncertain about what they should do. Some considered converting to Christianity, since British officials, who were Christian, seemed to be the only people in positions of authority who had tried in the past to help them. Due to the efforts of the local British government officials of the time, Parasuram and some of the other *chamars* in Chhattisgarh had been able to secure their own land for the purpose of cultivating and becoming self-sufficient. The group felt, however, that while secular British officials had assisted them, the missionaries often sought to associate with the upper caste as much as possible and thus looked down on Untouchables much as the *brahmans* had. Nevertheless, they ultimately decided that seeking justice through the British court system as their only viable option.

Parasuram and several of his landowning *chamar* followers sold most or all of what they owned and retained a British lawyer to take Singh and his hired hands to court. Aroused by this, some of the more influential *brahman* priests, who had actively objected to the Ramnamis, rallied behind the wealthy landowner. They supported what he had done, claiming his actions had scriptural sanction. To them, Singh was simply defending the Hindu religion and Lord Ram's sacred name from abuse and degradation. They cited scriptural evidence, such as the *Manusmṛti* and even the Valmiki *Rāmāyaṇa,* to "prove" that Untouchables are polluted and thus polluting.[57]

After several years of pretrial arguments and motions, the case finally went to court in 1910 and was heard by a British station judge in the city of Raipur. During the lengthy trial many spoke on behalf of Singh, while few outside the movement dared defend the Ramnamis. Because of all the postponements and delays, the trial lasted for two years. Finally, on October 12, 1912, the judge ruled that since Queen Victoria had passed a law declaring freedom of religion in India, caste Hindus had no legal right to prevent Ramnamis from worshipping any way they chose. He noted that since the Ramnamis made no effort to enter Hindu temples or worship Hindu images, there could be no grounds for objecting to their practices. The judge also warned the attackers that anyone trying to prevent Ramnamis from chanting or doing their worship would be severely dealt with by the government.

The previous year, the Ramnami Samaj had held its first annual *mela,* or festival, and during the three-day event caste Hindus had frequently disrupted their *bhajans*, or chanting. Aware of this, the judge further passed an ordinance requiring a police guard at all future Ramnami *mela*s in the province. Except for a twelve-year hiatus, this practice has continued up to present day.[58] As word of their victory spread, the Ramnami movement mushroomed. At their first festival in 1911, there was a relatively small gathering. The second festival was held several months after the court case, and it is said that more than three thousand tattooed Ramnamis attended.[59] It became not only a celebration of *Ramnam,* but also of the Untouchable sect and its triumph over the caste Hindus of the area. In commemoration of this, several of those in attendance had entire lines of *Ramnam* tattooed on their foreheads and on other parts of their bodies.

The court trial not only enhanced the *chamars'* and other oppressed groups' feelings toward and admiration for the British, it also gave the Ramnamis an abiding respect for the British government, which influenced their political feelings for decades to come. Another major consequence of the trial was a polarization of attitudes among the Ramnamis towards caste Hinduism. In the early days of the movement, Parasuram and his followers all felt themselves to be Hindu, albeit at its outermost fringes. The trial solidified their sense of independence. Many began to see themselves as a separate religious movement, no longer needing to follow the dictates of caste-Hindu doctrine. Along with this came an airing of their hostility toward the orthodox-Hindu tradition, since they had been successful in standing up to it. In turn, this led to a distancing of the Ramnamis from the Satnamis and Kabirpanthis, both of which were trying to court caste-Hindu acceptance and move their subcaste community into closer alignment with the brahmanical value system.

The first two "Bhajan Melas," as the yearly festivals have come to be called, took place in the village of Pirda, home of some of Parasuram's early disciples. Seeing the difficulties experienced by the host village in providing food and shelter for the many devotees who came, the elder Ramnamis decided the festival should move each year to a new location. Not only would this allow the burden and cost to be shared by other villages, but it also would make the *mela* and the *Ramnam bhajan* accessible to devotees in all parts of the region. Except for the first two years in Pirda, the annual *mela* has never been held in the same village twice.

It was not long after this that George W. Briggs did his study of the *chamars*, published in 1920. In it he includes a single paragraph devoted to the sect, whom he identifies as "Ram Ramis."

> The Rām Rāmīs are a small group organized about thirty years ago. They are found chiefly on the south side of the Mahānadī, in the Central Provinces. They carry a flute, put peacock feathers around their caps, and cry out "Rām, Rām." They mean always to keep Rām in mind. Their most distinguishing characteristic is that they have the couplet "Rām, Rām" tattooed all over their bodies.[60]

At the time of Parasuram's death in the early 1920s, there were nearly twenty thousand tattooed Ramnamis. Unlike the traditions attached to the previous founders of low-caste religious movements in Chhattisgarh, Parasuram chose no successor. Moreover, he had often told the Ramnamis to look upon him as a brother or father, not as a guru, for the only true teacher is Ram. He is said to have reminded them that the sole instruction they need is contained in *Ramnam* and the *Mānas*. Many of the current elders in the sect believe that Parasuram did not outright reject Hinduism, nor did he try to start his own movement. He simply sought the path of devotion to Ram, like many other *nirgun bhaktas*, and he saw it his calling to inspire others to follow the same path. Although he encouraged his followers to show respect to and learn from the *sadhus* who would visit the region, he strongly advocated the life of the householder over that of the renunciant, stressing the need for members of the *samaj* to work together as a family in developing their spirituality and passing on the tradition of *Ramnam* to their children. This was, to him, the only way the Untouchable could gain spiritual blessing and someday, hopefully, equality in the eyes of the caste-Hindu society. Apparently based on their clothing and practices, many people unfamiliar with the sect who see its members on pilgrimage assume they are renunciants. This may be what V. K. Sethi refers to in his book *Kabir: The Weaver of God's Name,* in which he mentions a "sect of sadhus, claiming to be direct spiritual descendants of Kabir, [who] even imprint the word *Ram* on their dress and often on their face and body."[61]

After the death of Parasuram, many in the sect felt lost without a leader. The vigor and enthusiasm that his presence and charisma inspired were deeply missed. A great deal of consideration was given to the problem, but Parasuram's words and his refusal to initiate a lineage of leaders were too fresh in their thoughts. Still, many of the younger Ramnamis felt the need for some form of human guidance. They looked to their elders for inspiration and direction, but the latter all agreed that no one person should determine the direction and fate of the movement. Consensus of all members must guide it.

Because the primary goal of the early Ramnamis was not the founding of an organization, but rather a banding together of low caste, uneducated people seeking to learn and practice the path of devotion, there were very few decisions requiring a leader that needed to be made. Anyone could become a Ramnami by taking a vow before others to chant *Ramnam,* abstaining from alcohol and meat as much as possible, and getting at least one tattoo on their forehead.

Eventually, however, it was realized that due to the growing size of the movement, some sort of organization and leadership were necessary. Ramnami elders from the various sections of Chhattisgarh were informally chosen as spokesmen for the members in their areas. The primary function of these spokesmen, called "*sadasyas*," was to determine where the yearly *mela* would be held. Also, they would be responsible for inspiring new practitioners and encouraging all Ramnamis, both new and old, to make a sincere effort to live a life of humility and devotion.

By the 1930s, the Satnami movement had become decidedly political and supported the Congress Party's efforts to oust the British from India. The Satnami leadership began urging all the low castes in the area, especially those of the *satnami* caste, to show their unanimous support for the Quit India movement. Ramnami elders, remembering all that the British had done to help them, resisted following Satnami political sentiments. The *sadasyas* were determined to avoid political battles, and this caused an even greater strain in the relationship between the two sects. The Satnamis began to apply a great deal of pressure on the Ramnamis, both individually and as a sect, to work for the Congress Party, warning that if they did not, there would surely be caste-Hindu reprisals against them and all the other Untouchables of the area once the British were forced out. The Satnamis saw this as a golden opportunity to gain some degree of recognition, respect, and clout in Chhattisgarhi society and politics. The Ramnami Samaj, on the other hand, viewed participation in the Quit India movement as a betrayal of those who had helped and protected them in the past.

As a whole, the *samaj* stood its ground, believing that to become embroiled in such a divisive and fateful political situation with the largely upper-caste Quit India movement would be antithetical to its own beliefs and values. The *sadasyas* decided that the safest course was to stay completely out of the politics of the time. Elders reminded the sect membership that their purpose was devotion to Ram and freedom of the spirit. Getting involved in politics would, in all likelihood, distract them from their real goal. Some of the current elders who were already members at that time explain that the decision was a hotly debated one that in itself threatened to split and even destroy the sect.

Prior to this, most Ramnamis had felt a deep and abiding connection with the Satnamis. Some even felt the Ramnami movement to be a sort of Satnami denomination and hence considered themselves as much Satnami as Ramnami. The political differences, however, caused a permanent schism in their relationship. Those active with the Satnamis stopped attending Ramnami festivals and barred Ramnamis wearing their sect's attire from taking part in Satnami gatherings. At the same time, the Ramnami *sadasyas* began encouraging their own sect's followers to adopt "Ramnami" as their surname, in order to distinguish themselves from the Satnamis. Some of the more adamant Satnami leaders sought to break off all relations with members of the Ramnami Samaj, even with respect to their *roti-beti* (food-daughter) exchange.[62] There are approximately sixty-five *gotras*, or clans, within the Chhattisgarhi *satnami* caste. Traditionally, there has been no discrimination between them in the areas of eating and marriage. The attempt to instigate such divisions brought loud cries of disapproval and rejection from members of both sects, and, for the most part, the idea was dropped. Nevertheless, there continue to be Satnamis who refuse to form marriage bonds with Ramnami families, but they constitute only a small minority of the sect. As a result of the differences between the two sects, however, all official relations were curtailed. This situation has persisted up to the present.

The Ramnami *sadasyas* saw a need to keep the focus of the movement on *Ramnam* and not to let social and political factionalism divide their sect as had happened with and to the Satnamis. In order to assure this, several resolutions were passed in the late 1930s as requirements for all *samaj* members. Heading the list was the daily practice of *Ramnam* and the chanting of *Mānas* verses as the center of Ramnami spiritual life. Vegetarianism, like abstinence from alcohol, became mandatory. An increase in *Ramnam* tattoos was encouraged, to show commitment both to Ram and to the sect. It was hoped that these rules would also discourage members from getting involved in the kind of social and political controversies that had become a seemingly integral part of the Satnami sect. Also, anyone in the future desiring to become a Ramnami would have to first find a sponsoring member to vouch for his or her sincerity.

The continued refusal of the sect to become political further angered activist Satnamis who called them traitors. In addition, caste-Hindu political activists claimed that the Ramnamis' failure to support the independence movement was, in essence, showing support for India's subjugation by a foreign power. Their failure to stand with other Hindus was seen by their critics as validating their low position in society. Through all of this, however, the Ramnami leadership remained firm. Membership continued to rise, as many Untouchables saw the movement as a source of strength and stability in the surrounding sea of social and political confusion and turmoil. The Ramnamis were one of the only religious groups in Chhattisgarh not involved in political disputes.

World War II brought increased economic hardships as well as fear of war within India itself. The movement sought to care for its own. More affluent Ramnamis were encouraged to feed their poorer brethren and help provide them with basic necessities. At the Bhajan Mela each year, the sect would collect as much food and clothing as possible to be distributed to the poor. Members were encouraged to fast one to two days per month and give that day's food to someone in greater need. Self-sacrifice for others' sake was promoted as an important virtue toward attaining Ram *bhakti*. Scores of low caste were attracted by this cohesiveness and charity, and the ranks of the *samaj* continued to swell.

After India's independence, there were occasional violent confrontations with caste Hindus that were believed to be reprisals against the Ramnamis for their failure to support and fight for India's political independence. The sect leadership realized the need to ameliorate their strained relationship with the upper-caste Chhattisgarhis who had been a part of the Quit India movement and were now the political leaders of the region. The police protection that had been given them under the British was halted, for in the eyes of the new government the Ramnami Samaj did not officially exist, since they had no official organization, nor had the great majority of them ever voted in state or federal elections. A small but vocal faction within the movement felt that not only should they become a legal organization, but they also should get involved in politics, at least to the point of openly showing support for Nehru and his Congress Party.

By this time the Satnami sect had members elected to the Madhya Pradesh State Legislature. The pro-political faction of Ramnamis warned that unless their own *samaj* became politically involved and declared itself on the side of the Congress Party, it would continue to be viewed as anti-government and would thus remain the object of abuse and harassment by police, government officials, and caste Hindus. Aligning themselves with those in power would, on the other hand, give them a protective umbrella under which they would be less susceptible to religious and social persecution.

Without denying the benefits of such an involvement, the majority of the elders felt that, while individuals should not be prevented from political activity, such as voting or even supporting candidates of their choice, the movement as a whole should not commit itself to any partisan group. Political participation and the factionalism that invariably occurs would threaten to undermine the philosophical foundation and cohesiveness of the movement, which puts its reliance completely on Ram as protector and ultimate authority. More pragmatically, the sect leaders also doubted that a government, consisting primarily of upper-caste politicians, could ever benefit or guarantee assistance to their sect.

The pros and cons of political involvement continued to be debated with little compromise in either direction. Finally, in 1960, the *sadasya* governing council, whose formation up until this time had been haphazard, decided that the *samaj* should at least seek official recognition as a religious sect from the Madhya Pradesh State Government. By-laws were drawn up, and fifty-two *sadasyas* were appointed by consensus from the districts of Raipur, Raigarh, and Bilaspur. From this council were chosen a leader, called *"adhyaksha,"* a director, or *"sanchalak,"* and a treasurer. The by-laws included the following rules:

1. Sect members are to eat only in the home of an initiated Ramnami, though they may invite anyone to their own home.

This rule stemmed from the Hindu view that vegetarian food cooked in the house of a non-vegetarian cannot be pure since all utensils there must have been used in the past to cook meat and have thereby become polluted. Therefore, to assure that one's food is completely pure, a vegetarian should eat only at home or in the house of another vegetarian. This rule was meant to impress upon Ramnamis the importance of pure diet.

2. All children born to a Ramnami family should be tattooed at least once by the age of two.

There were several reasons behind this rule. One was clearly the belief that the tattooed name has a spiritually protective effect on an individual, such as being able to protect a child against "the evil eye." Additionally, the *sadasya*s wanted to help assure that Ramnami children were raised within the tradition's beliefs and practices. This would obviously help in the perpetuation of the movement.

3. Anyone seeking to be married by the sect must also have at least one *Ramnam* tattoo and must agree to chant *Ramnam* daily.[63]

It was hoped that these rules would encourage current and prospective members to take the movement seriously and to realize that one seeking its benefits and protection also has a commitment and a responsibility to sustain the sect. As a show of support for the new rules and for the sect, many Ramnamis took the vow to tattoo their entire bodies. During the next fifteen years, more than ten thousand members did so.

Since the beginning of the *samaj,* the membership had been almost exclusively householders. From time to time, there were ascetic Ramnamis, but this was not the norm, nor had it ever been encouraged. After becoming an official organization, there was discussion by some of creating a *sadhu* wing, as had been done by both the Kabirpanthi and the Satnami sects. For a variety of reasons this was rejected, and while *sadhu*s were permitted to become members, as was anyone, lay members were discouraged from becoming *sadhus*. The general feeling was, and still is, that being a householder Ramnami adheres more closely to the teachings of Parasuram and stimulates greater practice of *Ramnam* among their community in Chhattisgarh. As *sadhus*, members are more likely to wander off or to live alone, and the benefits of their practice cannot be readily shared by those in their community. Currently, there are a few dozen *sadhu* Ramnamis in the *samaj,* but these are primarily widowers or physically disabled persons who have never been married. Most renunciant members have no land and are cared for by other members of the sect. A few important functions have evolved for the Ramnami *sadhus*, however. These include acting as official messengers and assisting in the organizing of various sect activities.[64] Still, while they are shown respect, the way of life is not at all encouraged.

The 1960s saw considerable growth of both the movement and its popularity throughout Chhattisgarh, especially in the eastern districts. It is said that by the early 1970s the number of initiated Ramnamis was over forty thousand, while the number of non-initiated devotees of the *samaj,* often having at least one "*RamRam*" tattoo themselves, exceeded one hundred fifty thousand. Members were found in the majority of northern and eastern Chhattisgarhi villages, and devotees in even more. There are still many villagers who feel a strong connection with the sect religiously, ideologically, or otherwise, but do not wish to take formal initiation, wear the Ramnami dress, or live up to the restrictions placed upon initiated members. To show their faith and support, however, many have tattoos on some other part of their body. They chant *Ramnam* in their homes, go to the *melas*, and most adhere to a vegetarian diet. *Samaj* members refer to them as "Ramnami *bhaktas*." Many are members of an initiate's family, and they make up the majority of those who attend Ramnami *melas*.

The Ramnamis have, for years, lived a relatively sheltered existence, independent of many of the social and political changes that are a frequent reality in twentieth-century urban India and the rest of the world. The Arab oil embargo of 1973, however, left few countries and peoples unscathed, and India felt its effect almost immediately. Fuel prices nearly tripled within six months, and the Indian government had to increase its export of grains, sugar, and other essential commodities to help offset the increasing fuel and energy costs. As a consequence, rice in the market place became scarce and expensive. In addition, Chhattisgarh experienced a severe drought during the next rice growing season, ruining much of the expected crop. This forced countless numbers of villagers to buy rice in an attempt to supplement their minimal harvest. Highly inflated prices made it impossible for a great many to meet their needs, and thus they were forced to travel outside Chhattisgarh and even outside Madhya Pradesh in search of work and food. In previous years, small numbers of Ramnamis and other villagers had gone outside their region to seek employment in times of scarcity, but this was the first time that most could remember when such a large percentage of the population had to leave in order to feed their families.

During the Bhajan Mela of 1975 the governing council of *sadasyas* realized the gravity of the situation as they had to confront the extreme economic plight of many Ramnamis and its effect upon the movement. They knew that the situation could, and most likely would, become worse before it improved, and they felt a moral obligation to help the Ramnamis and others in their community to survive this time of hardship. After much discussion and consideration, several decisions were made.

The foremost of these decisions, and one with immediate economic implications, concerned the goods being collected by villages seeking to host a *mela*. As the size of the yearly *melas* grew, so did the amount of food and other materials needed for a village to be able to host it. Several such villages had already amassed and stored large amounts of goods for the *mela*, including several tons of grains and beans, with commensurate amounts of firewood and other necessary materials. Now, however, their residents were facing shortages of such goods in their daily lives. Seeking to help relieve the villages' immediate problem, the Ramnami council, in conjunction with members from those villages, agreed that all supplies collected should be made available as a loan to villagers in need. The amount must then be repaid after the next growing season or as soon as possible. For many villagers this meant the difference between remaining in their village or leaving in search of work. Spurned on by the potential benefits of villages' having such a storehouse of supplies on hand, the council urged Ramnamis in other villages to create small *samaj* storehouses as well, where in times of plenty grains and other nonperishables could be donated and subsequently used to help offset the effects of famines in the future. Although times of plenty have been infrequent in the last several decades, several small Ramnami storehouses have been started in conjunction with other *satnamis* and have proven to be extremely beneficial.

Rules mandating tattooing and restricting Ramnami commensal practices were repealed (see Chapter 5 for current attitudes surrounding the practice of tattooing). Regarding the latter, it was decided by the governing council that Ramnamis should no longer be prohibited from eating in the homes of non-sect members. Moreover, vegetarianism, while strongly urged, should not be forced upon new members. For anyone desiring extensive body tattoos or appointed as a *sadasya*, however, vegetarian diet remained a must. All of these decisions were meant to keep the movement in line with the changing worldly needs of its members and devotees. But most of all, they show an attempt to reaffirm the basic concepts and ideals of Parasuram, who wanted his followers to be free from the rules and restrictions, that had separated them from the existing culture, and to have absolute faith in *Ramnam*.

As in previous decades, the 1980s provided new religious, social, and political challenges for the sect. In 1988, the Madhya Pradesh state government passed a law mandating that all villages in the region with at least 25 percent *harijan* residents be classified as "*harijan* wards." Further, in these wards only *harijans* could run for the position of village headman *(sarpanch)* in the 1989 local elections. This caused an uproar of political activity among the Satnamis, many of whom had actively worked for the law. The Ramnami Samaj was also affected. Without asking the *sadasya* council, more than a half dozen sect members—two of whom were *sadasyas*—made it known immediately that they would actively seek the office of headman in their respective villages. This was the first time in most villages that an Untouchable had ever attempted to compete in an election and the first time any Ramnami had done so. While the sect made no official endorsement of any candidate, it also made no objection to members running. Although only one sect member won in that election cycle, the opportunity to become actively involved in politics whetted the appetite of several of the younger Ramnamis, who began pushing harder than ever to get the sect officially involved in supporting sect candidates or any others who are sympathetic to Ramnami values and needs. Since that time, nearly a dozen Ramnamis have been elected *sarpanch* in their respective villages.

With a younger generation of Ramnami leaders coming to the forefront of the movement, it appears inevitable that some degree of political activity and participation will continue to be a fact of Ramnami life. Along with this, there is an increased awareness by the younger members of the *samaj* of the need to rethink its approaches to dealing with the new and more complex issues and problems that arise in the rapidly changing sociopolitical environment of contemporary Chhattisgarh. The next chapter, then, will consider some of these issues as it looks at the contemporary manifestations of the sect, including the ritual dress of the Ramnami, the organizational structure, and the annual Bhajan Mela.

A young Ramnami couple.

Chapter 5

The Ramnami Samaj: Its Contemporary Forms

A little more than a century has passed since the Ramnami Samaj began, and during that time it has played an important role in the evolving religious, social, and political consciousness of the *harijan* community in Chhattisgarh. Amidst all the changes that have taken place in that time, three unique structural aspects of the sect have evolved: its organizational makeup, its members' ritual dress, and its annual Bhajan Mela. A variety of specific developments, rooted in the *samaj*'s sociohistorical experiences and evolving religious philosophy, has led to the present-day shape of each of these.

Organizational Structure

Although the *samaj* has been in existence since the 1890s, it was not until after India's independence that its elders seriously considered obtaining any form of official recognition. Most considered the police acknowledgment and protection at the *samaj*'s annual *melas* as being sufficient government involvement. Due to various factors, however, Ramnami leaders applied for and received status as a religious organization in 1960. Since then, the degree of its official structure remains relatively minimal. There has been little added to the organizational makeup beyond what was created for the purpose of meeting the legal threshold and requirements to become a government-recognized religious body. For sect members, all social structures have an inherent hierarchy, and thus run the risk of creating inequality.

Throughout much of India, caste organizations have long served as fundamental governing and unifying bodies for the various *jatis*, or subcastes. Generally, all the members of a *jati* in a village or set of neighboring villages in a region collectively comprise a caste organization. These, in turn, are governed by a *panchayat,* or council of leaders, chosen formally or informally from among the elders of the subcaste.[1] Such organizations have been vital in looking after the interests of their caste membership. In Chhattisgarh as well, every caste-Hindu *jati* has had its own caste organization, but until recently, Untouchables were forbidden from having any such formal body. This prohibition served to impede whatever organizing efforts they might otherwise undertake in seeking to better their social, economic, or political situation. They were often less able to garner *jati* solidarity, especially in their dealings with their caste-Hindu neighbors. While such a ban did not prevent them from cooperating, it did limit the extent to which they could officially operate as a unit. Functionally, this caused the *harijans* in Chhattisgarh to be less dependent on their particular subcaste and more reliant on their own smaller clan groups. It also led them to seek alternative social and religious structures for gaining a sense of belonging and security. This is but one of several reasons for the proliferation of religious movements among the low caste in Chhattisgarh.

Since the early days of the Ramnami Samaj, there has been a reluctance to develop an elaborate organizational structure. Elders say this feeling came from Parasuram's frequent warnings against bureaucracy, hierarchy, and antagonizing the orthodox-caste Hindus of the region. He rejected the designation "guru" and a lineage to succeed him, because he had apparently seen how often persons in formal positions of power end up abusing their rank and authority. After his death, an informal ruling council of some of the more seasoned elders was chosen. The council, whose members came to be called "*sadasyas*," was organized primarily to help maintain a sense of cohesion. It was not empowered to establish a hierarchy, a sophisticated body of doctrine, or a comprehensive defined philosophy beyond the promotion of the practice of *Ramnam*.

In the early years, the only decisions the *sadasyas* had to make dealt with the preparations for and staging of the yearly *melas* and other occasional get-togethers. Other than regulations dealing with the festivals, the rules formulated in the 1930s mandating vegetarianism and abstinence from alcohol were some of the only laws passed by the ruling council prior to the sect's incorporation in 1960. Normally, the *sadasya* council has had little else to do and thus only meets officially two or three times each year. In times of crisis, such as during World War II, the 1974 Arab oil embargo, and extreme droughts, the council has had special meetings and drafted rules in attempting to deal with the situations and alleviate the ramifications of these events on the Ramnamis.

When the sect became an official organization in 1960, the Ramnamis had to create a set of written rules and doctrines for the first time. In addition to the *sadasya* council, three executive positions were established. Kunjram, one of the respected elders of the time, was appointed *adhyaksha* (lit. chairman) by the *sadasyas* to act as the *samaj*'s leader; a *sanchalak,* or director, was chosen to assist the *adhyaksha* in the running of the organization; and a treasurer was appointed to handle monetary arrangements for the annual *mela*. Prior to 1960, the number of *sadasyas* varied and the designation was relatively informal. At the time of creating the formal organization, the council number was designated at twenty-five. Each group of villages was given the power to designate its own representative or representatives to the council.

At the January 1973 Bhajan Mela, the *adhyaksha,* Kunjram, decided to step down, saying that it was time for someone else to lead the organization. A new *adhyaksha* was appointed by the *sadasya* council. At that time, it was also decided the number of *sadasya*s should be increased to reflect the increase in membership. Seventy new *sadasya*s were chosen, increasing the number to ninety-five. It was also decided that each area within Chhattisgarh, where Ramnamis live in any appreciable number, should have at least three representatives in the council. Their duties were designated as follows:

1. To live an exemplary Ramnami life, that is, chant *Ramnam* daily and adhere to the stated rules for members;
2. To encourage *Ramnam bhajan* in their area and have occasional get-togethers at their homes;
3. To keep the sect membership in their area up-to-date on the yearly and occasional *mela*s.

It was reiterated to all that being a *sadasya* incurs responsibility but does not in any way signify a higher status vis-à-vis the other members of the sect. As council members, they have particular functions, but other than those specific duties, they are to be treated no differently than any other Ramnami. Over time, however, because the most respected elders were usually the persons chosen as members, the council came to be viewed with great respect and anyone on it was shown some form of deference. Over the last decade, there has been a conscious attempt to alter the council membership so that it will reflect a broader spectrum of membership. As older *sadasya*s have retired, the council has increasingly become populated by younger members with vastly diverse and conflicting views of the sect and its future. On one hand, there is a strong vocal minority that tends to be more socially and politically confrontational, trying to push the sect toward increased political activity and participation. Many of these members look at the political successes of the Satnamis and feel the Ramnamis should do the same.

On the other hand, some of the more philosophically oriented sect members have warned of the pitfalls in political involvement, pointing to the ideological divisions and accompanying bitterness that have split the Satnamis. Instead, these Ramnamis want to see the sect move in the direction of an increased religious orientation, enhanced literacy of the membership, and the development of an elaborated unique Ramnami philosophy. At the same time, most of the remaining elders on the council and their supporters see both the above groups as wanting to move the sect away from its original roots and purpose, which they see as simply chanting *Ramnam* and helping each other to face the day-to-day world in which they live. During the last decade or so, the level of political rhetoric that takes place among *sadasya*s in council meetings has drastically increased. Conversely, the general respect that Ramnamis have traditionally shown council members has diminished. A few sect members even refer to the council now as "a bunch of politicians," a label clearly connoting a total lack of respect or admiration.

The primary function of *sadasyas* remains the overseeing of the yearly Bhajan Mela.[2] From time to time, new rules are formulated, but they are usually not widely promulgated, nor is there much of an attempt to enforce them. Consequently, many of the council-created policies are ignored, forgotten, or rescinded. The membership, *sadasyas* included, are clearly ambivalent about regulations. Ramnamis, like most Untouchables, tend to have a legitimate distrust of formalized doctrines and elaborate rules, clearly based on their experiences at the bottom of the caste system. This has caused many sect members to be skeptical of any organizational structure or doctrine that places certain individuals above or below others, for any reason.

An example of the 1983 rule, pertaining to the smoking of *bidis* (an indigenous cigarette), provides a good example for how Ramnamis tend to view most rules. A law was passed during the final day of the annual *mela* that prohibited sect members from smoking while wearing the Ramnami dress or sitting in *bhajan*. Nearly every *sadasya* present agreed the rule was a good compromise, for some members had been pushing hard to have smoking banned entirely, while others felt such a law was unnecessary and might drive away devotees who were also addicted to nicotine. After the meeting that evening, as many of the *sadasyas* were chanting *Ramnam,* several would, from time to time, light a *bidi*. No one appeared to pay the slightest attention. The following morning, when I asked several *sadasyas* who had been present the previous night about the situation, the general attitude expressed was that enforcing such a law might actually function to discourage the chanting of *Ramnam* or the wearing of the *Ramnam* cloth, and these were more important than any benefits that the prohibition might bring. It became quite clear that although the law had been passed, it was unlikely that anyone would seek to enforce it. Moreover, no one outside the council had even been told about the law. When queried as to the purpose of having the law then, one of the *sadasyas* who helped pass it replied, "But it is a good law." With little or no attempt to actually implement the regulation, the council rescinded it the following year. As a consequence of this approach to regulations, few sect laws presently exist. Other than those dealing specifically with *mela* events, the primary *samaj* rules are

1. Practicing *Ramnam* daily;
2. Treating all sect members with equality and respect;
3. Abstaining from alcohol;
4. Practicing vegetarianism;
5. Tattooing of "RamRam" at least once on the body;
6. Wearing a *Ramnam ordhni* during chanting, if one is owned.

The first three rules are considered of supreme importance, the next two of great importance, with the last one being encouraged but not compulsory. In addition, sect members are urged to read the *Mānas* and other texts dealing with the greatness of *nam*. Ramnamis are also expected to follow the moral rules of their community, such as practicing nonviolence, not lying or stealing, and so forth. Regulations regarding purity and pollution are significantly absent in the sect. Personal hygiene is left up to each individual; at the same time each is expected to adhere to local custom with respect to individual, but not ritual, cleanliness, if at all possible.

The Ramnamis will readily admit that they lack order and much of their organization is haphazard. The meetings of the governing council are seldom characterized by consistency or commitment to firm decision making. As mentioned earlier, few rules are ever made, and even fewer are ever enforced. Although this attitude often results in confusion, most sect members do not see this as necessarily negative. In reaction to the past and even present circumscriptions they have had to face in many of their interactions with caste-Hindu society, it is clear that for most members a sense of freedom and independence, even at the expense of order, is extremely dear, and they will apparently go to great lengths to maintain it.

The Visual Ramnami: *Ankit, Ordhni, Mukut,* and *Ghunghru*

The physical appearance of the Ramnamis is striking. With tattooed faces and bodies, long capes and shawls covered with *Ramnam,* tall peacock feather hats, and occasionally a set of bells strapped to their ankles, fully adorned Ramnamis stand out visually wherever they are. Early on in the development of their new movement, the Ramnamis sought to find their own unique identity, and the physical manifestation of this identity has become a trademark of the sect.

One of the major goals of the early Ramnami movement was to find a sense of social belonging and religious identity independent from the restricted social and religious environment in which they lived. As Untouchables, they had little or no rights of self-expression outside the boundaries forced upon them by the caste-Hindu society. All their lives they had been compelled to face the fact that their assigned status in relation to nearly every aspect of caste Hindu life was, and often still is, an inferior one. They were expected to accept the role of social subordinate and its restrictions and limitations without question. In the past, some Untouchables were made to wear particular markings, go without clothing above the waist, or even carry a bell so that caste Hindus could easily recognize and avoid them. As a consequence, most Untouchables today seek to minimize any visible distinctions between themselves and caste Hindus, in hopes of blending in and making social acceptance or integration more possible. They seldom have had reason to be proud of what they are or to stand out in the broader Hindu society.

The Ramnamis, on the other hand, have taken a different approach. From the beginning, the sect has made no attempt to be invisible in caste-Hindu society. It has found little reason to conform to the value system of the caste Hindu, and the Ramnami dress reflects and symbolizes that feeling. Generally speaking, the Ramnamis have a strong sense of pride in their movement. Time and again it has offered them security and support and has provided them their social and religious sense of self. When the movement first began, Ramnamis had few distinguishing rituals or marks. Over the years, as the *samaj* grew in size, strength, and respectability in Chhattisgarh, their dress also became more distinctive and noticeable. The three most striking facets of their appearance are their *Ramnam* tattoos *(ankit),* their *Ramnam* shawls *(ordhni),* and their peacock feather hats *(mukut).* A look at the evolution of each of these can help foster a greater understanding of the sect's growth and maturation.

Ankit ***(literally, mark, inscription)***

By far the most distinctive and unique physical feature of the Ramnamis is their *Ramnam* tattoos. Parasuram, founder of the Ramnami movement, was the first of the sect to be tattooed, but in India the concept and practice of wearing the name of God or other important religious and cultural symbols on the body date back to ancient times. Evidence of tattooing can be found as early as the third century B.C.E.[3] The use of tattoos or other forms of markings on the body may have come from the belief in the power of *yantras*, or sacred diagrams. Priyabala Shah believes that such marks were worn on the forehead and other parts of the body "in order to place the person under the protection of these powerful instruments and the divinities they represent."[4]

The Sanskrit term for the sacred marks used by many Hindu sects to identify themselves is *"tilaka."* Some religious sects in South India also refer to their marks as *"nama."* In the Ramanuja Sampraday, the *chakra* (wheel) and the *shankha* (conch shell) were commonly used symbols, identified with Vishnu. Certain orthodox schools within the sect developed the practice of branding their monastic initiates on their upper arms, the *chakra* on one, the *shankha* on the other. At certain holy places, Hindus have traditionally received tattoos or been branded to commemorate their pilgrimages there. Shah refers to these marks as "pilgrimage stamps." If the tattoo or branding stamp contained a name, it was usually *Ramnam* or some other Vaishnav name.[5] There used to be a relatively common tradition in Haridwar that Hindus journeying there for religious reasons would have "ॐ" *(om)* tattooed on the back of their right hands to signify that they had made this important pilgrimage. Tattoo artists can still be found near some of the *ghats* (bathing places along the river), ready to tattoo all those who wish to commemorate their journeys in this way.

During the last century, the practice of tattooing (*godna* in Hindi, *gurdai karna* in Chhattisgarhi) has been most prevalent in India at certain places of pilgrimage and by tribals and rural poor. Many tribal groups have long used tattooing for religious, beautification, social status, or identification purposes.[6] As a form of adornment, the practice has been almost exclusively found among poorer women, both rural and tribal. Tattooing has carried religious significance for some tribes, which believe their women must be tattooed so God would recognize their souls when they die.[7] Most tribes have their own characteristic markings that distinguish the members of their group. Young girls of several Central Indian tribes must be tattooed prior to their *gauna,* the ceremony when a girl is taken by her husband to his home. Girls of the Binjhwar and Dhanwar tribes believe that an un-tattooed girl is not pure, and men of the tribe should not eat food cooked by her.[8]

All its sections counted together, the Gonds are the largest tribal group in India, and many of them live in Madhya Pradesh and Chhattisgarh. Traditionally, both men and women were tattooed, but the practice among men has diminished greatly. Gond tattoos have both ornamental and religious significance and are probably the most elaborate of all the tribal groups in the region. Sorcerers in the tribe wear the symbol of a deity tattooed on their chest or right arm. Girls are tattooed upon reaching puberty, and as with many of the other tribes just before their *gauna.*[9] R. V. Russell believes that the Gonds attached magical significance to the tattoos, possibly for the purpose of warding off danger or evil spirits. Traditionally, both men and women may have an image of Hanuman tattooed on their arms, believing this will make them strong.[10]

The use of tattoos has not only been limited to tribals in Central India. In the early part of this century, many rural women, including those of the *brahman* caste, were tattooed with dots on the face and designs or symbols on the limbs.[11] Both men and women of the *gawari* caste, a *shudra* subcaste connected with the *ahirs*, had a tradition of tattooing to identify caste members. The men wore a vertical mark on the forehead, and the women had a pattern of straight and zigzag lines on their right lower arm.[12] This latter pattern is much like that found currently on *satnami* females. Tattooing was popular with other castes as well, but its practice has declined significantly in recent years. Nevertheless, it can still be found among several tribal groups and continues to be used by the low-caste poor.

Until ten or fifteen years ago it was a popular custom among *shudras* and *satnamis* in rural Chhattisgarh to tattoo young girls about to be married. The popularity of the practice is evident by the various folk songs mentioning tattooing that can still be heard in the region. The marks were seen as a form of beautification for the brides-to-be. The design usually consisted of dots on the chin and above the eyebrows. Occasionally, unmarried girls would get tattooed on their limbs as well, although this was usually reserved for married women. The designs were varied, depending upon the whim of the parents or of the tattooer. Women of the *devar* caste *(devarin)* traditionally do all the tattooing in the region. Even now, they will go from village to village and call out that they are there to tattoo. Women wanting more tattoos or wanting their daughters to be tattooed respond to them and express their desires. The tattoos are usually made with a large needle, and the ink is concocted from the ashes or soot of various plants or fires.[13] The fees currently charged by tattooers range from a few rupees, to some uncooked beans and rice, to a sari, depending on the wealth of the family and the extent of tattooing to be done. Nowadays, less than 20 percent of village girls are tattooed before marriage. Even these have very few tattoos as compared with what was common a generation ago.

For the Ramnamis, *Ramnam* tattoos have had varied significance throughout the sect's brief history, but they have always remained a vital part of the sect's tradition. For Parasuram, his tattoo was the result of his devotion and was also *prashad,* a divine gift, and an acknowledgment from Ram. For the first Ramnamis, their tattoos expressed their religious connection with Parasuram, signified their commitment to *Ramnam,* and furnished them with a common bond, which set them apart from others and linked them together in a permanent and visible way. After their persecution at the hands of intolerant caste Hindus, the Ramnamis saw their tattoos as symbolic of their struggle against oppression and their limited, but nonetheless significant, victory. Subsequently, *Ramnam* tattoos have become, for many members of the *samaj,* the epitome of their individuality, freedom of expression, and willingness to visibly manifest and display their personal and collective commitment to Ram, to their beliefs and practices, and to each other.

As mentioned above, tattooing has long been a custom in rural Chhattisgarh, although the practice has mostly involved women. From the beginning, however, the Ramnamis sought to present their tattoos in a very different light and distinguish theirs from the tattoos of the tribals and village women. Rather than using the prevalent local term *(gurdai karna)* to refer to the tattooing process, the Ramnamis chose the term *"ankit karna,"* meaning "to mark or inscribe." For the Ramnamis, then, their *Ramnam* tattoos are Ram's inscription or signature on their bodies. It identifies them as belonging to Ram. Shortly after first meeting the Ramnamis, I asked a group why the sect had chosen the term *"ankit."* One of them repeated a portion of a modified verse from the Valmiki *Rāmāyaṇa, "Dadau tasya tatah prītah Rāma [sva] nāmākopaśobhitam,"* which he then translated as, "He (Ram) joyously gave the mark *(anka)* of *Ramnam* as a decoration."[14] In order to come up with this translation, he had taken the first line of the verse out of its context, changed a word, and altered the grammatical structure. More interesting than his translation, however, was the ability of a semi-literate low-caste villager to reformulate a verse from a Sanskrit text in order to produce the meaning he wanted to express. Subsequently, I found this practice of altering verses from various sacred texts to be common among those

Ramnamis who participate in the form of *Ramnam bhajan* the sect calls *"takkar,"* which will be discussed in the following chapter. Not only does it show how the substitution of even one word in a verse can go a long way to transform its meaning, it also suggests the relative ease with which texts can be modified—and has often been the case, brahmanized—by one wishing to have verses express his own belief system, as opposed to that found in the original.[15]

Initially, the tattoos of each sect member was essentially limited to "Ram-Ram" on the forehead. Over the years, the number of tattoos gradually increased, so that by the 1920s some members of the sect had an appreciable number on their entire body. Nevertheless, current sect members say that at that time this was not yet a widespread practice. According to popular sect tradition, however, in January 1939, the approach to tattooing took on a new dimension. As the story goes, several days before the Ramnamis' annual Bhajan Mela was to take place in the Chhattisgarhi village of Tillapur, a young Ramnami resident, Rampriyabai, was visited in her dream by Hanuman, the monkey god, who is believed to be the greatest devotee of Ram. He blessed her and exhorted her never to give up repeating and depending upon *Ramnam.* On awaking the following morning, she discovered her entire body had been tattooed with *Ramnam.* During the *mela* that followed, nearly fifty Ramnamis, including Rampriyabai's brother and sister, had their entire bodies tattooed in honor of the miracle.

There is a definite significance to her alleged dream in the context of the socioreligious environment of Chhattisgarh. Hanuman is a tremendously popular deity in the region, among caste Hindus and *harijan*s alike. He can be found in every village, and in some, every dwelling has a small image of him either in the courtyard or on the outer wall. As is the case in many regions of North India, he is often referred to as "Bajarang Bali" (He whose body is strong like a thunderbolt), and as mentioned above, Gonds have had a tradition of tattooing his image on their forearms, so that they may draw on his great strength. Even though the Ramnamis formally reject the worship or veneration of all images and all deities other than Ram, in the eyes of many, Hanuman exists in a sort of mercurial status, outside the boundaries of normal worship practices and classifications.

Of major Vaishnav-related deities, Hanuman is the only one whose images do not require daily worship. He appears in countless forms, from a giant anthropomorphic monkey to a small shapeless stone, usually painted orange. Moreover, he can be seen as Vaishnav or Shaivite,[16] as a deity or a devotee (of Ram). Importantly, most see him as a deity who accepts devotion from everyone, caste and outcaste alike, in whatever form it is given. He is especially popular among Ram *bhakta*s, but can be found in the temples of most other deities as well. Although Ramnamis formally reject *sagun* devotional forms, many have pictures of Hanuman in their homes and justify it by saying that he is not there as a deity but because he is a Ram *bhakta,* he represents selfless devotion, and is also a part of the local culture. Some have pictures of Hanuman drawn entirely of *Ramnam.*[17] Thus, he serves as a sort of liminal deity, bridging the gap between castes, between denominations, and as with Ram, between *sagun* and *nirgun bhakti.*[18]

From the 1930s to the early 1970s, the number of initiated Ramnamis continued to increase, as did the extent of tattooing on individuals. The practice of child tattooing was also introduced sometime in the 1940s. Many Ramnamis began having "रामराम" tattooed on the forehead of their male children once they reached the age of two. Some sect members had the same done to their daughters as well, but the practice was far less common than for boys. Tattooing at the sect's annual festival became a frequent occurrence, as many sect members would get a new row or rows of *Ramnam* inscribed every year to commemorate their attendance; some would have their entire bodies tattooed. The tattoos functioned not only as a sign of their devotion, but also as a record of their membership and participation in the sect as well. By the late 1960s, the Ramnamis estimate that there were more than forty thousand sect members with a significant number of *Ramnam* tattoos on their body.

In 1974, the situation began to change rather rapidly. Reverberations of the Arab oil embargo reached Chhattisgarh, as the price of foodstuffs and other essential commodities drastically escalated.[19] Ramnamis were forced to look for seasonal employment outside their districts, and the presence of tattoos on their faces and limbs often caused ridicule and hindered their ability to find work. Ramnamis, especially males, have often been chided for their tattoos, since tattooing is generally considered to be a female adornment. In Chhattisgarh, where Ramnami presence is more commonplace, such abuse is, in recent times, minimal as compared to that faced by sect members who have moved to other districts and states. Those who leave in search of work usually relocate in urban areas, where employment is most likely to be found. To many city dwellers unfamiliar with the movement and its ways, visibly tattooed Ramnamis appear to be backward or strange. Their unusual appearance often makes it difficult for them to secure decent employment, even though they may be qualified. Their children, too, often become the objects of taunting and harassment by belligerent city youths.

The situation had often been the subject of concern and discussion by the *samaj,* which views it not only as a source of distress for the Ramnamis affected, but also as a mockery of *Ramnam,* which is held in the highest sanctity by sect members. In the wake of the embargo and subsequent economic crisis, it became apparent that more and more Ramnamis would have to leave Chhattisgarh in search of work, so the sect's governing council decided that the purpose and practice of *Ramnam* tattooing must be thoroughly discussed and re-evaluated. The resulting discussions have had a deep and abiding influence on the sect's future.

Much of the debate centered around the habit of child tattooing. Those who wanted the practice to remain warned that abandoning it could lead to serious consequences and harm the future of the movement. Their primary argument was that Hindus raise their children as Hindus, Muslims raise theirs as Muslims, and so forth. In this way, their beliefs and values are perpetuated. Ramnamis should do the same, and an important part of being a Ramnami is having a *Ramnam* tattoo. If it leads to pain, such as harassment, then the pain should be welcomed as *tapasya,* or religious austerity, that will foster humility and thereby cleanse the soul.

Those who opposed the practice, however, reiterated the original reason for getting tattooed: to show faith in Ram and commitment to the Ramnami movement. This can only be a conscious decision made by mature adults; it cannot be made by a two-year-old child or even an adolescent. These same elders also stressed that the need for inner faith and devotion is much more important than any outer form. Children should be brought up with the values and beliefs of the movement, but individuals must decide for themselves whether or not they wish to accept the external forms. After a great deal of discussion and dialogue, the organization's ruling body decided that no children should be tattooed until they are old enough to make the decision on their own. The council encouraged members to pay less attention to the number of tattoos they have and more to the extent of *Ramnam* they do. A general consensus was reached that if *Ramnam* tattoos are going to hamper the ability of sect members to support their families, then the sect must alter its stand on the practice.

The *sadasya*s, members of the ruling council, added to this view the point that tattooing should not be taken lightly by anyone, irrespective of age. The practice must be viewed with great deliberation, solemnity, and commitment. The council urged Ramnamis not to get full body tattoos all at once to show their faith. Any subsequent regrets of their impulsiveness might lead to a resentment of *Ramnam*. Full body tattoos, therefore, should be done over a period of years as other interests in life fade away and one's commitment and devotion to the movement and its practices grow.

Further, the council rescinded the long-standing rule mandating couples having a Ramnami-officiated marriage to be tattooed. The *sadasya*s continued to believe such persons should be encouraged to take part in Ramnami practices, especially the chanting of *Ramnam* and the *Mānas,* but they should not be forced to get *Ramnam* tattoos in order to obtain the benefit of a Ramnami marriage. Members against the repeal of these laws warned of an inevitable demise of the sect as a result of this retraction from what they saw as a fundamental part of the Ramnami tradition. For many, however, the importance and practice of tattooing are very much still alive and continues in present day, although in a much abated form.

Once the decision to be tattooed is made, a Ramnami or prospective initiate must choose a tattoo artist for the job. In the sect there are certain members who, due to their skill and steadiness of hand, are preferred for most of the tattooing. The choice is based on several factors, including familiarity with the artist and his work as well as his availability. Some artists, although not considered among the most talented, are picked out of respect. These are usually revered elders, and to be tattooed by them is considered auspicious.

The ideal ink used for the tattooing is made from camphor soot, but its cost is quite prohibitive. Instead, the primary ingredient used for most of the ink today is kerosene soot, collected in an inverted clay pot and then mixed with water in a coconut shell. This mixture can be stored in a glass jar up to one month, and Ramnami tattoo artists often bring the mixture with them to sect gatherings for anyone wishing to be tattooed. The instrument used for the actual tattooing is constructed of two large sewing needles bound together with thread and occasionally secured in a bamboo holder. The *Ramnam* design, several words at a time, is first drawn on the skin using a bamboo pen. The writing is then retraced with the needles and more ink. A talented artist can tattoo one small " राम " in approximately two minutes. If the tattoos are larger or elaborate, then the time it takes can increase severalfold.

When tattooing was at its height of popularity, Ramnamis would have their entire bodies done during a concentrated period of time. To cover an individual entirely with *Ramnam* tattoos could take anywhere from a week to a month, depending upon the tolerance of the individual, the speed of the artist, and the intricacy of the design. Some members have over five hundred tattoos on their face alone, requiring several days to complete. While there is no mention of any deaths from the practice, many who have had full body tattoos done in a condensed time period say they experienced intense bodily suffering, sometimes for up to a year or more afterwards. Although surprisingly little blood is lost during the normal tattooing process, rapid punctures to the skin can cause extreme swelling and can leave the tattooed person weak for days and even weeks at a time. With the diminished emphasis on tattoos, most Ramnamis today prefer getting only a few tattoos, or possibly a line of twenty-five to thirty repetitions of the name at any one time, either on the forehead or on an arm.

While individuals are free to choose the design of the tattoo, they often express a general preference and leave the details to the artist. If only a few tattoos are to be done, the process may take place during one of the Ramnamis' festivals. Nowadays, extensive tattooing is done at the individual's home, so that it may be followed by a period of convalescence. Until recently, tattooing always included at least one *"RamRam"* on the forehead. In the last fifteen years, however, the practice is no longer stressed, and it is common to find one's only tattoos on a somewhat less conspicuous part of the body, such as the neck, arm or chest. Female *Ramnam* devotees may have "Ram" tattooed in a small circle on their forehead, in place of the *bindi,* or holy spot, traditionally worn by caste-Hindu women. *Ramnam* may be tattooed around the neck, like the *tulsi kanthi* worn by Satnamis and caste Hindu Vaishnav *bhaktas*, or around the upper arm, where talismans are often worn. After Ramnami women get tattooed, they are supposed to cease wearing all other forms of jewelry, with the exception of wrist bangles (a sign their husbands are still alive) and a silver belt (of local cultural importance), if they possess one. *Ramnam* is seen as sufficient, superior ornamentation. Many female sect members continue to wear a nose pin (in one or both nostrils), but they say that this, like the bangles and belt, is a part of their culture, and therefore not jewelry.

Traditional Hindu purity/pollution restrictions prohibit the inscribing of the name of a divinity or other sacred mark below the waist, whether on the body or clothing, because of its possible contact with bodily excretions or other polluting substances. To wear a sacred symbol on the feet or shoes amounts to blasphemy in the eyes of many traditional Hindus. The Ramnamis see such regulations as contrary to the omnipotent and transformative power of the name of Ram. Thus, in tattooing their bodies, they see no part of themselves as prohibited. It is not uncommon to see tattoos all over the left, or "dirty," hand, on the legs and buttocks, and even on the feet.[20] In the past, such tattoos have raised the ire of many caste-Hindus and Satnamis as well, the former group seeing the practice as blasphemous, and the latter seeing it as creating more justification for caste-Hindu enmity against *satnamis*. In his defense, one *Ramnam* with tattoos all over his feet, asserted quite matter-of-factly, "*Ramnam* cannot be polluted. It is like the Ganges River: it purifies whatever it comes into contact with. Even my feet are clean because they have been purified with the name."

The psychological preparation and adjustments individuals must go through before getting themselves tattooed vary from person to person. Unlike joining a religious sect, getting tattooed as a Ramnami is a permanent, visible commitment. For this reason, even now some traditionalist Ramnamis are pressing for a renewed emphasis on tattooing. They feel this will weed out those potential members who are unwilling to make a lifelong commitment and strengthen those who do make it. Their view is that tattooing should be both a religious and a social statement of a Ramnamis' faith and commitment to Ram and to the Ramnami way of life. Anyone wishing to be a Ramnami should renounce attachment to worldly beauty and attainment in exchange for gaining the beauty, blessings, and power of *Ramnam*.

Initially, the practice of *Ramnam* tattooing by *samaj* members was done primarily as a means of giving up one's body, and by extension, one's life to Ram. Prior to the 1970s, it had come to be considered the greatest sign of *Ramnam bhakti* to cover one's face with tattoos while still young (in the teens or twenties). It was felt that this was the time when physical appearance is usually the most important to a person; thus, to adorn one's face with *Ramnam* at this stage of life is to offer one's looks to Ram and to make a great sacrifice.

With the change in attitude toward the practice over the last 25 years, the tradition of full-bodied tattooing of *Ramnam* has diminished greatly. It is estimated that less than a thousand members have done so. In fact, during the last decade, fewer than several hundred Ramnamis have been tattooed to any appreciable degree. As Ramnami youths are becoming educated and going outside their villages for school and work, they are being influenced by Western and urban concepts of fashion. These all put *Ramnam* tattooing in a negative light. It is seen as ruining one's looks. Even older Ramnamis who have full body tattoos generally discourage their children from getting any more than a minimal number.

As recently as twenty years ago, people getting tattooed at a *mela* was a common occurrence. Now it is a much rarer event, possibly happening only once during a three-day festival. Those in the last generation to be drawn to tattoos with any intensity are now in their fifties and sixties. For many of the younger participants in Ramnami *bhajan,* anything more than minimal tattooing is seen as something old fashioned, a part of the past. One of the most celebrated tattooers of the sect said recently that, for all intents and purposes, "The [tattooing] pen has ceased, it is no longer being used." While some Ramnamis view this as a decline in participation in and commitment to the movement, others see it more pragmatically, arguing that this allows those who do not wish to have extensive tattoos to take equal part in sect activities; the absence of tattoos is no longer a cause for anyone to feel inferior or less than a full member.

Ordhni ***(literally, covering)***

A *Ramnam ordhni,* the sect's ritual shawl, is a major part of Ramnami wardrobe. The shawls are generally made from thick pieces of white cotton cloth and are covered with *Ramnam,* written in *devanagari* script. Initially *ordhni*s were simple and had only one "*Ram*" on them ("रा" on the front, "म" on the back). Today, they vary in intricacy of design and can have *Ramnam* written on them more than thirty thousand times. Some of the dancing sect members wear a kaftan-like garment as well, called an *"olagi,"* which is also covered with *Ramnam.* All Ramnamis are encouraged to possess an *ordhni* and to wear it whenever they chant. The shawl is meant to symbolize the Ramnamis' devotion to Ram and their membership in the *samaj.* More importantly, it is used to wrap them in the name, as well as in a sheath of purity and protection provided through the power of the name.

According to tradition, the practice of writing on their clothing was started by Parasuram, who would scrawl *Ramnam* on everything he owned, including his clothing and turban. His followers soon began to do likewise. As the amount of tattooing increased in the sect, so did the extent of writing on clothing. The size of the writing gradually became smaller and smaller in order to accommodate greater numbers of *Ramnam* on the cloth. The practice has led to the evolution of the intricately hand printed *ordhni*s that have been popular during the last fifty years or so. When there were only one or a few repetitions of "Ram" on a cloth, nearly all the sect members were able to inscribe their own. As the writing diminished in size and became intricate, however, the demand for talented calligraphers arose, and Ramnamis who had both the ability and the time came to be in great demand as *ordhni* makers and tattooers. While extensive body tattooing has been greatly reduced, the practice of *Ramnam* shawl making has thrived, evolving into a definite art form.

The word *"ordhni"* itself reveals an interesting devotional dimension to the sect. In Chhattisgarh, the term specifically refers to a female's garment, such as a sari. Originally, many male Ramnamis told me that when they wear the Ramnami dress, consisting primarily of *mukut* and *ordhni,* they are Ram *rup,* that is, in the form of Ram. In answer to questions concerning the connotation of the term *"ordhni,"* others have said that it is because they practice *madhurya bhakti,* the form of devotion in which they see themselves as the female lovers of Ram, functionally making them closer to Sita *rup*. In actuality, both views are quite prevalent in the sect, the former being more philosophically Vedantic in orientation, the latter more in the direction of dualistic devotion. While the sect has sought to set certain theological and philosophical parameters with respect to its belief system, at the same time the door has been left open for members to develop their own beliefs and interpretations.

Until the mid-1980s, all printing of *Ramnam* shawls was done by hand, and members would typically have their *ordhni* prepared by one of the Ramnamis known for their penmanship. The writing utensil is a pencil-thick bamboo stick with an angled point. Like their tattoo ink, the ink used for printing shawls is made from kerosene lamp soot and water, but to this mixture is added the sap of the banana tree or one of a variety of other plants. These saps cause the ink to set into the cloth and make it permanent. Some Ramnamis have shawls that are more than fifteen years old and although washing and the sun have both contributed to the fading of the color, the writing on many of them is still quite sharp and distinct.

Ramnami men have traditionally preferred *ordhni*s with straight lines of *Ramnam,* with or without a simple border design. Women, if they can afford them, have often opted for shawls with more elaborate designs if they are available. Currently, older Ramnamis tend toward the more simple shawls, while younger members, both male and female, show a predilection for *ordhni*s with a variety of patterns. To have an *ordhni* made by a respected elder is considered auspicious, a sign of respect, and a connection to that elder. Some Ramnamis also believe that such cloth is then imbued with some of the spiritual power of the writer. A good artist with a steady hand and clear penmanship takes up to two hundred hours to complete one of the more elaborate shawls. Those who are known as skillful tattooers are nearly always good *ordhni* artists as well. Because the former task requires much more steadiness of hand and endurance on the part of the artist, however, such sect members usually continue to make shawls long after they cease to do tattooing.

In the mid-1980s, an inventive Ramnami experimented by carving a *Ramnam* woodblock with which to stamp *ordhni*s. Because of the relative ease with which he was able to complete the block-stamped shawl and the small amount of time that it required, he produced a few more to see if he could sell them. Initially, most sect members declined his creations, preferring the traditional handwritten variety instead. Over the years, this has gradually changed. With the continuing high level of poverty existent in Chhattisgarh and the greatly diminished cost to produce block-printed shawls in comparison to the freehand creations, many of the newer Ramnamis find it economically prohibitive to consider the older style. As a consequence, block-printed shawls make up nearly 40 percent of those currently in use and the vast majority of the new *ordhni*s being made.

When someone decides to become a member of the sect, the purchasing of an *ordhni* becomes the initiate's largest financial outlay. Prior to the introduction of the woodblock print, the acquisition of a shawl was an artful, almost ritualistic, process, and this is still the case with respect to the purchase of the old style cloth. Because the *ordhni* is covered with *Ramnam,* it is not something easily evaluated in monetary terms. Consequently, the practice of employing an intermediary to conduct the transaction evolved. A potential shawl customer will usually ascertain whether or not any of the artisans have a handwritten *ordhni* available for purchase, then request another Ramnami to act as go-between in the bargaining. The intermediary will ask the calligrapher such questions as how long it took him to prepare the shawl, if anyone else has expressed an interest in it, and how much it would normally cost to buy one of its quality. He will typically say something to the effect that "This *ordhni* must be worth at least Rs. 600 or more. It is too bad more Ramnamis cannot afford something so beautiful." The price mentioned will usually be generous. In reply, the artist will typically avoid attaching an exact monetary figure to his/her own work, saying things like, "*Ramnam* is sacred, how can one put a price upon it" or "The writing of *Ramnam* is a form of *sadhana* (religious practice). It is not the type of labor upon which a wage can be easily attached." The artisan may then mention the approximate length of time spent on the shawl's construction and then a price range he or she considers reasonable. It is then up to the intermediary Ramnami either to agree with him or to suggest a slightly higher—not lower—price, depending on his opinion of the quality of the work. He will then return to the Ramnami interested in the *ordhni* and reveal the amount he thinks should be given. The buyer will seldom quibble and will either purchase it at that price or not, depending on his or her economic situation. By carrying out purchase transactions in this manner, all the participants can be more frank about their desires, expectations, and financial situation, and there also is a diminished likelihood of hurt feelings on either part.

Depending on the extent of the artwork on the cloth, the time involved in making the ink and doing the actual writing, the entire project can take anywhere from a hundred to more than three to four hundred hours, and this makes a hand-written *ordhni* an expensive project, especially for villagers of the economic status of most Chhattisgarhi *harijans*. Shawl makers know that if their work is too expensive, the interested Ramnami may not be able to afford it. If, on the other hand, the artisan gets no compensation for his time and expenses, he will be less inclined to devote the energy required to make more *ordhnis*. Thus, the making of a deal is in everyone's interest, and usually a price is settled upon that considers all the concerns of the two parties, culminating with a purchase.

Ordhnis are definitely one of the most prized possessions of many Ramnamis, and, when properly cared for, they can last up to twenty years. Some wear their *ordhnis* everywhere they go, as their way of showing their commitment to the sect and also as their way of dressing up. Others don their *Ramnam* shawls only when they sit for *bhajan*. For the latter, economics seems to be the major reason for limiting the use of their *ordhni:* the cost of each shawl is such that they do not want to damage it or wear it out too quickly.

Nowadays at the *melas*, however, it is almost exclusively the woodblock shawls that are available for purchase, while the more traditional style seems only to be made as a gift or for special order. With respect to the former, there tends to be a more straightforward purchase process, with the price less ritually negotiated. This is because such a shawl can be printed in less than a day, once the ink is made, and there is far less skill and personal investment necessary on the part of the maker. These shawls also sell for a quarter or less of the price of the hand-designed cloth. Thus, while the woodblock *ordhni* is less valued, it is also far more affordable, and this encourages the wearing of the shawl more often. As a consequence, there are currently many shawl makers who produce the woodblock style of *ordhni,* and their creations are quite prevalent at the festivals.

Both types of shawls are attractive to many of the non-Ramnami visitors to the *samaj*'s festival. It is common to see spectators at *bhajan* gatherings, especially younger urban males, asking to put on an *ordhni* and a *mukut* (see below) so that a friend may take their picture while they are so attired. With the lower cost and increased availability of the woodblock printed cloths, there has been a rise in the sale of *ordhnis* to non-sect members as well. There used to be an unwritten rule against giving or selling an *ordhni* to anyone but another Ramnami, and there are still many sect members who believe only initiates should wear the cloth. They see it as an integral part of the *samaj*'s uniform and thus rightfully worn by members alone. Nowadays, however, there is less objection voiced to the practice of selling shawls to non-members. The prevalent feeling seems to be that no one wants to deny an *ordhni* maker the opportunity to earn some extra money, especially in the poor economic situation that the people of the region so often find themselves.

Since the artisans who have the ability and are willing to spend the time required to create the handwritten type are rapidly declining in number, this older variety is becoming even more expensive and harder to procure. Unfortunately, as the handprinted *ordhni*s disappear, the uniqueness that presently distinguishes each handmade shawls is a casualty of the change. As long as the sect remains, however, the *ordhni,* in whatever form it takes, will no doubt continue along with the *mukut,* to define the Ramnami ritual dress.

Mukut *(literally, crown)*

Along with their tattoos and *ordhni*s, the Ramnami's peacock feather hat, known as *"mukut,"* helps give *samaj* members a unique physical appearance. Like the tattoos and shawls, the *mukut* started out simple, but over the years has now become quite ornate. Currently, most *mukut*s consist of several hundred feathers and are elaborately constructed creations.

In Hindu devotional literature, the peacock feather is often associated with Vishnu or one of his *avatar*s, usually Krishna but also Ram. According to R. V. Russell, in the early part of this century, some of the *rajput*s of Chhattisgarh would use a bundle of peacock feathers to symbolize either Vishnu or the Sun god.[21] In those days wild peacocks were a common sight in Chhattisgarh. During the monsoon season, they would molt and their feathers could be found in the forest. To symbolize his devotion to Ram, Parasuram used to wear a peacock feather in his turban when he worked in his fields, and the members of his village soon began to call him *"pankhawala"* (literally the one with the feather). After his religious experience, his followers began to put a peacock feather in their own turbans, in remembrance of their teacher as well as of Ram.

Prior to the 1911 court case that gave Ramnamis official sanction and protection, most sect members only wore one or a few feathers in their turbans. This practice offended the more orthodox caste Hindus who associated a bundle of peacock feathers with Vishnu, for they viewed this Ramnami practice as a mockery of their deity.[22] After their court victory, sect members began to increase the number of feathers they wore. One feather led to many, and by the 1920s Ramnamis were wearing hats with more than one hundred feathers. Currently, the number of feathers used to make a standard *mukut* is somewhere between two hundred fifty and three hundred.

The feathers for making the hats have traditionally been collected during the monsoon season but have now become scarce. During the Ramnamis' annual *mela*s tribals from southern Chhattisgarh sell bundles of peacock feathers, found in more densely forested areas of the region. Most *mukut*s for the *samaj* are made by its *sadhu* members. Any Ramnami in need of a *mukut* must supply the feathers and the *sadhus*, or any other capable Ramnami, will make the hat at no cost.

When choosing the feathers with which to construct a *mukut,* artisans look for long feathers with deep blue and turquoise "eyes," for they say these are stronger, more beautiful, and longer lasting. The feathers are then divided into bundles, usually twelve to sixteen in number, depending on the size of the wearer's head. Optimally, each bundle has between fifteen and twenty feathers, all facing one way and layered together, somewhat in the shape of a fan. These bundles are then attached to a head band made from the lower half of the feather's stems. The bundles are spaced approximately one inch apart around the band, and then all are stood straight up and connected to a thick piece of wire at their midpoint. This keeps them all upright and creates a somewhat barrel-shaped hat. Finally, a small band of cloth, covered with *Ramnam,* is wrapped around the *mukut*'s midsection. A good craftsman can complete one *mukut* in fifteen to twenty hours.

Since the custom of wearing a *mukut* originated from the traditional male turban and its decorative peacock feathers are associated with a male deity, traditionally only Ramnami men wear them. Moreover, male Ramnamis are expected to wear their *mukut* when they are chanting. Formally, widows were the only women for whom wearing a *mukut* was considered proper. However, in the last decade or so several non-widowed Ramnami women have also begun wearing *mukut*s. While one hears occasional criticism of the practice, no actions have been taken to stop females from adorning themselves in this manner. Because the tradition confining the use of the headdress to males was one of the only elements of the *samaj* in which there was a differentiation based on gender, adherence to this seems more a basis of tradition than idealogy. As a consequence, it is quite possible that more females may begin to wear *mukut* as well, for they are unlikely to meet any real opposition.

There has been no formal attempt at any manner of standardization of style or form with respect to *mukut*s, *ordhni*s, and tattoos, for ideally these are meant to express each individual's unique personality and relationship with Ram. Practically speaking, only a handful of Ramnamis in any given area have "the hand"[23] to do tattooing, to make shawls, or to construct a *mukut.* Also, certain styles have come to be accepted as "traditional." While this has resulted in a similarity of design of the various elements of the Ramnamis' visual form, sect members are free to choose their own designs, resulting in some unique creations and forms.

Ghunghru *(Ankle bells)*

The Ramnamis use no musical instruments as such to accompany their chanting of *Ramnam*. Unlike the style of *bhajan* practiced by most Hindu devotional groups, the *samaj* has rejected the use of drums, harmoniums, cymbals, and other instruments for their chanting, saying that the only music they wish to hear is the sound of *Ramnam*. Throughout much of the history of the sect, however, members have used a set of handmade ankle bells, called *"ghunghru,"* for maintaining a beat during *bhajan*. While still somewhat a part of the Ramnami ritual dress, the *ghunghru* is rapidly becoming rare. Until fifteen years ago, they were a commonplace accessory of Ramnami attire. Today, only a minority of the membership possess them.

In the early 1920s, some Ramnamis had begun to incorporate a slow twirling dance into their *Ramnam bhajan,* inspired by pictures of Krishna dancing. In these pictures, he wore bells on his ankles, and the Ramnami dancers decided to do likewise. At first they used the small ankle bells commonly worn by women in the region. After a few years, Binduram, a young Ramnami of the *ghasiya* (drum maker) caste, began to fashion ankle bells by hand, as a form of *seva,* or service, for the sect. His artistry gained such popularity that his *ghunghru* soon defined the style used by the *samaj*. For many years he spent much of his free time making sets of *ghunghru* for sect members who would ask for them, never charging anyone for his creations. By the 1930s, his were the only ankle bells used by the sect.

Using a lost wax technique he had learned from his father, Binduram made bronze bells, much larger and heavier than had been prevalent. Each round bell, approximately a half inch in diameter, was individually fashioned, some with *Ramnam* on them in relief. A set generally consisted of forty to fifty bells, woven together onto a thick hemp ankle band. All those who danced would wear them on their ankles, while seated Ramnamis tapped them on the ground in a slow, steady beat. Nearly all sect members sought to have at least one set of *ghunghru,* and Binduram devoted himself to fill each and every request. His bells were so well made that, despite extensive use, some have lasted more than thirty years.

In the late 1970s Binduram died, and it was realized that no one in the sect had learned how to make *ghunghru* the way he did. Although he had taught his son, the latter was not interested in following his father's profession and refused to make any. For nearly ten years, there were no new *ghunghru*s in the sect. Each time there was a new initiate, existing *samaj* members who had *ghunghru*s would give up some of their bells to fashion an ankle band for the newcomer. As a result, at present, the number of *ghunghru* has decreased drastically. Some Ramnamis have begun to use ready-made bells bought in the bazaar, but most do not like them. In the late 1980s, Binduram's son said that he would begin to make the bells, but since that time he has only produced a few sets. While the use of ankle bells will probably continue to some extent, the unique style and sound that had long been a part of the sect will, like the tattoos and handwritten *ordhni*s, most likely become a part of the past.

Bhajan Mela

Melas, or religious fairs and festivals, are of central importance in popular Hinduism. Most villagers have little experience or recognition of Vedic scriptures, elaborate brahmanical ritual performances, or the complex theology that serves as the theoretical foundations of the orthodox religion. Most do not live near, nor are able to frequent ashrams or temples where such activities usually occur. In short, most Hindus live outside of the centers, both geographically and socially, where the practice of orthodox Hinduism takes place. Instead, their predominant exposure to and experience of the religion that exists outside the confines of their local environs is through religious festivals. *Melas* are more within the grasp of most villagers' experience and understanding. While the larger festivals, such as Ramnaumi, Holi, and Shivratri, that are celebrated throughout India often serve to help villagers feel a sense of continuity and identity with the more widespread normative religious tradition, the smaller regional *melas* tend to inspire in participants a connection with the religion and culture of their particular region. By inspiring in participants a perception of unity and validation of their beliefs and faith, festivals encourage continued adherence to the value system espoused by the prevailing belief systems. In this way, festivals serve to promote both the popular and orthodox traditions.

Larger *melas* often have their roots in the mythological past, through their association with ancient personalities, deities, or events. Upper-caste-prescribed normative religious beliefs and practices tend to dominate at such festivals, and participants, attracted from distant as well as nearby areas, are exposed to the more orthodox and national interpretations of Hinduism. These *melas* are often the only place where many villagers have the occasion to experience firsthand traditional orthodox elements such as brahman priests chanting Vedic scriptures, performing elaborate fire rituals, or lecturing on religious topics.

Regional festivals, on the other hand, are usually inspired by local deities, figures, events, ritual practices, or religious movements. Because of the closer geographic and cultural proximity between these *melas* and those who attend them, these smaller events serve to promote and perpetuate various local traditions and practices, as well as to provide villagers with a sense of continuity and identity with the religious and cultural heritage of their particular region, caste, and/or ethnic group. Nevertheless, both national and local *melas*, not only inspire in participants a perception of solidarity and a validation of traditions and practices, but also encourage continued adherence to the value systems being espoused.

Chhattisgarh has a varied festival calendar, most gatherings taking place between fall and spring. Because of the diverse tribal groups, sectarian movements, and peoples from surrounding states that now reside in the region, the festivals exhibit an array of ethno-cultural traditions and religious beliefs and practices. *Melas* often provide the only opportunities for Chhattisgarhi villagers to leave the confines of their daily rural existence and to witness the diversity of religious practitioners, activities, and entertainment found at such gatherings. Because of the incredible assortment of people who attend and the various goods available at even small local *melas*, these festivals also provide participants one of the few occasions they have to make contact with the world beyond their immediate locale and its ways.

Traditionally, *melas* are held at places considered sacred. These include natural formations such as bodies of water, hilltops, temples, or historic sites. Such places are often pilgrimage spots as well. The site adds sanctity to the festival, and at the same time, staging festivals there also serves to popularize and sanctify the location. Thus, place and performance interact to promote one another. The Ramnamis have their own *mela* and their own unique approach to staging it.

The primary festival for the sect is its yearly Bhajan Mela, and it is the group's most important gathering. As mentioned earlier, the first such gathering took place in 1911, and tradition has it that one hundred fifty to two hundred people attended that initial festival. During the three days of the 2001 Bhajan Mela, over seventy-five thousand people attended. Unlike most other *melas* in India, the Bhajan Mela moves every year; moreover, Ramnami rules prohibit it from returning to any spot where it has already been held. There are two reasons for this. Primarily, the rule was meant to pass on the burden and expense, as well as opportunity, of hosting a *mela* to a different village or town each year. Also, it is felt that the *mela*'s purpose is to spread the chanting of *Ramnam,* and this can best be done by taking the *mela* throughout the region.

Ramnamis can be found in nearly thirty-five hundred villages spread throughout northern and eastern Chhattisgarh. Most of these are small villages, so many sect members have few other Ramnamis nearby with whom they are able to meet on a regular basis for *bhajan.* As a result, the Bhajan Mela provides one of the few opportunities for many Ramnamis to get together and spend any length of time with other members of the sect. It is the one time the majority of the sect gathers together to function as a unit. Ramnamis often count their time in the *samaj* by how many annual *melas* they have attended.

The Bhajan Mela is an important event for the people of eastern Chhattisgarh, not just for Ramnamis. Its increasing popularity has caused it to become a focus of energy and activity, and it is anticipated by many from all over the region. As none of the other religious sects in rural Chhattisgarh has as large a gathering, the *mela* enhances the Ramnamis' popularity and credibility in the eyes of many villagers. The *mela* serves as a sign of stability and continuity, and thus it enhances the status of the sect. The *mela* also gives Ramnamis an opportunity to reaffirm their commitment to the movement and its goals, to come into contact with people from all over the region and to celebrate. For many it is also a time to forget for a few days the problems and worries that so often plague daily existence. At the *mela* it is easy to become involved in the visual, emotional, and religious activities and fervor, thus allowing the daily difficulties to fade from thought and concern.

Although the traditional Hindu New Year is in the spring (March–April), for many Ramnamis and devotees in the region the *mela* begins the new year. New vows are taken, in initiation and in marriage; new families and friends are made; old vows are reaffirmed. A year has gone by since the last festival, and all that has transpired is now in the past. Spring will soon be approaching and with it the season to begin planting rice. Already, thoughts of the coming *mela* will be on the minds of many, since preparation for the *mela* actually begins on the last day of the previous year's festival.

On that day, a committee consisting of *sadasya*s is chosen by the *adhyaksha* with the sole purpose of deciding the location of the following year's festival.[24] Representatives from each village seeking to host the *mela* must be present at the time the committee members are picked. Each village submits a written request to the committee to be put on the list of contenders. At the same time, a coconut is offered and a token monetary offering made. This procedure must be repeated every year by each village requesting the *mela,* until it is chosen. Failure to do so results in removal of the village's name from the list and is viewed poorly by the committee with respect to any future consideration of that village as a potential *mela* site. The committee then takes the list of represented villages and goes to a secluded place to make its decision. In the process of selecting the *mela* site, six factors are carefully examined.

First, the length of time a village has been consistently requesting the *mela* is considered. Every year, fifteen to twenty villages ask to host the following year's festival. Consequently, they must be put on a waiting list, and at present they must have been on this list at least ten to twelve years before being given serious consideration. Villages picked as festival sites during the last decade have been on the waiting list an average of fifteen years. Occasionally the time is shorter, but it can also be much longer. For example, the village that served as host for the 1990 *mela* was chosen after thirty-one consecutive years of requesting it.

Second, the location of a village along the Mahanadi River, which traverses Chhattisgarh, is taken into account. By the 1940s, the *mela* had become so popular throughout Chhattisgarh that many villages began to request the chance to host it. Since most Ramnamis live in the eastern portion of the region, the selection committees preferred that area, causing sect members and devotees from other areas to raise objections. In 1945, it was decided that in order to give all areas an equal opportunity, each year the *mela* should be held on the opposite side of the Mahanadi from the previous year, since at that time the river divided the Ramnami population into two roughly equal portions. Currently, however, nearly 70 percent of the *samaj* live on the southeastern side of the river, but this method of choosing remains in effect.

Third, the material capacity of the requesting village is examined. Since the hosts must make all preparations and provisions for the staging of the *mela* and for the basic needs of sect members who attend, a great deal of material goods must be collected and arrangements made well in advance. Due to the amount of goods currently necessary, such preparatory work requires years of gathering and storing of the required items. In the 1940s, the selection committee made a list of *minimum* supplies needed to support a *mela*. From time to time the list has been updated in accordance with increasing *mela* size and attendance. For the 2001 festival, the major items on the list included:

1. 6,000 kg. of rice
2. 1,000 kg. of wheat
3. 2,000 kg. of beans
4. 1,500 tons of wood (for burning)
5. 4,000 clay pots (for cooking)
6. 1000 long poles for setting up tents, boundaries, and so forth
7. 500 kg. of kerosene
8. 400 kg. of potatoes
9. 100 kg. of coconuts
10. 200 kg. of sugar
11. 100 kg. of cooking oil
12. 50 kg. lamp oil
13. 10,000 kg. of hay (for sleeping on and feeding animals)
14. Rs. 2,500 (to be donated to the sect)

In addition to the above, the village must also provide a sufficiently large, open area to accommodate the festival.[25] There must be an adequate water supply nearby to sustain up to fifty thousand people for three days. The village must also arrange for some sort of transportation from the village to the nearest town, in case of any emergencies, and it must provide, before and during the *mela,* housing, care, and assistance for any *sadasya*s who come early to supervise and oversee final preparations.

The last and currently most costly of the individual material requirements is the building of a permanent *Ramnam stambha* at the site of the festival. This is a structure adorned with *Ramnam* and around which the *mela* takes place. Its presence and use has its roots in the Satnami practice of constructing a *stambha* to mark their annual festival spot. However, *stambha* forms and uses for the Ramnamis have evolved well beyond the significance afforded them by the Satnamis.

During the first few decades of the Ramnami Samaj, a simple wooden pole was used for the *stambha,* like that used by the Satnamis. Then in the mid-1930s, the practice of building permanent structures began. Many of the Ramnamis felt that the *stambha* should represent the abiding presence of *Ramnam* at the place where a *mela* has been held. Then, any Ramnamis not being able to attend the yearly *mela* can at least congregate at a nearby *stambha* and chant *Ramnam* there during the time of the festival. It was thus hoped that the increasing presence of *stambhas* in Chhattisgarh would inspire *Ramnam* chanting at various sites throughout the region. At present there are more than sixty-five *stambhas* visible in Chhattisgarh, and they exist as a reminder to many of the continuing presence of the Ramnamis.

The first permanent *stambha* was built out of rock and cement, and like all subsequent *stambhas*, it remains standing today. Gradually, the design of the structure began to vary, as it was left up to the inclination of the hosting village. The only guidelines given to the host village is that the *stambha* not be made to house any images, that it have *Ramnam* written on it, that it be made as a permanent structure, and that there be a place at its pinnacle for a *kalash,* a brass ornament shaped like a stack of water pots that adorns the peak of most Hindu temples.[26] The form of early *stambhas* was relatively simple, mostly monolithic in shape. Many of these resemble miniature Washington monuments and range in height from fifteen to thirty feet.

Then in the early 1970s, one village sought to make sure its *stambha* stood out from the others as a lasting remembrance to its hosting of the *mela.* In the process, it spent nearly Rs. 4,000 to have one built, which was quite expensive at the time in comparison to previous structures. This began several decades during which time many villages apparently sought to outdo previous ones in the construction of their *stambhas*. As a consequence, by 1992 the village that hosted the festival spent nearly Rs. 70,000 for its structure, which is an ornate, temple-like creation, complete with small minarets.

At the same time, however, during the 1990s one of the Ramnamis who is known for his artistic talent has been called upon by several villages to design and oversee the construction of their *stambhas*. His creations reflect a desire to move the style away from the ornateness that has marked so many of the more recent *stambhas* and return to a more simple form like those built in earlier years. The *sadasya* council also made known its strong support for the building of simple *stambhas,* but refused to put any further restrictions on the host village's design preference. Since that time many of the villages have opted for a more simple style. However, with the inflation that has occurred. even these have become expensive, by village standards. The 1996 *mela stambha,* for example, is relatively simple, but even then it cost nearly Rs. 35,000 to construct (approximately $900 at the time). Then in 2001, because the recently appointed Chief Minister of the new state of Chhattisgarh agreed to attend the opening of the 2001 *mela,* the host village again opted for lavishness and spent nearly Rs. 80,000 for its *stambha.* The village council's justification was that the structure should represent the permanency and importance of the *samaj.*

Formal requests by villages wishing to host the Bhajan Mela are given to the *sadasya* selection committee each year. These must contain an assessment of the supplies that have been collected by the village up to that time, since this is a major factor in the decision-making process. In order to put the impact of these material requirements into perspective, it should be noted that if the entire list above had to be bought in the market place, currently the cost would exceed Rs. 350,000.[27] Most villages that host a *mela* have less than 350 to 400 families, the great majority of whom have no source of income other than the food they grow for their own personal consumption. Moreover, the few paying jobs are typically held by caste Hindus who are less likely to strongly support the festival, although some do. Add to this the fact that the last two decades the region has experienced drought conditions and crop failures during at least six of the monsoon seasons, and most families only survive season to season with much sacrifice, the difficulty involved in collecting such a list of goods should be obvious. It is for this reason that it takes so long for a village to be ready to host a *mela,* if at all.

Most villages take years to accumulate such surpluses, and the fact that they do so shows the Ramnamis their devotion, willingness, and commitment to sacrifice in order to have the *mela.* Obviously, not all villages can even dream of gathering such a storehouse, so in some instances several nearby villages join together for such an undertaking. Of the six factors examined in making the choice for the *mela* site, this third requirement is the most difficult to fulfill.

Fourth, because of the size and cost of the *mela,* as well as the potential burden on a village, there must be unanimous approval by the village *panchayat,* the ruling body of the village. Before giving its consent, this body must consider multiple factors, including financial burden, responsibility for making all the preparations, and consideration for members of the village who may not want the *mela* there. In some villages in the region there is a sizable Muslim community, but objection to hosting the *mela* is rare. The 1983 *mela,* for example, was held in a village whose population is nearly 40 percent Muslim. Not only did the latter not object, but several helped to provide goods and many visited the festival to watch and listen.

Fifth, the village wanting to serve as host must have at least five initiated Ramnamis, whose duty it will be to direct the *arti* that is carried through the streets to mark the beginning of the festival.[28] A village without five initiates can request the *mela* and begin the process of gathering goods and preparing for the festival. But before the *mela* is actually awarded to a particular village, at least five of its members must become tattooed Ramnamis. Also, all Ramnami residents in that village and their families must take a vow to become vegetarians from that point onward.[29]

Finally, once a village submits a formal request for the *mela, sadasyas* from that area watch to see how often and how many members of that village attend the yearly festivals. If sufficient faith in and devotion to the *melas* and the movement are not shown, then there is little chance the village will get selected, irrespective of the level of preparations made.

During the last decade or so, the entire selection process is being watched more carefully by the membership as a whole. This has come about since the mid-1980s, when representatives of some of the requesting villages were charged by other village representatives with bribing *sadasyas* in order to have their village chosen. While nothing could be proven, many sect members feel certain that this had in fact taken place.[30] The subsequent *mela* at one of the highly suspected villages was a near disaster due to rains and flooding. Ramnami elders could not remember such a calamity ever happening during a festival, and a general feeling among sect members was that this was Ram's way of punishing the village for its "dishonesty" in obtaining the *mela*.

A variety of factors inspire a village to seek the opportunity to host a Bhajan Mela. For its residents who are Ramnamis or *Ramnam* devotees, this may be an expression of their faith or of a desire to give their entire village an experience of the sect and its *Ramnam bhajan*. They may also see this as a way to gain status in the sect, their village, or their caste community. Also, the presence of the *mela* allows many villagers to experience a holy festival that comes to them rather than they having to go to it, yet it carries in the mind of most who attend it the same religious virtue that is gained by traveling to one of the traditional pilgrimage spots or attending larger holy festivals.

For other residents, there are economic interests and agendas. Whenever there is a massive accumulation of goods and material, there is always an opportunity for some people to make a profit. Increasingly, retailers, hawkers, portable cinema houses, magicians, and other performers seek a role in and a place at the *melas* and are willing to pay to get it. Also, with an influx of up to fifty to seventy-five thousand outsiders at such a festival (most are not sect members), there is an enormous demand for essential commodities and the prices of such merchandise will drastically inflate during those few days. With a little advanced planning and the ability to secure such goods prior to the *mela,* some village entrepreneurs have been able to makes thousands of rupees during the three-day event.

As soon as a village is selected, work begins toward assuring that all material requirements will be met by the time the *mela* begins the following year. Representatives of the village may be chosen to seek the aid of nearby villages in filling their needs. In some cases, resident Ramnamis have sold jewelry and even land in order to assure material preparedness for a *mela*.

Just before the monsoon season in late May, another committee of ten *sadasyas* is appointed to oversee *mela* preparations. At this time the committee visits the upcoming festival site. To be sure that everything will be ready by January, they check on the progress of preparations and the amount of goods collected. In October, the *sadasya* committee, accompanied by the sect leaders, meets in the village to ascertain once again its readiness and to be assured that construction of the *Ramnam stambha* has begun. If at any time during the year the village has failed to make sufficient progress in all its commitments, the committee can change the *mela* site and give it to another village. Practically speaking, however, this has never happened, nor is it expected.

After the October gathering in the village, the *adhyaksha* calls a meeting of one or several *sadhu* Ramnamis from each of four districts within Chhattisgarh.[31] They are given the responsibility of finding villages willing to serve as rest stops for Ramnamis and other devotees traveling to the *mela* from the outer sections of the region. The group first plans four basic routes to the host village, starting anywhere from fifteen to as many as fifty kilometers from the actual *mela* site, and then each group goes to villages along or near the routes to find those willing to participate as *bhajan* and rest stops along the route. Because the processions to the *mela* begin one week before the actual festival, there must be a host village for each night along the route. Villages agreeing to act as halting sites must provide shelter for all Ramnamis and others making the pilgrimage, a place for all to gather for all-night *bhajan,* welcoming refreshments, an evening meal, and breakfast on the following morning.

Arranging routes and rest stops serves several important functions. Originally, the route system was initiated to facilitate the journey to the *mela* for those devotees living in outlying areas of Chhattisgarh. Until the late 1960s, public transportation in the region was predominantly confined to the area around a few urban centers. Villagers, traveling in other parts of the region, did so either by private vehicle, such as an oxcart, or on foot. Consequently, a trip to the *mela* required a minimum of several days for most of those who wished to attend. With the establishment of routes and rest points, pilgrims could join the procession at the place closest to their homes and then travel with others without having to worry about food and lodging.

This seven-day procession has become such an important and integral part of the annual *mela* that despite the prevalence of improved and relatively convenient public transportation, many Ramnamis prefer to participate in the procession as a part of the festival experience. It gives them an opportunity to visit new villages, spend time with friends whom they may see only during this annual occasion, and enjoy a week of nightly chanting prior to the *mela* itself. More importantly for the sect, however, the procession allows it to perform *bhajan* and make its presence felt in many villages that might not otherwise come in direct contact with the sect. The appearance and performance of the Ramnamis in such villages along the procession route have inspired several such villages to subsequently initiate the process of offering coconuts in an effort to become a future host village.

Once the *sadhus* have chosen the villages along the route, they inform the *adhyaksha*. He, in turn, notifies all the *sadasya*s, who then let the Ramnamis in their areas know of the established routes. The processions begin on the fourth day after the new moon in the month of Pau (December–January). That afternoon, a small group of Ramnamis arrive at the first village on each of the four routes. They are given refreshments and a place to rest. The village prepares a *bhajan sthal,* the place where an all-night *bhajan* will occur, by laying down straw and erecting a canvas tarp for a roof. Usually by late afternoon the chanting begins. On this first day, only ten or twenty Ramnamis may be present, but as word spreads through the village that *bhajan* has begun, many residents converge as spectators or participants. Some of these may already be Ramnami devotees. For others, this may be their first experience of the sect and their chanting.

As it gets dark, individual villagers begin arriving at the *bhajan sthal* and invite participating Ramnamis home for an evening meal. Not all *samaj* members go, as some prefer to stay and continue chanting. By nine o'clock, the *bhajan* is once again in full swing. As the evening wears on, most villagers will return to their homes, leaving only a few to stay awake with the Ramnamis. Throughout the night *chai,* black tea with sugar and milk, is served to help participants remain awake. Not all sect members stay up the entire night to chant, but most try to do so. Some may sleep for a few hours and then return to the *bhajan sthal* and continue chanting. Early morning finds a few villagers returning for the last few hours of *bhajan,* often bringing *chai* with them for the chanters who are awake.

Just after sunrise, the chanting draws to a close. Participants are all fed a meal consisting of *chai* and rice cooked with beans or made with sugar. Shortly thereafter, the pilgrims begin their journey to the next rest stop on the route, which may be anywhere from three to ten miles away. Small groups walk at a slow pace through empty rice fields or on dusty footpaths to the next village. Cloudless January skies offer no relief from the sun's intensity, and although it is winter, the noon temperature can reach ninety degrees. Once they arrive at the next village, the travelers are given refreshments and a place to rest until the evening *bhajan* commences.

With each new day and each new stop the number of Ramnamis and devotees in attendance increases, and by the seventh day as many as five hundred pilgrims may have joined each procession.[32] By this time, some of the participants may have walked fifty kilometers or more and had less than two or three hours sleep each night. The psychological state induced by such sleep deprivation mimics a state of intoxication, in which thoughts of home and worldly matters wane. Those who follow the routes and partake in the *bhajans* tend to relinquish themselves to the experience and become absorbed, instead, in chanting, dancing, reading, or listening to the *Mānas* with other participants.

The *adhyaksha, sanchalak,* and most of the *sadasyas* are expected to arrive at the host village several days before the beginning of the *mela,* to assure that all last minute arrangements are being made and to help ready the camps. The group of ten sadasyas chosen before the monsoons to oversee *mela* arrangements will have been at the site for at least a week. Village distribution points at strategic places near the mela grounds are supplied with firewood, kerosene, food, and clay pots to be portioned out to each Ramnami camp. Village heads organize groups of resident volunteers to staff these centers and assure that goods are given only to those who are actually participating in the festival. During the last decade or so, oversight of these distribution points has become increasingly necessary. This is because many of the small time merchants, who set up shop in the bazaar that inevitably accompanies the festival wherever it is held, also attempt to procure the free items while they are still available and then use or even sell them in their shops. Although the situation is well-known to *samaj* officials, and villages volunteers look to them for advice on how to curb the problem, the *sadasyas* do not seem to pay it a great deal of attention. Instead, they say they are there to chant, not to do policing, and that whatever happens at the *mela* is in Ram's hands.

The Bhajan Mela begins on Paush *ekadashi,* the eleventh day after the new moon (usually four days before the first full moon in January) and a day normally set aside by orthodox Hindus for fasting. Sometime during midmorning the *adhyaksha* and several of the *sadasya*s of the festival committee officially bring out the *kalash* and take it on procession through the village to signify the arrival of the spirit of Ram to the *mela.* As it passes through the streets and alleyways, women from various castes emerge from their homes and perform *arti* to the *kalash* and to a copy of the *Mānas,* both of which are carried in the front of the procession by the resident Ramnamis. As the procession passes, many of the village residents pick up some of the dust on the path just treaded and sprinkle it on their homes as a sign of faith and devotion.

When the *kalash* finally reaches the *mela* site, it is taken to the newly constructed *Ramnam stambha* in the center of the festival grounds. Here, *kalash* and *Mānas* are taken on seven counterclockwise *parikram*s, or circumambulations, around the *stambha.*[33] One or two of the resident Ramnamis join the *adhyaksha* in ascending the *stambha* by ladder to affix the *kalash* as its crown. This marks the official beginning of the festival. At least five Ramnami residents of the village must be present during the entire procession to make sure the ritual is performed correctly, as this is one of the few formal rituals to which the sect advocates strict adherence.

All through the first day, Ramnamis, devotees, and others arrive from remoter parts of the region. Traveling merchants, showmen, and hustlers set up makeshift stands on the perimeters of the festival grounds to peddle their goods and talents. *Chai,* food, costume jewelry, clothing, and housewares are sold to meet the needs and desires of the villagers. Dentists, with a few pairs of pliers and a pile of old teeth—proof of their experience—await anyone in need of an extraction. Fortune-tellers and magicians hustle audiences. Additionally, every year since the mid-1980s a temporary movie house has been set up on the periphery of the festival grounds, and its loud speakers incessantly blare out garish Indian film music to entice naive villagers away from chanting and into its own cheap thrills. Thus, such festivals offer many villagers their greatest and easiest access to an experience of the sight, sounds, and seduction of the outside world.

In the midst of the festival grounds, loosely arranged around the central *stambha* are a hundred or more *chandnis,* or canopies, that are erected by sect members to serve both as their place to do *bhajan* as well as their shelter during the *mela. Chandnis* are constructed of light-weight, white-colored, canvas cloth and are about 20' × 20' in size. Many of the canopies have been covered with the name of Ram, much like the designs on the *samaj* shawls. While these are usually collectively owned by the Ramnamis of a particular village for use by its residents, in keeping with the general Ramnami approach to life, all members are allowed to use any canopy as their place of rest and activity during the *mela.* Also, because most Indians have long had to learn to share limited space and limited resources with others, it is not uncommon during any particular evening at the festival to see 30 to 40 chanters sitting together doing *bhajan* in the front section of a *chandni* and nearly that many more individuals sleeping or resting under the back of the canopy.

By sunset, *Ramnam* chanting has already begun under many of the canopies. At first there may be a half dozen participants, but soon thereafter more join in. *Bhajan* participants sit in a semicircle around a copy of the *Mānas.* The front few rows are reserved for Ramnamis in their ritual dress, and behind them sits anyone else who wishes to take part. This practice of sitting in groups, on hay spread out under a *chandni,* around copies of the *Mānas,* dates back to the early gatherings in front of the home of Parasuram. There has been talk of making a few enormous canopies so that larger groups can sit together and do *bhajan,* but the general feeling among the Ramnamis is that the small groups inspire a more intimate atmosphere and are more conducive to feelings of devotion and to the Ramnami style of *bhajan.* Moreover, large gatherings diminish the number of persons who take an active part and, as one Ramnami reflected quite pragmatically, "Who would carry such a large *chandni*?"

Since the canopies also serve as shelter for the Ramnamis and their possessions during the *mela,* space underneath is always limited, and many are forced to sit outside or to sit only when there is room. Those who do participate sit very closely together, knees often overlapping, hands in another's lap. Except for the front few rows of chanters, there is no separation between sect members and others. There is absolutely no separation of the sexes in seating or sleeping arrangements. Many couples sleep together, and it is not uncommon to find them sharing a blanket and embracing, a public show of affection one would be hard pressed to find in most of rural India.

Bhajan continues through the night, a chorus of *Ramnam* is interspersed with various verses from the *Mānas,* and increasingly from other texts as well.

Additionally, some Ramnamis have developed a unique process whereby, during chanting, they use *Mānas* verses to converse with each other and also to debate various philosophical ideas. This process is discussed at length in the section on *"Takkar"* in the next chapter. If there is a Ramnami elder or a *vidvan (learned person) present,* then he may be asked to give commentary on a section of the text, ranging anywhere from two to about five or six pages in length. This process will begin with a period of *bhajan* in which a few of the verses to be commented upon will be inserted in the chanting. Then the speaker will rise to discuss one or two verses. Again, there will be *bhajan* for ten to fifteen minutes, followed by commentary. In this way, one speaker can continue for several hours at a time. Some of the more popular speakers are asked to talk at several of the canopies. They may thereby spend the entire evening going from one chandni to another giving commentary on the *Mānas.*

When participants feel sleepy, they may move to the rear of the covered area to rest, but will often try to get a cup of *chai* first if available, to help keep them awake. Some sect members spend all evening under one *chandni* doing *Ramnam bhajan*. Others will make the rounds to different camps to get fresh air and listen to their *bhajan* styles. Since the Ramnamis come from many different areas in the region, a variety of *bhajan* rhythms has evolved. They all follow the same basic style, but differ in the melodies used and, to a certain extent, in the texts from which chanted verses are drawn.

The mood of the night is light and festive. Old friends sit and talk; impromptu *satsangs* take place at all-night *chai* stands in the nearby makeshift bazaar; on the spot marriage arrangements for children may be finalized. Nearly half the Ramnamis remain awake nearly the entire night, chanting, listening, or walking around. Most of these are men and older women, since many of the younger women are with their children. By seven o'clock in the morning most *bhajans* stop, so people may rest, relieve themselves, or clean up. Men go to the distribution points to collect food and firewood for the day, and as the fires are started, the women begin preparing the midday meal.

The second day is important for organizational meetings. *Sadasyas* gather under a central *chandni* to discuss any problems or matters essential to the sect. Any Ramnami having a grievance against the *samaj* or another Ramnami can bring it up. It is here that such matters are vented, addressed, and usually resolved. The council reflects upon events and activities that have transpired throughout the region during the previous year and makes plans or suggests activities for the future. At some of the other tents intermittent chanting continues throughout the day, but many Ramnamis use this time to rest, shop, have *satsang,* or chat with fellow members or devotees.

Until recently this day was important to hundreds of poor families annually throughout the region for yet another reason: the performance of Ramnami marriages would begin. Throughout much of India, the dowry system has financially ruined many families, and although among the low caste of Chhattisgarh, bride price—paying for a bride for one's son—is the common practice, the social coercion for the daughter's family to spend lavishly on a wedding can be overwhelming. Even though the expectation for poor families is relatively small, for those who have next to nothing, even a moderate size wedding can strip them of what they own. The Ramnami Samaj has forbidden its members from seeking a dowry or bride price in the marriages of their children. Nonetheless, many Ramnamis negotiate marriages with non-Ramnami families who may make financial demands.

In the 1950s, in order to help make marriages more affordable to the rural masses in the region, the sect instituted the practice of performing marriages during the *mela* and encouraged all of its members to have their son's or daughter's marriage ceremony done at this time. Priests were appointed from among the sadasyas to act as marriage officiants during the festival. In the early days of the movement, only the offspring of Ramnami families were married in this non-traditional manner, but eventually the practice was opened to anyone wishing to be married without the constraints of the more expensive traditional system. For many families, this was the only kind of marriage they could afford, and during the *mela* as many as four hundred weddings were performed every year. It was not uncommon for a family to come to the *mela,* child in hand, looking to find a match and complete a marriage, all within the space of the three-day event.

The marriage ceremony was quite simple, devoid of the pageantry associated with traditional Hindu weddings. Generally, the parents of the couple to be wed would first ask permission from the Ramnami priests, who seldom had any reason to refuse. The bride and groom would be ritually cleansed with tumeric paste, a common Chhattisgarhi practice usually performed for three days before the marriage. In the wedding ritual, the bride and groom were accompanied by their parents, and they carried with them the articles for performing *arti* to the *Mānas.* First, they would circumambulate in a counterclockwise direction seven times around the *Ramnam stambha,* then enter the central *chandni,* where the Ramnami priests sat with an open copy of the *Mānas* and a register book. After finishing *arti* to the text, the couple would take a vow to be loyal to each other and to God. They would then sign or put their thumbprint in the register and pay a token five rupees each to the priests. With this, their marriage became official, recognized by both their community and the state government.

However, in 1999, the practice was abruptly ended. For several years, there had been growing concern that many of the youths married in this fashion were not happy with their mates, or more often in the case of females, with their in-laws. The *samaj* elders realized that so many poor families were arranging marriages for their daughters into families about which they knew very little, and many of these families were not sect members and did not share the same set of values. By the mid-1990s, an increasing number of recently married girls from Ramnami families were leaving their husbands and returning to their ancestral homes, alleging unresolvable problems with their mother-in-laws. The *sadasyas* met to discuss the situation several times during 1998, and they resolved to put strict limitations on the practice. They decreed that only those families who had already visited each other's homes and had become sufficiently acquainted with each other could have their children married at the *mela*. As a consequence, there were no weddings that took place during the 1999 festival and only a few at the 2000 event. In 2001, the *sadasyas* officially halted the practice altogether, saying that the benefits of the process were not worth the problems that arose.

In the late afternoon of the second day, the chanting begins once again under every canopy, and by sunset the celebrations intensify as the chanting, reading, and dancing increase. Nearly all the Ramnamis try to stay awake this evening since for many it is their last night at the *mela*. For some this is also the ninth consecutive night of chanting and keeping awake. The excitement of the festival, coupled with their lack of sleep, arouses their emotions, blurring the distinction between physical experience and mental imagining. This state of inebriated fervor is a desirable one—often seen as an end in itself. Some have hallucinations; some have visions; for some, reality becomes narrowly defined by their immediate experiences; some become sick and pass out.

On the morning of the third day, the chanting officially ends, but the excitement does not: this is the day the *sadasyas* will choose the site for next year's festival and there will be distribution of *mela prashad* (blessed food) to all those present. By midmorning, the *sadasyas* gather under a side canopy, cleared for the occasion. Representatives of the requesting villages submit a formal petition in writing, asking to be able to host the following year's *mela*. They must do this, even if their village is on the same side of the Mahanadi as the present festival, thereby disqualifying them from being able to host the next *mela*. The *adhyaksha* chooses the group who will vote on the villages under consideration from among the *sadasyas* present. The chosen ones then proceed to a private place, far from the ears and eyes of the *mela* crowds, and go through the process of selection. This often takes several hours, as the *sadasyas* go over the records of the status of material collection by the various villages, the length of time they have been requesting the *mela,* and the other points to be considered. They may call other *sadasyas* from the various areas in which the requesting villages reside to get input on the status of *Ramnam* practice in a particular village.

In the meantime, everyone's attention is on the central tent as they await the decision of the *sadasyas* to be announced. Invariably, local politicians arrive at this time of the festival to take advantage of the opportunity to get the attention of a waiting, joyous crowd. They go to the *Ramnam stambha* and usually make an offering, then to the central canopy to greet Ramnami officials and praise the festival. The politicians usually give short speeches to rouse support for an upcoming election or to convince the villagers and Ramnamis that they, the politicians, are working for the betterment of their constituency. It seems the audience they are seeking are not actually the Ramnamis as a group but naive villagers who may easily be swayed by their promises and any charisma they may have. This is because the traditional Ramnami distrust of most politicians, who are predominately high caste, is well known in the region. Although this attitude is slowly changing, most sect members continue to pay little attention to these political orators, especially during *mela* time.

In the meantime, members of the host village busy themselves with preparing the *prashad* (sacred food) which, in this case, is a boiled concoction made from all the leftover grains and beans that *mela* participants have donated for this purpose. Although the food is usually ready by noon, it cannot be distributed until the site of next year's *mela* has been decided and made public. Unlike most forms of *prashad,* no special rituals or prayers are done over this food to bless it. Instead, it is believed that the food has become sanctified simply by being in the *mela* where thousands of people have been chanting Ramnam. Thus, when the *prashad* is ready, those who prepared it shout *"RamRam"* and it is considered fully sanctified and ready for distribution. Once the *sadasya*s announce the location of the next *mela,* word spreads rapidly through the camps, and everyone rushes to get *prashad.* Many of the participants believe this holy food purifies those who partake of it, and, more importantly, that anyone who leaves the *mela* without first having *prashad* will lose the virtue or blessing gained by attending. Other *samaj* members reject this as superstition, saying it is, after all, just food, and only *Ramnam* can grant wisdom and liberation, not something one eats or does not eat.

The passing out of *prashad* officially ends the *mela,* and the majority of the participants leave, as does the temporary bazaar that inevitably shows up whenever there is a festival. Many Ramnamis remain until the next day, so they can have one last night of *bhajan* without all the noise and distractions of the shops and spectators. The chanting on this final night usually moves into the host village and is a lively affair, with many of the residents taking an active part. Once again, as on the procession routes, villagers will take individual Ramnamis back to their homes for dinner before the evening *bhajan* gets into full swing. Any leftover grains from the *mela* distribution centers are given to the sect members present to take home, and residents occasionally make a final monetary offering to the sect or to individual members whom they have come to know.

When those attending finally set out on their journey homeward, they will return by bus, jeep, oxcart, or bicycle, although most will walk. Participants who live far away are often invited by friends or other villagers, whose homes are along the route, to spend the night and break up the trip home. By the time they reach their respective villages, many will have been gone for two weeks or more. Although the pilgrimage provided insufficient sleep and little physical comfort, most look upon the experience with a great deal of gratification, for the journey affords the opportunity to escape the concerns of everyday life for a time and provides them the chance to participate in a holy festival. The informality associated with the *mela* gives the villagers a chance to take an active part in the entire festival rather than be passive spectators, as would be the case for them in any brahmanized event.

For the Ramnamis, the Bhajan Mela is truly special. In present day, the Ramnamis appear backward and outdated to many of the Westernized and secularized Indians who encounter them. The practice of tattooing is increasingly looked down upon by many, and it often makes the Ramnamis the object of jest and ridicule. However, at the *mela* they are in their own element. They are the center of attention and attraction, observed doing what they do best; they are viewed with respect and admiration by the majority of those who attend. Ramnamis find tremendous inspiration at the *mela* and return home having reaffirmed their commitment to the sect, to their way of life, and to the practice of *Ramnam*.

Chapter 6

Ramnamis' Contemporary Use of the Mānas *and* Ramnam

Two principal elements of the contemporary Ram *bhakti* tradition have been incorporated into the orthodox Hindu value system: the *Rāmcaritmānas* and the practice of *Ramnam*. The *Mānas* has been accepted and given legitimacy as a sacred text, while the practice of *Ramnam* has been acknowledged as a valid and effective form of *sadhana* for Kali Yug, the age of darkness all of existence to be currently immersed. In brahmanizing these practices, the orthodox elite have attempted to place ritual restrictions around the reading of the text and to attach purity stipulations to the use of the name. The Ramnamis' approach to these two, however, provides both an alternative and a challenge to the brahmanical efforts. This chapter will look first at the contemporary status of the *Mānas* and *Ramnam,* and then at how the Ramnamis have adopted and adapted them to meet their own needs and beliefs.

Mānas *as* Shruti *and* Smriti

When Tulsidas wrote his now famous *Rāmcaritmānas,* the religious orthodoxy of the time saw it as blasphemous, suggesting that the Ram story was already viewed by them as a part of the brahmanical religion. With the increasing popularity of this vernacular rendering of the story, it, too, was eventually brought under the umbrella of the orthodox value system. The process through which a text is elevated in status within the hierarchy of sacred texts has been termed "vedacization."[1] Unlike brahmanization, this process does not involve a modification of textual content but rather of attributed status. The dual processes of brahmanization and vedacization of numerous sectarian works in Hinduism have led to the evolution of a new scriptural category that subsumes the categories of *shruti* and *smriti,*[2] encompassing characteristics of both. Briefly, the category of *shruti* traditionally contains the Vedic texts, which are generally held to be eternal and uncreated emanations of truth. They have no authors, human or divine, and their sounds, or *mantras,* carry more power than do their meanings. *Smriti,* on the other hand, is an open-ended category of texts, including the

Chanters circumambulating a Ramnam *kambha* during an annual festival.

Finishing touches on a new *mukut*.

Dharma-Shastras, Epics, Puranas, and so forth. These texts are believed to have been composed by personal authors, either human or divine, and a study of their meanings is seen as vital.

Most writings deemed sacred in Hinduism enter the scriptural hierarchy at the level of *smriti,* being the preferred text for a particular religious movement or sect. As the movement gains adherents and the ritual importance of the text increases, the latter tends to be ascribed additional sanctity by its followers. Eventually, it may bridge the gap between *shruti* and *smriti* attribution, taking on dimensions of both categories. Lutgendorf refers to a text that undergoes this transformation as an "upwardly-mobile scripture."[3]

The multivalent status and role of the *Mānas* in North India provides an excellent example of the elevation of a text to the point that has assumed characteristics of both *shruti* and *smriti.* On the one hand, the *Mānas* has the attributes of a *smriti* text in that it was composed by a human author, Tulsidas, and is written in Avadhi, a regional dialect of Hindi, rather than in Sanskrit, the language of the Vedas. Moreover, the content of the text, as the source of the Ram story, is considered by the majority of its adherents to be as important as its sound value. In this context as *smriti,* modification of the text, in its written form as well as in oral presentation, forms a part of the process of continual reinterpretation and recreation of the story.[4] At the same time, the *Mānas* clearly has attained *shruti* status in the eyes of many North Indians. Its verses are believed to be efficacious *mantras*, the chanting of which can induce blessings, cure illness, remove obstacles, and even grant powers.[5] Like the Vedas, the *Mānas* has generated a sizable body of literature that imitates, interprets, and expands on the text. Moreover, even many *brahman* priests today, albeit some begrudgingly, grant a *shruti*-like position to the *Mānas* and use it ritually as such.[6] Philip Lutgendorf has described the process of vedacization in Banaras and other urban centers of North India through which the *Mānas* has come to be regarded as the "Hindi Veda," and *Mānas* recitation rituals have been transformed into Vedic *yagyas* (sacrifices) performed by *brahman* priests.[8]

The Ramnamis and the *Mānas*

While the "official" scripture of the Ramnami Samaj is the *Rāmcaritmānas,* an examination of the movement's history and practices reveals the presence and growing importance of oral variants of the *Mānas,* based on Tulsidas's telling of the Ram story, yet distinct from it. Increasingly, these oral variants have a dominant role in circumscribing the Ram story for the Ramnamis.

In the early days of the *samaj,* the *Mānas* became its central text on three different levels. On the material level, the physical text was revered as the sect's chosen deity, apparent in the still common practice of positioning a copy of the text, preferably on a book stand, in the center of the group during *bhajan* and treating it as a deity, to which the recited hymns are offered. Also during *bhajan,* village women often perform *arti* to the text, usually followed by offerings of food or money to the chanters.[8] On the level of sound, the *Mānas* has always been celebrated as a repository of *Ramnam*. Further, its verses are viewed as *mantras* possessing transformative power and as being spiritually efficacious, whether or not their meaning is understood. Like other North Indian Ram *bhaktas*, Ramnamis may use verses from the text in seeking to remove various obstacles in their lives or to accomplish various tasks.[9] On the level of meaning, the *Mānas* has been cherished by the Ramnamis as a repository of great spiritual wisdom and devotion and as their primary source of the Ram story, although actual recitation as a narrative has never been stressed.

For the first several decades of the movement, the Ramnamis focused primarily on the first two levels, paying little attention to the text's meaning, since the vast majority of members were illiterate. Moreover, the level of literacy in the region has long been one of the lowest in India. At the onset of the *samaj,* the literacy rate was less than 10 percent, most of which were in urban areas. Illiteracy among village *harijans* most likely exceeded 95 percent. Even for those Ramnamis who can read, understanding the *Mānas* can be difficult, for although the medieval dialect of Avadhi of the text and the Chhattisgarhi dialect are considered to have similar roots, the former is sufficiently different from most current Hindi dialects so as to discourage most contemporary speakers from gaining more than a cursory understanding of the *Mānas* in its original language. Consequently, when North Indians are reading the text specifically for content, they typically use a version that provides a contemporary Hindi translation of each verse.[10]

At first, Parasuram, the sect's founder, could not actually understand the language of the *Mānas* either, but he could read the script and had memorized large portions of the text that he would recite to his followers, occasionally giving them what he understood the meaning to be. At this stage in the *samaj's* development, the *Mānas* enjoyed a quasi-*shruti* status in that it was revered primarily as a recited text containing potent *mantras* that need not be understood in order to be efficacious. The text had already attained this status among many North India Ram *bhaktas*, so the Ramnamis view of the text was consistent with prevalent sentiment.

Since the majority of the sect could neither recite from memory nor understand the *Mānas,* the original focus of group *bhajans* centered almost exclusively on the chanting of *Ramnam* rather than on actual recitation of *Mānas* verses. Because of the primacy accorded repetition of *Ramnam* in group *bhajans,* the Name gradually came to supersede the *Mānas* in importance as the central focus of the sect.[11] It became not only the quintessential *mantra* that was the core of Ramnami devotional chanting, but its written form came to be regarded as a ritual diagram, or *yantra,* that members inscribed on their homes, their clothing, their possessions, and their bodies.

In time, followers began to memorize various *Mānas* verses as well. Although they often did not have a clear understanding of these, the participants would integrate the verses into their *Ramnam* chanting. While sect members would eventually learn the meanings of some memorized verses, such understanding was not viewed as necessary. Because the verses were regarded as sacred *mantras*, their power was believed to be activated through recitation, independent of understanding.

The desire to memorize verses eventually led to an increase in literacy, which in turn led to a greater understanding of the chanted portions of the text. As long as the Ramnamis were not familiar with the total content of the *Mānas,* they believed its teachings were based solely on *gyan* (wisdom, religious knowledge), *bhakti* (devotion), and the greatness of *Ramnam*. Over time, however, their understanding of memorized verses increased, and a number of sect members began to realize that the text also contains many verses supporting orthodox-Hindu beliefs regarding the social and religious superiority of the *brahmans* and the inferiority of low castes and women. The Ramnamis were thus confronted with a religious dilemma, for the text they had been taught to revere as scripture also includes teachings diametrically opposed to their own beliefs and apparently supportive of their social and religious suppression.

This situation inspired a move by many of the younger Ramnamis to become literate so that they could understand the meaning of the growing number of verses being integrated into group *bhajans*. The purpose of this effort was twofold. First, it would allow them to sift through the existing collection of verses and eliminate those that were contrary to the sect's developing belief system. Second, it would aid in the establishment of a selection criteria to be employed in the building of a corpus of chanted verses, which would in turn help give definition to the sect's philosophy and values. In this way the corpus of memorized verses and the sect's beliefs came to exist in a dynamic interchange, each affecting the development of the other.

As the focus shifted from rote recitation of *Mānas* verses to an understanding of the recited text, from an emphasis on sound to an emphasis on meaning, the status of the *Mānas* began to shift away from *shruti* in the direction of *smriti,* in many ways a de-sacralization of the text. Verses were no longer accepted as powerful *mantras* simply because they were from the *Mānas,* and the text itself was no longer viewed as a bounded, inviolable scripture. It came instead to be seen as open-ended, capable of being interpreted, elaborated, and when necessary, even altered. The Ramnamis began both to reinterpret and expand on the text, emphasizing certain verses that were in accordance with their values while ignoring others that violated their belief system. Thus, the *Mānas* became the basis and point of departure for the development of the sect's own tellings of the Ram story, which draw not only on the *Mānas* but on a variety of additional texts.

Retelling the Ram Story

In the early days of the Ramnami movement, the *Mānas* clearly had a sacrosanct and authoritative status as the preeminent text used in the sect's devotional practices. Until the 1920s, the *Mānas* was the only text from which verses were extracted for use in Ramnami *bhajans*. With the growing realization that the *Mānas* also contains teachings antithetical to the sect's own philosophy and values, as described above, the Ramnamis were forced to reevaluate the role of the text in their religious life. This increased awareness of the contents of the *Mānas* subsequently opened the door for the inclusion in their chanting sessions of verses from other texts and alternate tellings of the Ram story. Another pivotal factor influencing the inclusion of supplemental textual material seems to have been the presence and influence in Chhattisgarh of Kabirpanthis. Praise of *Ramnam* is a recurring theme in much of Kabir's poetry, and the Ramnamis, as devotees of the Name, eventually began to incorporate several of Kabir's couplets into their *bhajans*. Once verses from Kabir became a part of the sect's chanting, it was not long before the Ramnamis began to incorporate verses from a variety of other texts as well. In the process, the Ramnamis began developing their own rendering of the Ram story, their own Ramayan, created from the editing and adaption of existing versions and verses.

Although the *Mānas* has gradually lost its position as the sole repository of verses used in *bhajan,* it is still the major source for most Ramnamis. A corpus of approximately five to six hundred *Mānas* verses constitute more than half of the sect's chanted Ramayan. Added to this are nearly two hundred verses from an assortment of different texts that have also become an integral part of the group *bhajan.* Use of these latter verses vary relative to the particular Ramnamis who happen to be chanting. Author and antiquity play little or no role in the selection of alternative texts or verses to be used. On the contrary, many of the Ramnamis are entirely unaware of the origin of numerous verses they commonly use in chanting.[12] In their view, the authoritativeness of a verse or text is determined, not by its author but rather by its content. Sect members cite the example of Ravan, the demon king of Lanka, who on occasion in the *Mānas* speaks words of great wisdom, thus illustrating that even demons can speak truth. The Ramnamis say that ultimately it is truth they seek, irrespective of its source.

Two major criteria are used to determine whether or not a verse may be included in the Ramnamis' *bhajan.* First, its metrical form must be either *doha* or *chaupai,* the meters in which the majority of the *Mānas* is written.[13] Second, its content must generally pertain to Ram, *Ramnam,* wisdom, or devotion, although in certain situations this rule can be suspended (see "*Takkar*" section below). The secondary texts that meet these criteria and are consequently drawn upon for use in chanting include well-known writings like Tulsidas's *Dohāvalī* and Kabir's *Bījak,* as well as lesser known texts like *Gyan Prakāś, Gyan*

Sāgar,[14] *Viśrām Sāgar, Sukh Sāgar,*[15] *Vraj Vilās,*[16] *Brahmānand Bhakta,*[17] and Sabal Singh Chauhan's Hindi version of the *Mahābhārata.* Most of the supplemental writings used by the Ramnamis are in fact obscure texts, discovered by various sect members, with regional popularity at best. Verses become popular in the *samaj,* because their ideology and meter happen to make them suitable for chanting. The most popular of these auxiliary texts is the *Viśrām Sāgar,* and over the years it has earned such a position of respect among Ramnamis that it is second only to the *Mānas* in terms of the number of its verses that are included in Ramnami *bhajan.*

The Ramnamis' compilation of *dohas* and *chaupais* from the *Mānas* and other texts represents the sect's own, ever evolving and maturing telling of the Ram story. It emphasizes aspects of the story that give expression to their particular beliefs and values while ignoring verses presenting doctrine and narrative with which the sect disagrees. Consequently, the sections of the *Mānas* and other texts most consonant with the Ramnamis' philosophy receive the greatest attention. Conspicuous by their absence are nearly all references to *brahmans*, adherence to caste distinctions, criticism of low castes and women, ritual observances, image worship, and devotion to deities other than Ram. Most sect members simply ignore such verses, although some have gone to the point of actually crossing out offensive couplets from their personal copies of the text. Others will simply alter such verses while chanting them, so that it reflects *samaj* belief.

The Ramnamis' telling of the Ram story is, then, crafted around teachings concerning *gyan,* various dimensions of *bhakti,* and *Ramnam.* In this context, the only narrative material in the life of Ram that figures in the sect's chanting centers on those events that tend to emphasize his impartial love, compassion, and forgiveness. Other than Ram, the most frequently appearing characters in the Ramnamis' version of the Ram story are Sita (Ram's wife), Bharat and Lakshman (his brothers), Hanuman, Guha (a low caste chieftain), and Vibhishan (the brother of Ravan and a demon devotee of Ram). All of these characters have special devotional relationships with Ram and thus assume important roles in the sect's rendering of the story. Many of the verses used in *bhajan* are either words spoken by these characters or words addressed by Ram to one of them. The ways in which these figures relate to Ram are viewed by Ramnamis as ideal manifestations of devotion to him. The last three, Hanuman, Guha, and Vibhishan, are of special significance to the sect because in their respective roles as a monkey, a *harijan,* and a demon, they testify to the belief that any being can take refuge in, have an intimate relationship with, and ultimately attain union with Ram.[18]

In summary, to the early Ramnamis the *Mānas* had a quasi-*shruti* status, but as they gradually came to understand its meaning, the status of the text itself began to shift. Although the sect still tends to assign the *Mānas* a special status, makes it the centerpiece of their group *bhajans*, and uses its verses as *mantras*, at the same time its members add to and take away from it as they please, praising some sections, denouncing others. The implications of this change in attitude towards the text will be explored more fully below.

Ramnami *Bhajan*

Members of the Ramnami Samaj are spread throughout the northern and eastern districts of Chhattisgarh. It is one of the least developed and poorest regions of the North Indian plains, thus travel tends to be infrequent and arduous. As a result, group *bhajans*, especially those connected with the Bhajan Mela but also smaller local gatherings, afford the only opportunities many of the sect's members have to get together. Like the Ramnami dress and the annual gatherings, the style of group *bhajan* has gone through a variety of modifications and elaborations since the formation of the sect. Both its formative process and its present state reveal much about the *samaj* and the individuality of the membership.

Whenever they sit to chant, the Ramnamis place a copy of the *Mānas* before them, usually elevated on a small wooden book stand. If no book stand is available, the text will be placed instead on a piece of cloth or simply placed directly on the ground in front of the seating area where the Ramnamis have gathered to chant. As long as the chanting continues, the text will remain open in its place, although it may never be actually read from. The physical text exists in their midst as the symbolic source of *Ramnam* and a repository of teachings concerning *gyan, bhakti,* and the glories of the Name. Once the chanting has ended, however, so has any reverence shown the physical text.[19] The book is then generally handled and stored by the Ramnamis as any other book would be.

Although *Ramnam* remains the central focus of the Ramnamis' *bhajan,* the gradual introduction of random verses into the practice has resulted in the evolution of the sect's distinctive style of chanting: a chorus of *Ramnam* interspersed with verses primarily from the *Mānas* and increasingly from other texts. The refrain of *Ramnam* used in the chanting is approximately forty-eight beats in length and, for the most part, consists of twenty-eight repetitions of the name of Ram, using various melodies. The chorus is repeated over and over, until a chanter wishes to add to it a *doha* or *chaupai* from the *Mānas* or other text. To do so, he or she will notify the other *bhajan* participants that a verse is forthcoming by vocalizing an extra *"RamRam"* more loudly, during a fixed point in the latter part of the refrain. At the end of the chorus, the person presenting the couplet recites alone all but the last line of the introduced verse, then all those familiar with the verse being chanted will join in its conclusion. The inserted couplet is then followed by recitation of the *Ramnam* refrain. During the last few decades, the number of inserted verses has increased to the point that nearly every refrain is followed by one. Moreover, the Ramnami repertoire of verses has grown so large that during any particular *bhajan* sitting—unless it is an all-night event—very few verses are ever chanted twice.

In addition to selecting only verses they deem ideologically and metrically appropriate for their chanting, Ramnamis further individualize their oral Ramayan by modifying *Mānas* verses themselves. The most common form of modification is the insertion of "RamRam" or "Ramnami" into verses, either on their own or as substitutes for alternate names or epithets of Ram. Thus, "Ramchandra" becomes "RamRam" or "RamRamnami," "Raghuvir" becomes "RamRamvir," "Ramu" and "Ramahi" become "RamRam" or "Ramnami," and so on. "Sita Ram" is often replaced with "RamRamnami," and, where the meter allows, even "Ram" may be replaced by "RamRam" or "Ramnami."[20] Such substitutions are the Ramnamis' way of demonstrating where their devotion actually lies: not with the person of Ram, a human incarnation of the divine, but with *Ramnam,* their link to the formless Ram, the Absolute.

Another form of verse modification of *Mānas* couplets involves replacing the words *"brahman"* or *"vipra"* with *"Ramnam."* This is often sufficient to recast verses originally containing praise of *brahmans* and the brahmanical value system to form verses that praise the practice of *Ramnam* instead. Consider the following examples from the *Mānas.* In its original form, the verse gives the reasons why Ram incarnated in human form:

> The Lord took human form to help *brahmans*, cows, gods, and holy men.[21]

A small change by the Ramnamis (see following endnote) gives the verse a meaning much more consistent with their particular beliefs:

> The Lord took human form to help gods and holy men by giving them [the practice of] *Ramnam.*[22]

In the following *Mānas* verse, Ram is speaking to a demon who had been cursed by a *brahman* sage:

> He who sincerely serves the gods on earth [*brahmans*] in thought, word, and deed.
> Enamors all divinities, including Brahma, Shiva, and me.[23]

With the replacement of one word, *"bhusur"* (gods on earth) with *"Ramnam,"* the verse proclaims:

> He who is sincerely devoted to *Ramnam* in thought, word, and deed . . . [24]

The processes of text and verse alteration have opened up the practice of Ramnami *bhajan* and allowed the sect as a whole, as well as individual members, to become creative in their use of the Ram story. As a consequence of this flexibility, several variant styles of *bhajan* have evolved that have inspired the development of individualized Ramayans and that reveal the direction and maturation of the sect and its philosophy. These will be discussed below.

Individualizing the *Mānas*

The creativity with which the Ramnamis have approached the process of *bhajan* has added new dimensions to the sect's chanting and oral performance of the Ram story. Two formats have been the most influential in increasing the Ramnamis' understanding of, and memorized repertoire from, the *Mānas* and other texts. The first of these involves the insertion of conversation in verse form within the *bhajan* process itself. This is a common practice on the part of many members of the sect. The second format is a specialized type of philosophical dialogue or interchange, engaged in by a small but growing number of Ramnamis. The participants in this stylized interchange refer to the practice as *"Takkar"* (literally, collision, quarrel).

Conversation

To the Ramnamis, *Ramnam bhajan* is both a religious practice and a form of entertainment. As a religious practice, it is the focus of their individual spiritual lives as well as of their shared life of devotion as a community. In this context, it is to be taken quite seriously and to be practiced every day. At the same time, however, *Ramnam bhajan* gatherings, especially the larger periodic ones, are the only time many Ramnamis have the opportunity to see each other and to experience a temporary escape from troubles and concerns of daily life. Thus, group chanting sessions are also a time of joy and celebration. It is in this context that *bhajan* is viewed as a source of entertainment, involving at times lighthearted conversation, jesting, and joking among the Ramnamis.

Besides the corpus of verses from the *Mānas* and other texts that have been incorporated in *Ramnam bhajan,* there is also a vast array of other *Mānas* verses that cover a broad range of subjects. Although these do not directly apply to the common *bhajan* topics, they are often quite useful for the purpose of actually conversing with one another while chanting. Sect members will occasionally interject such verses into the actual chanting as a means of greeting one other, joking, complaining about the difficulties of family life, speaking irreverently about priests, politicians, and wealthy landowners, and so on.

During chanting, for example, a Ramnami may spot a friend he has not seen for a long time and may nod an acknowledgment of the other's presence, while reciting the following *Mānas* verse. The words are those of a sage greeting Ram upon his arrival at the former's hermitage:

> With deep concentration, day and night I've watched the road.
> Upon seeing (you) my Lord, my heart has been consoled.

Lord, I have no reason to be worthy.
Yet you've graced me (with your presence), knowing me as your devotee.[25]

A fitting reply to the welcoming couplet might be:

Now, Hanuman, I have faith the Lord's blessings are upon me.
For without it, I could not encounter one so holy.[26]

If an unknown member of the sect arrives to take part in a particular *bhajan* gathering, a Ramnami may want to show hospitality and inquire as to the identity of the stranger. At the same time he may wish to ascertain if the stranger is aware of the conversation style and his level of cleverness:

Are you one of the Lord's servants? Loving feelings fill my heart.
Or maybe you are Ram, Friend of the poor, with blessings to impart.[27]

The newcomer might use the following brief reply to show his humility, his awareness of the conversation, and knowledge of how to respond:

Lord, I am [Vibhishan] the brother of the ten-headed Ravan.
O Protector of the gods, I was born in the family of demons.[29]

In turn, such a statement may prompt the reply:

Praises, praises, praises for Vibhishan.
You have become the jewel of all demons.[29]

Another common way to greet an unknown Ramnami is with the following verse:

Who are you (two), light and dark in color,
wandering the forest, dressed as warriors?[30]

At the first Bhajan Mela I attended, I entered the *chandni* and sat down amidst the chanting taking place. One of the Ramnamis modified the above *doha* as his greeting to me:

Who are you, light complexioned foreigner,
in the forest, dressed as a *sadhu* wanderer?[31]

Because I was as yet unaware of this unique style of chanting and use of verses for conversation, I was cognizant only that he was acknowledging my presence, not that he had altered a *bhajan* verse to greet me. Afterwards, one of my Ramnami acquaintances informed me of what had taken place.

Over the years, I have seen a variety of conversations and commentaries on life occur during chanting. While they are generally light and cordial, they also may contain an element of melancholy or even a little cynicism. During one evening *bhajan*, a Ramnami appeared who, due to domestic difficulties, had not been to the local gatherings for some time. On seeing him, one of his friends recited a verse commonly used for greeting:

> With deep concentration day and night I've watched the road.
> My heart has been soothed upon seeing (you) my Lord.[32]

In suggesting a reason for his absence, the first Ramnami replied:

> Every man, O Lord, is controlled by a lady.
> Forced to dance, like a trained circus monkey.[33]

Since the establishment of "*harijan* wards" in 1988, Ramnamis have increasingly begun to look to the possibility of political involvement as a means of upliftment for their community or themselves, but most are still skeptical that any real benefits can be gained in this way. Moreover, many feel that those who do go into politics must sacrifice their ethics and values in order to be successful. In this context, many a Ramnami with political ambitions has been the subject of comments during *bhajans*. Recently, a *sadasya* had boasted in a council meeting of his political connections, aspirations in an upcoming local election for *sarpanch,* and "assurance" of his imminent victory. Later that evening, he arrived at a *chandni* where *bhajan* was in progress. Two Ramnami chanters who had heard the *sadasya*'s earlier self-touting, offered a few verses (the latter, a modified one) as the *sadasya* made a place for himself in the front of the tent:

> Let me tell you of Ram's true nature, he will not allow pride in His devotees.
> Pride is the root of suffering and rebirth, and the vast host of miseries.[34]
> For his devotee's sake, *Ramnam swami* will surely take away his vanity.
> *Brother Ramnami,* how can you not worship such a Lord, giving up all falsity.[35]

The *sadasya* seemed sufficiently distracted in seeking to position himself for all to see so as not to notice the commentary being directed at him. In this manner, the Ramnamis combine *bhajan* and conversation, and the process often seems more like a competition to see who can be more clever in seeking out verses to apply to a variety of situations. When a verse used in conversation is replied to, a dialogue may begin and this, in turn, may lead into another stylistic variant of Ramnami *bhajan* called *"takkar."*

Takkar

Nearly all Ramnamis know something about the use of *Mānas* verses in conversation, and many of them practice it. Barely half, on the other hand, are even aware of the *bhajan* style known as *"takkar"* (lit. quarrel, collision), and not more than 20 percent actually take an active part in it. Nevertheless, *takkar* and its practitioners, currently referred to in the sect as *gyanis* (exponents of wisdom), provide perhaps the greatest formative influence in contemporary times on the future direction of the beliefs and practices of the Ramnami Samaj.[36]

The Ramnamis' gradual growth in literacy and ability to understand *Mānas* verses has led to their realization of the need to sift through and evaluate the text in order to avoid those verses and sections that are discordant with their own beliefs. The designation *"gyani"* was initially and informally given to those Ramnamis who particularly dedicated themselves to deepening their comprehension of the *Mānas*. They did this to gain a foundational knowledge on the basis of discerning which verses from the *Mānas* and other texts are in accordance with the Ramnamis' philosophy. In this way, they selected verses they would then incorporate into their *bhajans*. Although the *gyanis* constitute only about 20 percent of the sect, they have had a tremendous influence as the architects of the sect's philosophy, giving shape and direction to the Ramnamis' beliefs and *bhajan* practices. The vehicle the *gyanis* employ for the expression and dissemination of their particular philosophical perspectives is *"takkar."*

As understood by the Ramnamis, *takkar* is a form of dialogue or interchange between *gyanis* that takes place during chanting. The language of these interchanges consists entirely of couplets from the corpus of verses and texts collected by the *gyanis*. The *takkar* process evolved as a direct result of both the conversation style of *bhajan* and the freedom allowed each individual Ramnami in selecting of verses to be memorized for use in *bhajan*. The more literate sect members tended to seek out primarily those verses consistent with their own personal philosophical viewpoint.[37] In time, differences as well as similarities in the perspectives of the various sect members became apparent on the basis of the particular verses favored by each member in the *bhajan* sessions. For example, a Ramnami, finding himself agreeing with a verse interjected into the chanting by another sect member, may choose to display his consensus by offering a verse consonant in spirit with the previous one. At the same time, however, a sect member may choose to counter a verse, either because it was objectionable or simply as a game, and this could be accomplished by reciting an opposing couplet. In time this back and forth process of responding to recited verses became formalized in *"takkar."*

Although the term *"takkar"* normally suggests a combative disagreement and is often spoken of as a form of philosophical debate, the process here more closely resembles a school debate or a game. *Takkars* do not always involve *dohas* and *chaupais* with opposing viewpoints. In fact, many *gyanis* prefer to recite *samarthak* (which means both supporting and conclusive) verses as opposed to conflicting ones. In these *takkars*, the goal is often to see who can be the most creative in seeking out verses dealing with the particular topic at hand. Topics of these *takkars* are usually devotion-oriented and generally consist of verses dealing with Ram's blessings or grace, his devotees, various forms of devotion, methods of gaining and practicing non-attachment, the role of wisdom, and so forth.

On the other hand, some *gyanis* are known to be highly combative when involved in a *takkar*. Many of these are quite intelligent and clever individuals who possess a large repertoire of verses from which to draw. The ability to get one of these more aggressive *gyanis* to respond with a *samarthak* verse during a *takkar* is considered highly praiseworthy. While younger *gyanis* incline towards combative *takkars*, seeing them as being the most intellectually challenging, older *gyanis* prefer *samarthak takkars* instead. The latter say that combative participants run the risk of becoming egotistical and arrogant with their knowledge, as well as offended if anyone "cuts" their verse with a more convincing one. Such attitudes will in turn lead them away from the goal of their practices: love and knowledge of God and humility in dealing with the world.

One *gyani* stated that the main reason he and his companions participate in *takkars* is to plumb "the depths of each other's knowledge and devotion." In a gaming spirit, as they intellectually and philosophically joust with one another, Ramnami *gyanis* may set parameters or rules for each *takkar*. One type of parameter might be to limit the subject matter of the *takkar*, the preferred topics being *gyan*, *bhakti*, and *Ramnami*. Another type of restriction might involve limiting the verses used in a *takkar* to those drawn from a particular section of the *Mānas*, or from a particular alternate text. These limitations are seldom formally set before *bhajan* but generally evolve out of an ensuing interchange. For example, after a *gyani* recites a particular verse, a responding Ramnami may choose a verse from the same text or section of text with which to reply. In this way, *takkar* parameters may become established.

At any time during *Ramnam bhajan*, *takkars* can take place. Since the vast majority of *bhajan* gatherings involve mostly non-*gyanis*, then short *takkars*, generally lasting only a few verses or minutes, will occasionally take place between the *gyanis* present. Such dialogues often pass unnoticed by the majority of Ramnamis present. When, on the other hand, a large number of *gyanis* gather together, then a much greater percentage of the *bhajan* will be in the form of *takkar* exchanges of one type or another.[38] Although *takkar* sessions can last hours, the length of each individual *takkar* varies greatly. Combative *takkars* are generally no more than ten to twenty verses in length, although a series of them can last over an hour. Supportive *takkars* and those whose parameters simply consist of limiting verses to a particular chapter of the *Mānas* or to another text can easily go on for hours, since some of the *gyanis* have literally memorized the entire *Mānas*, as well as countless non-*Mānas* verses.

An amazingly high percentage of Ramnamis—perhaps as high as 40 percent—are oblivious to the existence of the *takkar* process itself, and an even greater number are generally unaware when such interchanges are actually occurring during the *bhajan*. Those Ramnamis who are least aware of the *takkar* process tend to be the women and the older men, the two groups in which illiteracy is the highest. Their ignorance of *takkars* results from the fact that most illiterate Ramnamis have simply memorized verses they chant through listening to their frequent repetition during *bhajans*, without any real attempt to understand what is being chanted. Consequently, their actual comprehension of most verses is minimal and is generally limited to only the most commonly repeated ones from the *Mānas*. As was the case in the early days of the movement, such sect members simply have faith that the verses they are listening to or repeating are about Ram, or deal with *gyan, bhakti,* or *Ramnam,* and that is sufficient for them.

On the other hand, many of the younger males, and a few of the younger females, have had at least a few years of schooling and have attained at least a certain degree of literacy. These sect members tend to have a greater curiosity with respect to what is being repeated, and thus have a greater capacity to understand recited couplets. In addition, they also have a greater ability to read the *Mānas* and other texts to search out new *bhajan* verses on their own. It is, therefore, from among this group of Ramnamis that the greatest number of new *gyanis* come.[39]

The *takkars* have stimulated the *gyanis* to undertake an in-depth study not only of the *Mānas,* but also of various other texts—including Hindi translations of some Sanskrit scriptures—in order to improve their understanding of classical and contemporary Hindu thought as well as to find verses with which to fuel and energize their debates. This study is not necessarily confined to those texts and verses used in *bhajan* but can also extend to Hindi translations of such works as the Upanishads, the *Bhagavad Gītā,* Puranas, various *stotras,* and even portions of the Vedic Samhitas. If a text is found that is in *doha* or *chaupai* meter, then it will be culled for verses applicable to *takkar*. More often than not, however, Hindi translations of classical texts are in prose rather than verse form and so cannot be used in chanting.[40] Thus, although the initial impetus for such research might have been simply a desire to increase the repertoire of verses useful for *takkars*, the purpose of study for many *gyanis* extends beyond collecting verses for *bhajans*.

In the eyes of many of the *gyanis*, the purpose of their textual study is not only to deepen their own understanding of *gyan, bhakti,* and *Ramnam,* but also to provide them with a storehouse of knowledge from which they can draw in order to continually enrich, renew, and invigorate both the sect's as well as their own recitations, and conceptions, of the Ramayan and of Ram. It is not uncommon to see two or more Ramnamis sitting and discussing spiritual philosophy with one another and in the process reciting verses from a variety of Sanskrit texts or attempting to elaborate upon or critique one of the traditional philosophical schools. Such study has greatly increased the awareness and appreciation of certain aspects of classical Hindu thought by many of the *gyanis*. This process has inspired several *gyanis* to find themselves closely identifying with Hinduism as a religion, while simply rejecting its brahmanical orthodox elements as but aberrations of the tradition.

During the early 1970s, three *gyanis* published a collection of verses entitled *Rām Rasik Gītā*.[41] Most of the couplets are either original and are interspersed with verses from various texts used by the sect. Of the latter, many are modified by the authors, in much the same way as is done for *bhajan*. The compilers maintained that their text was for use both in *bhajans* as well as non-*bhajan* discussions and debates. The first five pages of this fifty-eight page booklet are entirely in Sanskrit, drawn primarily from the Valmiki *Rāmāyaṇa*. This is followed by a Hindi *phalashruti,* which states:

> Contained in this *Rām Rasik Gītā* is the eternal greatness and praise of *Ramnam*. Who reads or listens to it with faith will become free of sin and a knower of all things.[42]

The remainder of verses are in Hindi. Without presenting a history of the sect as such, many of the booklet's original verses refer to events in the life of the *samaj*. One verse, for example, tells of the Ramnamis' court victory in 1912; another gives a brief lineage of Parasuram's family; yet another tells of the miracle at Tillapur, and so forth. Some verses also express the philosophy and doctrines of the sect, such as the necessity of the daily practice of *Ramnam,* the significance of having *Ramnam* tattoos, or the importance of abstaining from alcohol.

For a variety of reasons, the reception of the publication by sect members was muted. Because the authors stated that it was a text for use in *bhajan* and discussion, but used only Sanskrit verses in the first pages, and then devoted most of the remainder to their own writings, this raised the ire of many sect members, who viewed the booklet as a form of self-aggrandizement. Although some sect members refuse to acknowledge the text as having any benefit, the *Rām Rasik Gītā* has nevertheless become a useful source of verses for Ramnamis who cannot afford to buy books or who are unable to obtain copies of the original texts from which part of the booklet's contents is drawn.

Most *gyanis*, however, prefer to seek out their own verses and develop their own individualized repertoire of *dohas* and *chaupais* to be used in the performance of *takkar*. Thus, the particular form a *takkar* takes depends to a large extent on both the subject matter and the *gyanis* present. *Gyanis* with a large repertoire of verses and a deep knowledge of their subject matter can generate lively interchanges. In *gyan takkars*, *gyanis* may deliberately take opposing stands on various philosophical issues, such as the impersonal *vs.* personal understanding of God, the dualism/monism debate, and disagreement concerning the relationship between God and *maya*. In *bhakti* and *nam takkars*, the range of viewpoints represented is less diversified since most discussions concerning these topics find relative consensus among the *gyanis*, and all the verses used for such *takkars* are usually in accord with one another. The object of this type of *takkar*, then, seems to be more in pitting one's cleverness and the breadth and diversity of one's repertoire of verses against that of the other *gyanis* more than in refuting another's specific philosophical or theological viewpoints.

Following is a portion of a *gyan takkar* that took place during the 1989 Ramnami Bhajan Mela. Several thousand Ramnamis had gathered for the three-day festival.[43] One evening, a young *gyani* recited the following verse while eyeing another *gyani* seated nearby:

> According to the Vedas, Itihasas, and Puranas,
> God's creation is filled with both good and evil.[44]

Accepting the challenge, a second *gyani* replied:

> God created all existence as a mixture of goodness and corruption.
> Swan-like saints drink the nectar of goodness and leave the water of imperfection.[45]

Stimulated by the response, the first *gyani* offered two verses consecutively, the second intended to bolster the view presented in the first:

> The use of planets, plants, water, wind, and clothing depends on their association.
> Only a clever and thoughtful person can truly make the distinction.
> Only when the Creator gives one discriminative wisdom does the mind turn from sin to goodness.[46]

The second *gyani*'s rejoinder was a verse commonly heard in chanting:

> Knowing *Ramnam* [Sita and Ram] permeates the universe,
> I join both palms and make humble obeisance.[47]

In the above interchange the challenging Ramnami puts forth the view that the world is dualistic, containing both good and evil. As he goes on to point out, wisdom and discrimination are necessary in order for one to be able to reject its sinister side. The initial reply by the respondent seems to accept this view, further suggesting that a holy person absorbs the good and is not bothered by the bad. Ultimately, however, he implies that in reality there is no evil, for the world is permeated by none other than Ram's Name. Such a reply is referred to as *"samarthak,"* (here meaning conclusive), in that there can be no rebuttal, only agreement. While the previous verse is one commonly repeated in *bhajans*, in the context of this particular *takkar*, it was seen as a valid rejoinder, and not just an uninspired retreat into platitudes, as it might have been viewed if used in some other *takkars*.

An intriguing feature of this particular interchange is that the verses are all taken from within the same three pages of the *Mānas*. The ability to conduct a *takkar* with *dohas* and *chaupais* drawn entirely, or even predominantly, from the one episode in the text is considered by the *gyanis* to be a sign of both knowledge and cleverness. It suggests that the participants in the *takkar* are sufficiently knowledgeable of the particular event and the various concepts present in it to be able to glean verses from a common narrative to support opposing viewpoints.

A *gyani* may also begin a *takkar* with a verse antithetical to his or her own belief system in order to compel a reply. If a respondent recites a verse in support, the initiating Ramnami may then take the opposing viewpoint. If the respondent's verse had been a rebuttal, then the first *gyani* would continue couplets supporting the opening verse. Thus, *takkar* participants can put forth a variety of viewpoints, and while the *gyanis* generally present verses consistent with their personal views, this is not always the case, for the purpose of the *takkar* may simply be to challenge the others present. A *gyani* may also initiate a particular *takkar* simply for the sake of *"leela,"* or play.

What I term "*leela takkars*" (*takkars* in the form of a *leela:* play or drama) are a relatively recent variant of the *takkar* form and add a new dimension to the Ramnamis' *bhajan* process. During chanting, a *gyani* may adopt the role of one of the figures in Tulsidas' Ram story, from Ram himself to Ravan, the ten-headed demon king who is Ram's staunchest adversary. To indicate his choice, the *gyani* recites several verses spoken by that character in the *Mānas,* casting challenging glances at one or more of the other *gyanis* present. It is expected that at least one of them will accept the challenge and take on the role of an opposing character.

A *takkar* that took place during one Bhajan Mela serves as a good illustration of the dynamic interchange between opposing characters that distinguishes this form of *takkar.* On the second evening of the festival, nearly seventy-five Ramnamis were assembled in and around one of the many open-sided *chandnis* set up for the gathering. As the chanting proceeded one *gyani* recited several *Mānas* verses attributed to Ravan, the ten-headed demon king of Lanka, all the while looking quite intently at a *gyani* seated nearby. The latter soon acknowledged the challenge and replied with two verses spoken by Angad, a monkey member of Ram's army who, in the *Mānas,* engages in a philosophical argument with Ravan immediately prior to the war in Lanka. Their roles firmly established, the participants in the *leela takkar* were now free to recite any verses they chose in order to help further their respective positions in the debate. Among the verses recited by "Ravan," who is both a demon and a *brahman,* were several spoken by Ram extolling the greatness of *brahmans*. Here the recitation of verses glorifying *brahmans* was in order because the speaker was playing the role of a demon. "Angad," on the other hand, quoted from Marich, a demon friend of

Ravan, celebrating Ram's power. Soon the discussion left the *Mānas* entirely and concentrated on verses from another text. Ultimately the *leela takkar* returned to the *Mānas,* and the *gyani,* playing the role of Ravan, spoke of his great sacrifices:

> I have removed my lotus-like heads in many a situation,
> And countless times given them to Shiva as offerings.[48]

The "Angad" Ramnami's response was a modified statement of Shiva to his wife on the importance of Ram *bhakti:*

> Uma, let me tell you my own realization.
> *Ramnam* [Vishnu] *bhajan* is truth, all else is illusion.[49]

The *gyani* who initiated the *takkar* as Ravan then joined in with a *samarthak* verse praising *Ramnam,* thereby acknowledging the ultimate validity of the previous verse, concluding the dialogue, and making "Angad" the winner of the debate—an inevitable outcome. Figures such as Ravan, Bali, and others whose roles in Tulsidas's telling are generally negative, never win such debates, but then winning is not the purpose of the *leela.* It is a sport, a game, in which the *gyanis* display their mastery of relevant verses and their understanding of various texts and their teachings.

In the above interchange, it was important for "Ravan" to give the final verse, for it is considered *anuchit,* or improper, for the "winner" of a *takkar* to have the last say. Ramnamis give two reasons for this. First, it is seen as a sign of arrogance to want to "have the last word," especially if one has just succeeded in elucidating a verse of agreement from a *gyani* with whom one was involved in a *takkar.* Second, *gyanis* say it comes from the belief that no one tenet or philosophical viewpoint can fully delineate the divine. All verses presented in a *takkar,* even those by "defeated" participants, have validity, and even after countless ideas have been expressed—some of which will contradict each other—there is still no way to plumb the depths of God. Thus, no *takkar* can ever really end, in the sense of being the final word. Furthermore, it is said that a *gyani* can only really understand a verse when he or she knows all the possible replies to it beforehand, and the one who gives the reply must also have a deep understanding of the viewpoint to which he has chosen to reply. Thus, participation in a *takkar* implies that one has a grasp of the various points of view with respect to the verses being presented and realizes that viewpoint and context usually determine a verse's validity. For the sake of discussion and *satsang,* however, the speaker has chosen to present one side while encouraging others to express another. As a result, when a particular *gyani's* viewpoint has "won out" in a *takkar,* then it is considered proper to let the final verse come from another *takkar* participant.

The final verse(s) used to conclude a combative *takkar* may be of several types. They may support the viewpoint of the preceding couplet, express humility and thereby suggest the recognition of defeat, or praise the greatness of

Ram or *Ramnam* and the infinity of his *leela.* One may choose to show humility by reciting the following modified verse:

> Knowing myself to devoid of knowledge, I recall *Ramnam's greatness* [son of the Wind].
> Bless me with strength and wisdom and please remove all my distress.[50]

A *gyani* wanting to add a *samarthak* praising *satsang* might say:

> Without *satsang* God's tales are not heard; ignorance will not retreat.
> Unless it is gone, one cannot attain deep love for Ram's holy feet.[51]

The ending of one *takkar* may be followed immediately by the beginning of another, or the *gyanis* present may return to regular *Ramnam bhajan* for a time. Once *takkars* have begun in a *bhajan* session, however, they will most likely occur throughout the sitting, since for many *gyanis, takkars* are their favorite form of *bhajan.*

Ramnami *gyanis* have evolved a system of labeling verses used in *takkars.* While *samarthak* verses either support the previous verse or end a *takkar,* a verse that has been successfully countered or refuted *(khandit hua)* by another's couplet is termed *"asphal,"* or "fruitless." When certain verses are in close resonance with Ramnami beliefs and values, they are often referred to as *"akatya,"* or "that which cannot be cut." Once agreement with a verse clearly dominates whenever that particular verse is used in *takkar,* then it becomes a part of Ramnami *siddhant,* or doctrine. Such verses are often called either *"siddhant kavita"* (doctrinal verse) or *"gyan ki bharati"* (lit. lord of wisdom). In this way, not only does the involvement in *takkars* encourage Ramnamis to study various scriptures and develop a deeper understanding of spiritual philosophy, but the process itself functions to hone the philosophy of both the individuals involved and the sect as a whole.

The most immediate correlative to this debate process that comes to mind in the Hindu context is the philosophical debates that were a part of the Upanishadic and post-Upanishadic ages that led to the development of the various schools of classical Indian philosophy (*darshanas*), both orthodox and heterodox (for example, Nyaya, Vaisheshika, Mimamsa, the early Buddhist schools, etc.). It also calls to mind the ritual contests in the ancient Vedic traditions. In discussing the importance of the proper recitation of *mantras* for the early *brahman* priests, Ellison Banks Findly says that ritual contests involving proper pronunciation, knowledge of verses, and insight was a part of the Vedic priest's ritual life.[52] She adds that such contests were very important to the participants:

> The priestly competition, then, is the vehicle by which the seer's identity is established, an identity based as much upon his ability to play with words as it is upon his powers of infusing them with an inspiration that is ritually effective.[54]

Similarly, the Ramnami *gyanis* establish their individual intellectual reputations and philosophical identities through their performance in *takkar*. Like the early contests, the *gyanis* use *takkar* to match their "artistic dexterity and literary cleverness."[54]

An interesting consequence of the practice of *takkar* and the extent of scriptural study that it has inspired among the *gyanis* is that many are becoming known in their villages as "*pandits*," a title which aptly fits them, though it has long been used solely to refer to *brahmans*. I have heard many non-Ramnami *satnamis* refer to certain *gyanis* in their own villages as "*pandit ji*." Some *harijans* in the area even look to them as their priests, and they are called on to officiate at a variety of ritual occasions. This clearly irritates many caste Hindus in the region, especially *shudras* who have long depended on *brahman* priests to perform their rituals. Some *harijans* have developed their own religious practices and identity, their own Hinduism, that does not depend upon the blessings and support of the caste Hindus. Moreover, because of the direction of much of caste Hindu society today, emulation of the high caste has increasingly come to mean westernization. Thus, Untouchable religious movements do not have contemporary upper-caste religious traditions to emulate, because so many of the upper caste are leaving aside their religious beliefs and practices. In some ways, this frees lower-caste religious movements to grow in their own direction, and not feel as great a need to use the upper castes as a model.

The number of Ramnamis has been declining rapidly during the last decade, essentially because the number of deaths of elder sect members far exceeds the number of new initiates. At the same time, however, the percentage of *gyanis* is increasing because many of the new, younger members are relatively more literate and are thus encouraged by the older *gyanis* to study various texts and take part in the *takkars*. As their numbers increase, many *gyanis* are gravitating toward smaller *bhajan* gatherings at which they make up the majority of participants, so that their *takkars* are not "interrupted" by the interjection of random verses from sect members unaware of the interchange process taking place.

The increase in the number of *gyanis* and their practice of *takkar* has led to the creation of two levels of oral Ramayan within the sect: the Ramayan of the general membership and the individual Ramayans of the various *gyanis*. In some ways, this is dividing the sect, yet at the same time each level performs an important function. Through group performance, the shared Ramayan of the sect unifies it and defines its beliefs. It provides the sect with an oral scripture, whose parameters and philosophy are constructed around the specific beliefs of the sect. For the *gyanis*, the freedom to develop in their own directions, intellectually and philosophically, invigorates them and gives them a sense of personal achievement. In doing their individual studies of various texts, both to search for new *takkar* material as well as to expand their own private understanding of *gyan* and *bhakti, gyanis* create personalized repertoires of verses that alter their own tellings and make each of them a unique creation. This process inspires a great deal of experimentation and growth for many of the *gyanis*. It also provides a diversity of directions and an ever-changing treasury of new verse material for the future growth of the shared Ramayan of the sect. It assures the continual fluid nature of the Ramnamis' telling of the Ram story as well as the intellectual and philosophical development of the sect and the individual.

Chapter 7

The Ramnami Life: Six Biographic Sketches

Whatever [the Untouchable] is reflects on the larger society and its values. Although he is now more studied and talked about, he himself remains a social enigma. This is so because he is too readily stereotyped by others while he himself often remains remote and silent . . . Once we prepare ourselves to consider the Untouchable on his own terms, after penetrating certain stereotypes, his arguments for alternative self-evaluation begin to surface.

—R. S. Khare, *The Untouchable as Himself*

One of the more often voiced criticisms of organized religions is that they tend to inhibit individuality and create passive followers rather than independent thinkers, individuals, and leaders. Such a statement is too simplistic to be accurate. What can be said historically as well as in the present day is that religious affiliation is the consequence of birth and thus requires little or no forethought. Further, one's inherited religious beliefs are also often intimately connected with one's cultural traditions, which also rarely involve conscious selection. Where individuality tends to manifest in such cases is the degree of active involvement or lack thereof. For religious converts, however, an adopted sectarian alliance is typically the result of deliberate decision making. Typically, political, economic, social, and cultural considerations influence people's choice of religion as much as religious motivation does. All of these factors can be seen to have motivated various Untouchables and Untouchable groups to convert to Christianity, Buddhism, and Islam. The November 2001 conversion of an estimated 50,000 Dalits to Buddhism as a protest against the caste system is an example of this.

The *samaj* comprises mostly persons who made a conscious and voluntary choice to participate. Only a small percentage of the initiated membership was actually born into the sect. Moreover, the philosophy of the *samaj* does not encourage impulsive or unreflective membership, and during the past several decades it has even denied membership to Ramnami children from an unthinking and casual following of their parent's religious preference. On one hand, this attitude has functioned to inhibit a large congregation, but at the same time it has served the sect in that, for the most part, its membership is comprised of persons who are Ramnamis because of an intentional and reflective commitment. This

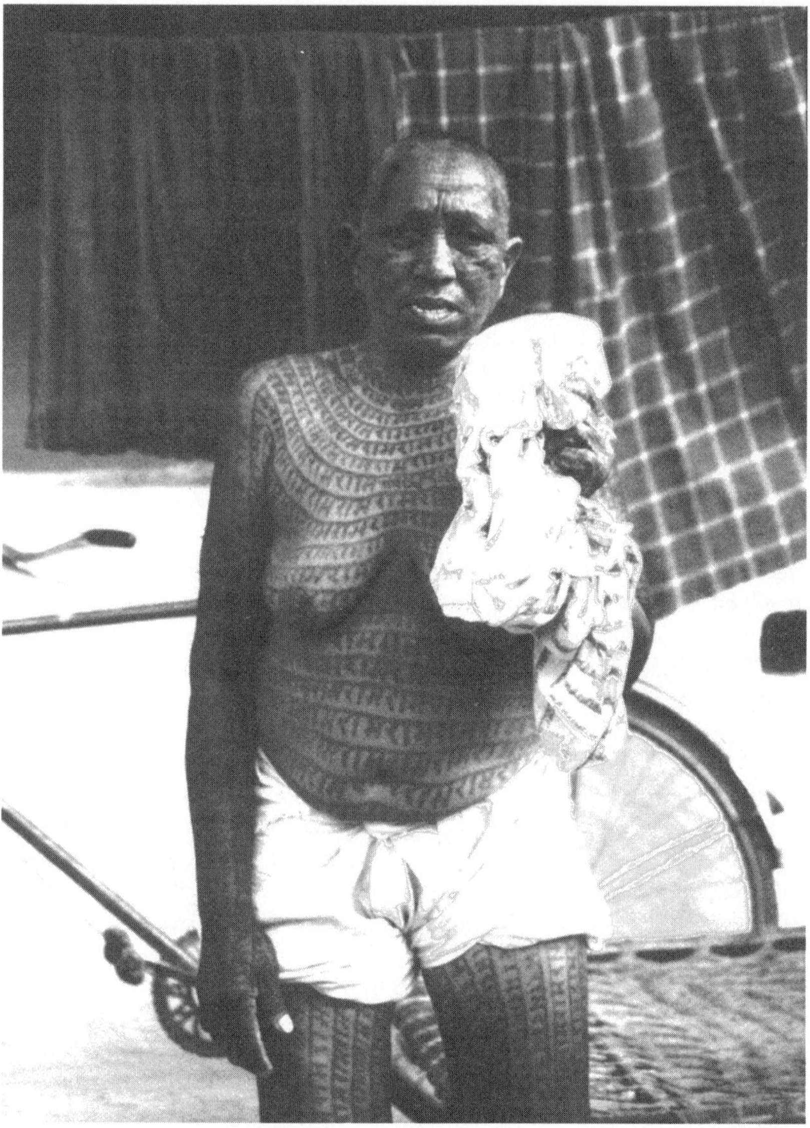

One of the oldest active Ramnamis, proud to show off her full body tattoos.

fact clearly influences both the functioning and ethos of the movement. The short biographical portraits below introduce six Chhattisgarhi villagers who have been involved with the sect, five current members and one ex-member. Their differing experiences and relationships with the *samaj* should help reveal something about the range of influence the sect has on the life of individual Chhattisgarhis and vice versa. From these life sketches, hopefully the reader can recognize the great diversity of individuals found in the Ramnami Samaj, and appreciate the degree to which each is able to determine his/her own relationship to both the sect and the practice of Ramnam.

Ramtaram

The months of December and January comprise a relatively relaxed time period for Chhattisgarhi villagers. Rice crops have been harvested, beans are in mid-season, and there is little work to do in the fields. It is also the time for various religious festivals in the region, including the Ramnami Bhajan Mela. The morning air in Chhattisgarh during that time is crisp with a chill that invariably finds Ramtaram huddling near the wood fire his wife, Kosalbai, makes for him nearly every dawn in the corner of their mud and rock home. His sweater, once brightly striped but now faded into soft hues, is his only piece of woolen clothing. Most men here in Devpur, a small village in Bilaspur District, are farmers and like to bathe early before starting their day's work. Ramtaram, however, prefers to spend those first few chilly hours sitting by the fire sipping *chai*. To him, God made midmorning a better time to bathe.

Even at this hour, the village women are busy preparing meals on their small wood fires set into the mud and cowdung floor of their kitchens, feeding children, and fetching water for the morning's activities. Although there are a few wells in the village, most of the drinking water comes from a two-acre man-made pond nearby. Lines of women carrying large brass water-pots on their heads lead to and from the water. The pond is a gathering place in the early morning: women bathe, fill their water vessels, and converse; men, assembled on their own section of the bank, bathe, sit quietly, and watch young boys playing and learning to swim in the reservoir.

Now in his mid-seventies, Ramtaram is still relatively strong and healthy but seldom works the fields with his brothers and his eldest son. Compared with the other men in the village, he has spent little time farming; for much of his life he has wandered throughout Madhya Pradesh and other parts of North India. While engaged in home-related work, he would rather go to the forest in search of firewood or dig rocks in a nearby quarry to build a new cowshed. Ramtaram prefers these kinds of undertakings to doing farming with the other males in his family, since he can remain his own boss and determine his own pace; more importantly, he can conclude the day's efforts whenever he wishes. Such work is also less monotonous than farming, and it gives him time alone to be with his thoughts and, no doubt, memories of his many travels and experiences.

By ten o'clock in the morning, Ramtaram has bathed, read from the *Mānas,* done some *Ramnam,* and is ready to begin the day's work. Because he no longer has field chores, what he will do depends entirely upon his whim. He may just as likely decide to take a walk to a nearby village to see friends and have *satsang*. Of course, he will certainly tell his wife first of some important errand to which he must immediately attend. The declaration to her is mostly a formality, however, for she has long known that, more often than not, his journey is down old roads.

Ramtaram was born in 1927 to one of the more economically secure *satnami* families in Devpur. At the time, his family owned twenty acres of land, enough to support his parents, grandparents, aunts and uncles, and the many children who shared their home. Ramtaram was the second of four boys in a family of six children. As he was growing up, there were no schools in the area, so young boys spent their days helping their fathers in the rice fields, tending to any animals their families might have, or looking for ways to amuse themselves. One popular amusement was watching the performance of wandering troupes, called "*mandalis*," that used to regularly roam throughout Chhattisgarh to entertain village audiences.

The *mandalis* are a major form of entertainment for villagers throughout much of India, especially in Chhattisgarh. Two kinds of troupes most commonly perform in the region, *Bhajan mandalis* and *leela mandalis*. The former are small bands of musicians who travel from village to village playing and singing devotional songs in temples, homes, or at local *melas*. They may stay from one day to several days at each place, depending on the reception and hospitality they receive from the villagers, who are expected to offer them food, lodging, and money. Such troupes are often formed by the members of one family, and it is not unusual to find up to three generations in one group. The *leela mandalis* are larger troupes of only male performers—mostly pre-pubescent—who dance, sing, and act out stories from the Puranas and the Epics, accompanied by musicians and singers. Males play the roles of boys and girls, men and women, demons and deities. Ram *leela mandalis* use the *Mānas* as the basis for their plays but also draw from other *Ramkathas* and mythological sources to enhance their stories. The Ras *lila mandalis* deal predominantly with stories of Krishna taken from the *Bhāgavata Purāna* and the *Mahābhārata*. The larger, better known *leela mandalis* are from cities, especially those pilgrimage centers sacred to Ram and Krishna, and attempt to remain faithful to the scriptures they portray. The smaller village *mandalis*, on the other hand, exercise a great deal of freedom in their renditions; frequently they tend to insert material extraneous to the story line, and often give performances that are little more than comedy routines with a thin veneer of scriptural adherence or serious devotion.

Ramtaram's exposure to the many *mandalis* that frequented Devpur fostered in him an interest in music and dance. That he was not the oldest son in his family made it easier for him to pursue such interests instead of having to devote his time learning to be a farmer like his father. In his community, as well as throughout much of India, the firstborn son is responsible for following in the footsteps of his father and pursuing the parent's profession, eventually taking over and caring for the family's land or business and the elders who live in the home.

Like most village children, Ramtaram anticipated the arrival of the *mandalis*, especially the *leela mandalis*. By the age of five, he was a regular spectator, and whenever a troupe performed nearby, he would abandon the few responsibilities he might have and would watch the performances with rapt attention. In addition, he was a regular spectator at any function in his village where there was music, singing, or dancing, including marriages, births, or other religious ceremonies. The young Ramtaram often gathered several friends together to imitate the actors in the *leelas* they had seen. His parents realized their son had more than just a passing interest in music, so they allowed him to begin playing the harmonium—a small, box-shaped keyboard instrument with accordion-like bellows—and to learn to sing with one of his uncles in the village. Ramtaram enjoyed music to such an extent that he went to his teacher's house to practice and sing whenever the opportunity presented itself.

Because he was a handsome child with musical talent, Ramtaram was quickly spotted by several *leela mandalis* as a potential actor of female roles. Over the next few years, his parents were approached a number of times by *mandali* managers seeking to draft the youth into their troupes. Ramtaram's mother, however, was extremely reluctant and refused to give her permission, fearing she may never see her son again. Villagers in Chhattisgarh are said to fear the kidnapping of their sons by monks, *mandalis*, or marauders, all supposedly on the lookout for young boys to swell their ranks. In reality, boys are seldom stolen. None of the villagers with whom I have spoken could recall such a kidnapping actually taking place in their environs and few seem to believe it would actually occur; yet, the fear persists in the hearts of many.

When Ramtaram came to know that he had been sought by some *mandalis* and that his parents had refused to let him join, he was greatly disappointed. To him, joining a troupe would not only be an opportunity to learn music, dance, and drama, but it was also a rare occasion to travel beyond the limits of his village and to experience the great world outside. Moreover, having been named Ramtaram (lit. wandering lord), he felt it was his destiny to join a *mandali* and to travel. He made the decision to himself that someday, with or without his mother's blessings, he would become part of a troupe.

When he was eight years old, Ramtaram's parents arranged his betrothal to a five-year-old girl from a nearby village.[1] Their action was motivated by their desire to change the boy's mind about joining a *mandali* and traveling. However, Ramtaram paid little attention to the fact that a family life was already being prepared for him. He was not deterred and remained adamant about joining a troupe someday. This quality of determination marks much of Ramtaram's life, as will become apparent.

Over the next several years, Ramtaram continued his musical interests and studies. Music and dance are much desired additions to any festive occasion, especially marriages and other rites of celebration, but few in his community had such talent, instruments, or the money to hire musicians. Consequently, Ramtaram and his uncle were often invited to sing and dance whenever there was a festival. The youth enjoyed the opportunity to perform and did so whenever asked. Their paying patrons were usually caste Hindus, as it is common for the latter to hire *harijan* musicians and dancers for festive occasions, and also because Ramtaram and his uncle were reticent about charging members of their own caste community for their performances.

Ramtaram became particularly attracted to one Ram *leela* troupe that performed in a large village near Devpur twice a year during the two nine-day Navaratri festivals in spring and fall. His musician-uncle knew the manager of the *mandali,* and the two of them would stay together in the village whenever the troupe was there. In 1938, when he was eleven, Ramtaram finally succeeded in gaining his parents' approval to join and travel with this *mandali.* Because of his looks and the fact that he had already learned many of the troupe's songs and routines, the youth immediately began training to play the role of a female. The *mandali* heads had Ramtaram's nose and ears pierced and started dressing him in saris, the typical dress of most Hindu women. The boy had little difficulty accepting and adjusting to his grooming as a female, because boys chosen for such roles are rarely looked down upon or mocked by their peers. Like people everywhere, village youths of the region usually admire anyone who has a role as an entertainer. Moreover, little concerned Ramtaram, who was delighted that he had finally gotten the chance to learn the music he enjoyed and the opportunity to travel and experience the world beyond the confines of his village.

The *mandali* traveled throughout Madhya Pradesh, and Ramtaram quickly and easily adapted to this new transient, nomadic life-style. With the exception of the monsoon season, the troupe spent nearly the entire year on the road. Every few months Ramtaram was able to return home for short visits, and each time he did, he would give his family most of the money he had earned and bring them gifts from places he had visited. This tremendously aided their financial situation and gave the boy a higher status in his family, in his caste community, and even among many of the caste Hindu youth of the village. It also boosted his own self-confidence and esteem. The vast majority of villagers in rural Chhattisgarh are sustenance farmers, growing much of what they eat—sometimes less, rarely more. When working for someone else to supplement their crop yield, these farmers usually receive their pay in the form of grain. Consequently, few ever have cash to save or to spend on luxuries. Thus, Ramtaram's financial independence and monetary contribution to his family not only accorded him great respect but allowed his family to purchase several acres of quality land and increase their annual harvest.

In his own village Ramtaram became something of a celebrity, and his visits home were met with excitement and joy. Even caste Hindus would approach him and ask about his travels and adventures. His family and friends, too, relished in his fame and they basked in his limelight. For these relatively immobile and isolated villagers, the young performer became a link to the world beyond and a source of news and information about what life was like in the greater world. Then, too, Ramtaram's training had made him a good storyteller who could entertain relatives, friends, and onlookers for hours on end with his worldly tales. As mentioned earlier, the storyteller in India has long been as important to the existence and the continuity of the social, religious, and cultural traditions and mythologies as the ritual priest, the philosopher, and the historian. At an early age, Ramtaram had become an active part of this tradition and process.

During the next five years, Ramtaram immersed himself in learning his new profession. Interested in every aspect of his expanding world, he constantly asked questions about what he saw and experienced. He became increasingly curious and critical about the constraints his own culture forced upon him as an Untouchable. Although he enjoyed the freedom his association with the *mandali* allowed him, he nevertheless grew to resent the caste prohibitions under which he was expected to live. As with other *harijan*s in the *mandali,* he was told by his managers, themselves caste Hindus, to lie about his caste background so that the troupe could more readily participate in caste-Hindu festivals and be invited into temples and homes. On stage, he often played the part of a goddess, and people would touch his feet to ask for blessings. Off stage he had to continue to act the part of a caste Hindu, lest he be shunned. He gradually came to blame such hypocrisy and deceit on brahmanical Hinduism itself and found it increasingly difficult to see through his feelings and recognize any sincerity in the caste Hindus with whom he associated. Thus, his early years were charged with joy and freedom on one hand and turmoil and growing bitterness on the other. On several occasions he considered quitting the *mandali* altogether, so that he could cease such close affiliation with caste Hindus. At other times, however, he would meet caste Hindus who treated him with genuine sincerity and love, and this, coupled with the many joys he felt as a member of the troupe, would displace thoughts of abandoning the *mandali.*

By the time he was sixteen, Ramtaram's physical maturity forced him to quit playing female roles. However, because he had acquired a large repertoire of *bhajan*s, he became one of the *mandali* musicians and began to assist in managing the troupe as well. Although he missed acting, he enjoyed his new responsibilities, which included creating and directing new scenes and episodes for the troupe's *leelas*. As its reputation and popularity grew, the *mandali* began to travel into those areas of the bordering state Uttar Pradesh where there were no language barriers. Although Hindi is the official language of both states and is used by *mandali*s, the diversity of dialects sometimes inhibits communication and comprehension. Thus the *mandali* had to limit its travels to those areas in which the majority of the populace could understand their dialect sufficiently to follow lines and get their jokes.

When Ramtaram was eighteen, his parents decided to finalize his marriage and formally bring his bride, Kosalbai, to their home. Although he accepted their decision, he made it clear to them that he had no intention of leaving the *mandali* or giving up traveling. After the marriage, he began to spend more time in Devpur but still spent half the year on the road. As a manager, his salary increased and his family was able to buy additional land. His wife's family, on the other hand, was quite poor and had little land, so Ramtaram brought his two younger brothers-in-law to live with his family and help in the fields. Ramtaram's own younger brother, Ghoomram, also took an early and avid interest in music and had longed to follow in his brother's footsteps. Ramtaram had encouraged him in this direction and even bought him a harmonium when the boy was only six. Two years later, Ghoomram began to travel with the *mandali* and learn the profession from his brother.

Ramtaram attended his first Ramnami Bhajan Mela when he was twenty-three. Prior to this, he had heard about the movement for several years but had never been in the vicinity of one of their *mela*s or had any previous contact with sect members. Moreover, several of his Satnami acquaintances had spoken ill of the sect and its ways to him, blaming it at least in part for the continuing low status of the *satnami*s in the region. However, his first direct experience with the Ramnamis obliterated any apprehensions he had about the group, and he began what would become his lifelong association with the movement. The event took place in a village not far from Devpur. Ramtaram attended a Bhajan Mela and was immediately enamored by the singing and dancing, and he appreciated the Ramnamis spontaneity and what he perceived to be a strong camaraderie among members. Although the Ramnamis were—and still are—predominantly *satnami* by caste, they did not seem to feel ashamed of their status—nor did they attempt to disguise their social rank. This was the first time Ramtaram had encountered a group of *harijan*s who were openly proud of their roots and showed no overt indication of striving for caste-Hindu status or acceptance.

Throughout his travels, Ramtaram had come into close contact with many upper-caste Hindus and found little difference between their physical cleanliness and moral makeup and that of the lower castes, especially those with whom he had grown up and lived. Caste Hindus who knew he was *satnami* would still listen to him sing songs of devotion, watch him play the roles of gods and goddesses, and offer him food and money. But once he was off stage they rarely shared the hospitality of their homes and did not treat him as an equal in any way. He felt caste Hindus perceived and treated him in much the same way they would a monkey or dog trained to do tricks. Such experiences fueled and intesnsified his resentment of caste Hindus during his years in the *mandali*. When singing *bhajans* Ramtaram felt a love for and close connection with Hindu beliefs, but when he experienced discrimination he despised Hindus and anything to do with their religion. This dichotomy of feelings affected his emotions deeply.

The Ramnamis, on the other hand, appeared to care little about the condescension or disdain of caste Hindus, instead seeking solidarity and fulfillment within their own community. Although he felt a strong attraction to the sect, Ramtaram objected to their lack of overt resentment at and criticism of the hypocrisy he himself had seen and hated. Nevertheless, his first encounter inspired him to seek a better understanding of the sect, their ideas, and their way of life. For the next two decades, he participated in their annual festivals whenever possible, and became a frequent observer at Ramnami functions. There were two respected *samaj* elders living in villages near his own, and he began to spend time with them whenever he returned to Devpur from his travels with the *mandali*. The elders convinced him to chant *Ramnam* daily and to read the *Mānas*. Although Ramtaram had read and memorized many passages of the book to recite with the *mandali* in performances, he had done so in a rote manner with little thought of their meaning. At the inspiration of these elders, he slowly started to view the text differently and came to use it as a source of personal guidance and instruction.

The *mandali* attended various and diverse religious *melas* throughout Madhya Pradesh, from small village events to large urban affairs. At some of these festivals, traditional Hindu fire rituals also were performed with *brahman* priests officiating. On occasion, there would also be religious conferences with teachers and scholars from all over the state attending. Ramtaram savored the opportunity to sit and listen to the different speakers and the diverse philosophies espoused, and he gradually developed a broader understanding of the varieties of Hindu religious thought. He also came to perceive in Hinduism more than the lifeless dogma and the social bigotry and prejudice that characterized his previous understanding of the religious tradition.

At these gatherings he listened intently whenever someone spoke on the *Mānas*. Eventually, he began to give short talks himself on the Ram story when his troupe visited villages. Ramtaram had never attended school or been trained in giving discourses like those often presented at the conferences he attended, but he was inspired by them and began to fashion his own style of presentation, blending philosophy with storytelling and a little comedy. Although the scholarly discourses were always in the official Hindi dialect, Ramtaram gave his expositions in the Chhattisgarhi dialect, often attracting a broad audience of listeners. His enthusiasm, devotion, and charisma made him popular with village crowds. At Ramnami gatherings, he was called upon to speak as well, and many of the sect members enjoyed listening to his discourses. His talks were invariably spiced with jokes, antics, singing, and dancing. For example, Ramtaram would assume an evil look and make frightful faces when he described the demons who play such a large role in Hindu myths. When describing a warrior, he would puff out his chest with exaggerated cockiness, and when he related the exploits of Hanuman, he would hop from side to side mimicking the deity's humble but confident demeanor. Some Ramnamis even approached him to learn how to give discourses on the *Mānas*. Although he had not yet become an initiate in the *samaj,* many members considered him one of them.

Finally, in 1965, after more than twenty-five years of traveling with the *mandali* Ramtaram decided to leave the troupe to spend more time with his family and with the Ramnamis. Kosalbai had never asked him to leave the *mandali,* but he had long known of her wish. He also now had two young sons and an infant daughter, and his responsibilities to family and farm took increasing precedence over his life in the troupe. His father had died the previous year, and although Ramtaram had an older brother, the family looked more to Ramtaram as its primary elder. As a result of the division of his family's land between his father and his uncle several years prior—an almost inescapable situation with the maturing of each new generation in India—Ramtaram and his three brothers now had only five acres of land between them with which to support their families. In order to ease both the congestion and the constraints of his ancestral home and farm, caused by the increasing size of the four families, Ramtaram purchased a small parcel of fertile government land on the outskirts of his village with some of his *mandali* savings. There he set up a separate household and farm, and he, Kosalbai, and their children settled in to working their new land, more than sufficient to supply them with rice and various other small crops.

Soon after this, Ramtaram decided to take initiation as a Ramnami and make his relationship with the sect official. His wife had also been a frequent participant at Ramnami gatherings—the movement encourages family rather than individual participation—so on learning of his decision, she expressed the same desire and they both became Ramnamis. At this time, each had several lines of *Ramnam* inscribed on their faces in honor of the decision and their commitment. Ramtaram already had a reputation in the sect as a good speaker, and he often received invitations to various festivals and functions throughout his district. Because he had become so accustomed to a nomadic life-style, Ramtaram enjoyed the opportunities to travel once again. As soon as their sons could farm the land on their own, he and his wife took advantage of their freedom and started going on pilgrimages and attending as many Ramnami functions as possible.

Pilgrimages are an important aspect of the Hindu religious practice and have long been popular throughout India. However, due to illiteracy, poverty, and unfamiliarity with the world outside their region, most villagers are reluctant and incapable of venturing out on long journeys. Many sect members longed for the ability to experience even once the kind of journey that Ramtaram had done so often and that he knew how to undertake so well. When word spread within the *samaj* that Ramtaram and Kosalbai were planning a pilgrimage to sites sacred in the Ram story, a number of Ramnamis sought to accompany the couple, pleading with him to take them along. His presence was a catalyst for many sect members to act on unfulfilled desires to make such trips. In all, eleven Ramnamis from his district made the first pilgrimage with them. The group traveled by train to Haridwar, in the Himalayan foothills. From there they set out on foot, and after another eight days the group arrived at Gangotri, almost eight hundred miles from their home.

When they returned, the travelers were the envy of their neighbors and fellow sect members, and soon Ramtaram was besieged with requests by others wanting to go on pilgrimage. He began taking small groups of Ramnamis on journeys to sacred places and *mela*s in North India several times a year. Officially, the Ramnami Samaj discounts the belief in a special sanctity attached to particular places, asserting instead that God is omnipresent and thus every place is sacred. Further, the presence of *Ramnam* makes the divine become manifest wherever it is chanted. Nevertheless, the popularity of such journeys increased in the sect. Initially, several *sadasya*s had misgivings about the development, but in discussing the situation the collective sadasya group decided that it was not harmful to the *samaj*. Moreover, it gave Ramnamis increased opportunities to take part in *bhajan*s and *satsang* with others—a common occurrence at pilgrimage places—and an increased occasion for others to hear the sect's chanting of *Ramnam*.

In the villages throughout Chhattisgarh, there are countless devotees and admirers of the Ramnami movement, although only a small percentage actually take initiation and become tattooed. Such was the case in Devpur. While there had been admirers of the sect for many years, Ramtaram and Kosalbai were the first to become initiated members. Their involvement increased interest in the activities of the sect in that area and soon more Devpur residents joined it as well. One of these was Binduram, a childhood companion of Ramtaram. The two friends shared the joy of traveling, and after the latter's initiation, he, Ramtaram, and their wives, began attending every Ramnami function and festival they could.

In January 1977, Ramtaram helped organize a pilgrimage of more than three hundred Ramnamis to take part in the Kumbha Mela at Prayag (Allahabad, U.P.), the confluence of the Ganges and the Jamuna Rivers. Of the four places designated for Kumbha Melas,[2] Prayag is considered the most sacred, and on that occasion nearly five hundred thousand pilgrims from all parts of India and foreign countries camped on the river's bank for an entire month. On the main bathing day, the new moon in January, it is estimated that over twelve million people attended. The *mela* grounds covered approximately three thousand acres of the river bed, left dry by the receded water of the Ganges in the winter. At these festivals, participants usually live in canvas tents or coverings, straw huts, or in the open air. Numerous religious teachers, various sects, and countless religious organizations set up camps for their followers. At some of these campsites, there are daily *leela* performances, *bhajans*, or lectures on any of a variety of texts and topics. Other sites are meant only to house pilgrims.

On their arrival to Prayag, the Ramnamis set up two large open tents under which they kept their belongings, chanted, prayed, and slept. During the twenty-five days they stayed at Prayag, they performed their *bhajan* in front of their campsite for four or five hours each day, drawing large crowds of listeners fascinated by their appearance and their unique style of chanting. As word of their presence and chanting spread throughout the *mela,* the Ramnamis began to receive invitations to visit various campsites to perform their *bhajan*. At each one, they received offerings of food, clothing, and money. To their surprise, sect members were seldom asked about their caste, neither were they turned away or shunned when other pilgrims learned they were *harijans*.

During the *mela,* Ramtaram spent much of his free time watching the various Ram *leela mandali*s perform, and he listened to the religious speakers who spoke on the *Mānas*. He was attracted to one speaker in particular, a Ramanandi *sadhu* called Tyagi Ji, who gave daily discourses on various aspects of the Ram story. Ramtaram took other Ramnamis to listen as well. After two weeks of hearing the monk's lectures, Ramtaram approached him, hoping for some personal spiritual guidance. He also told the *sadhu* of his caste background. Tyagi Ji agreed to teach Ramtaram some religious practices and told him that if he would perform them daily as directed, then the following year he would consider accepting Ramtaram as a disciple. Although this was a surprise to Ramtaram, it was not a unique occurrence. Of all the major Hindu monastic orders, Ramanandis are most likely to disregard caste barriers, allowing people to join regardless of background, provided the new members adhere to Ramanandi beliefs and practices, especially with respect to devotion, cleanliness, diet, and so forth.

Since that time, many of Ramtaram's family and more than a dozen other sect members have visited Tyagi Ji and become his disciples. Traditionally in most schools of Hindu thought, a spiritual teacher is believed to be necessary for one to progress on the path to enlightenment. Such a guru-disciple relationship has generally been closed off to Untouchables, however, for most teachers are upper caste and are unwilling to accept Untouchables as disciples. While his relationship with Tyagi Ji has been a source of inspiration and new experiences for

Ramtaram, it has also met with opposition within the Ramnami Samaj. The sect officially rejects the concept of a guru-disciple relationship as traditionally understood in Hinduism. They view it as establishing a religious hierarchy between peoples, and they consider any such hierarchy as negative. Within the sect, a Ramnami who sponsors a new member and instructs him or her in the practice of *Ramnam* is called "guru," but he/she is not accorded the veneration usually bestowed upon one's religious initiation teacher in India. The religious oppression that sect members have experienced as Untouchables has made the Ramnamis acutely sensitive to anyone claiming religious superiority. Nevertheless, Ramtaram and the other Ramnamis initiated by Tyagi Ji continue to look to him for spiritual guidance as their guru, and those in the sect who object are in the minority and are generally silent about it.

Today, Ramtaram is considered by many Ramnamis to be one of the respected elders of the sect as well as one of the most knowledgeable of the current *gyanis* (see section on *Takkar* in chap. 6). Because his eldest son has taken over the maintenance of the family farm, Ramtaram spends a great deal of his time with the *samaj*. He is an active participant in *takkars* and is partially responsible for the practice's growing popularity. He encourages philosophical debates with the young men of his village, and through his efforts several have become Ramnamis and are learning the technique of *takkar*. Since 1980, Ramtaram has been a *sadasya,* but primarily in name only, for he seldom attends their meetings. Although he is committed to the sect and does what he can to assure its continuance, nevertheless, he would rather leave the politics and official business to others. As he put it:

> I did not join the *samaj* to work and organize.
> I came to chant and fraternize.[3]

Motibai

Among Ramnami couples, one member may be much more involved in *samaj* activities than his or her spouse. However, the sect encourages couples to practice together and share their involvement so that participation does not come between them. For many couples, it has become one of the major focal points of their lives. A good example of this was the case of Motibai and Siddharam. Motibai and her husband, Siddharam, were among my first close acquaintances within the Ramnami Samaj. A quite outgoing and personable couple, they immediately set about helping to make me feel welcome. They were relatively well-educated, and they matched my inquisitiveness about the *samaj* with their own curiosity about the world outside Chhattisgarh—and even outside India. In this way, they were somewhat uncommon for their time, since most villagers I met in those days had a simple bifurcated view of the world: "Chhattisgarh," which they saw as their homeland, and "outside Chhattisgarh," which they tended to view collectively as *videsh,* or "foreign land."

Within a short time, Siddharam and I developed a brotherly relationship, and whenever we were together, our discussions would span everything from religion and culture to politics, economics, and science. Moti, the first Ramnami woman whose extensive tattoos appeared to me as a real mark of beauty, loved to join in our conversations, and in the process my relationship with her also began to develop. In the traditional culture of the region, it is not uncommon for a married woman to have a close friendship with a non-related male, provided the parameters of that relationship are clear. This often takes the form of a brother/sister relationship, and there is even a ritual to formalize it. Moti, however, saw our relationship as one of mother and son, even though she is actually several years younger than me. Whenever she would see me, she would immediately hug and kiss me and then set about making sure that all my needs and desires of the moment were being met. She would take any soiled clothing I might have and make sure it was washed. If I appeared to her to be hungry, even if I was not, she would make or bring me food. If I appeared tired, she would force me to stop whatever I was doing and lay down, even laying down with me sometimes to make sure I would not get up until I had rested. As a result, we had many long and personal conversations over the years, and we came to know a great deal about each other.

Moti was not born to a wealthy or well-educated family, but her father had a deep philosophical bent which he passed on to his only daughter. When she was old enough, he was insistent that she go to school and get an education. This was at a time when few village girls did so. He likely realized that with the innate intelligence and independent personality she so strongly possessed from early childhood, she would probably find personal fulfillment and happiness in marriage with a more educated mate, who would hopefully enjoy and appreciate these qualities in her. She always felt close to her father as a child. Even though she wanted to have a family and children, a part of her also desired to remain unmarried, to stay with her parents and to care for them when they got old. From an early age, she learned to cook, to understand the family's finances, and to shop in the bazaar, the latter of which she loved to do on her own. It made her feel independent and grown-up. Those who knew her then said she learned the knack of bargaining quite quickly.

When Moti was thirteen years of age, her parents were approached by a relatively well-to-do couple in search of a bride for their educated eighteen-year-old son. They had heard about her through a relative. Moti's parents were curious why a family of their economic status would be interested in a girl from a poor family such as theirs. The boy's parents replied that their son had made only one request regarding his bride-to-be, that she be educated. The fact that Moti had already completed sixth grade clearly made her one of the most educated single girls in their caste community at that time. Sensing the boy's family to be loving and stable, Moti's parents approved. They immediately told her of the inquiry, and they asked her to accept their decision. She agreed to go along with their plans, as long as she was allowed to visit home as often as she wished.

From the outset, her in-laws treated her with love and respect; Moti felt comfortable in their home. At the same time, she found that she and Siddharam had many interests in common, and the new couple became good friends rather quickly. As is common in India, Siddharam's younger brother looked up to his new sister-in-law as a mother, and she relished that relationship. All in all, Moti felt comfortable and happy in her new home and village, situated only a few miles from her birth village. The proximity to her parents' home, as well as the openness of her husband and in-laws, afforded her the opportunity of frequent visits to her parents. In certain communities in India, young brides are discouraged from visiting their parents' home, except on certain special occasions, since such visits are viewed as a sign of the girl's dissatisfaction with her new family. However, this is clearly not the case in the *satnami* community, and Moti and Siddharam were frequent visitors at the home of her parents.

Siddharam's parents had long been members of Ramnami Samaj, and they often took the young couple with them when they went to sect gatherings. Moti enjoyed participating in the activities, and the couple became regular participants whenever there was a nearby *bhajan* taking place. Within a year or so of their marriage, both Moti and Siddharam took initiation into the *samaj*. Because so many other members lived in or near their village, and because the family's economic status allowed them to have servants to perform many of the daily chores, *samaj* activities soon became an integral part of both their lives. Within a few years of their initiation, they both began to increase the number of *Ramnam* tattoos that adorned their bodies. By the time Moti was twenty-one, both were nearly covered in Ram tattoos.

As happy and content as Moti was with her new family and life, she had a growing sadness: regardless of regular efforts, she had not yet become pregnant. Traditionally in Chhattisgarh, as well as in many other areas of India, a pregnancy soon after marriage is seen as both a blessing as well as an auspicious omen for the future of the family. Conversely, a lack of early pregnancy is seen as an unfavorable sign. As months turned into years, both she and Siddharam became increasingly concerned. When I first met them, they had already been married nearly four years without any signs of a pregnancy, and within a few weeks, they confided in me and told of various efforts they had undertaken to diagnose and solve the problem. They also asked me if I knew of any medicines, prayers, rituals, or talismans that might help Moti to conceive. Since they had already gone to several *vaidya*s, or ayurvedic doctors, in the area without any success, I suggested they visit an allopathic, Western-style, doctor in the city about a day's bus ride from their village. Although they said they would consider it, their inaction in that regard suggested a lack of faith in that approach. Apparently, they thought that becoming more involved in the *Ramnam* and *samaj* activities might help, and they increasingly made the practice and group functions a larger part of their lives. In addition, they continued to add Ram tattoos wherever they could.

After more than a dozen years of marriage, the couple remained childless. Frustrated and increasingly despondent, Moti finally asked Siddharam to take another wife. At first, he was adamantly opposed to her suggestion, telling her that he would simply live by Ram Ji's decision as to whether they should have a child or not. Moti, however, saw the situation differently. She felt it was God's way to test her love for Siddharam, to see if she could open her home and heart to another woman who might be able to produce a child for the family. Even today, in much of rural India, it is a somewhat common and acceptable practice for a Hindu man to take a second wife if his first is barren. As with Moti, in Chhattisgarh the barren wife may even initiate the idea and play a role in the picking of this second wife. Because compatibility between wives is extremely important, the first wife's approval of the second is essential. In the case of Motibai, she would search for someone with whom she and Siddharam would enjoy sharing their home.

Several months went by without their discussing the matter again, although the silence did not mean inaction. Then one day, Moti told Siddharam that she had found a young girl from her birth village whom she felt would be both a good companion for her and a fertile wife for him. The girl she chose was from a very poor family, and her parents saw this as an opportunity for their daughter to have a financially secure future. After continued insistence on her part, Siddharam finally accepted Moti's wishes, and soon the new wife, Sitabai, became a part of their family. Moti felt secure in her choice, and she was proud that she had found such a healthy, attractive, and willing mate for the man she loved. She also felt confident that they would soon have a child in their home.

The next time I visited the region, Moti was excited to introduce me to her young "co-wife." After spending a few days with them, it appeared to me that the relationship between the two women was warm and amicable, while at the same time Sitabai clearly showed great respect and deference to Moti, nearly a dozen years her senior. At first, Siddharam found the new arrangement rather uncomfortable, often fearing that Moti might interpret any overt affection he showed Sitabai as a rejection of her. Eventually, they all seemed to settle into the new relationship.

After nearly two years, Sitabai had not become pregnant, and both Moti and Siddharam again became extremely concerned . . . and very worried. What were they to do? What was the solution? Impulsively, Moti decided that Siddharam should take a third wife. He was very much against this, confiding in me around that time that he felt he was probably the reason neither wife had conceived. However, Moti was not about to give up. There was a recently widowed sixteen-year-old in their village from a very poor family, and Moti convinced the girl's parents to allow their daughter to become part of her and Siddharam's family. Moti had long been praying daily that she, or Sitabai, would get pregnant, and now she was putting all her hopes in Kiran, the new girl. Siddharam surrendered to his goddess's wishes. However, it was not to be, and after barely a year with the family, an unpregnant Kiran decided to return to her parents. After she left, the couple gradually came to acknowledge what he had long suspected and feared: the lack of a pregnancy in the home was due to Siddharam. On occasion, we talked about adoption, but neither seemed to see it as an option. Moreover, it is not a popular practice in Chhattisgarhi culture, except when the child is the offspring of a sibling or close relative.

Within a year of Kiran's departure Siddharam became ill, and he was subsequently diagnosed with prostate cancer. He sought out various doctors in the region, but none was able to provide much relief for his condition. Within two years, he died, but not before guaranteeing Moti and Sitabai his half of his family's home and land.[4] Depending on caste, region, cultural community, and individual situation in India, a childless widow's status in her in-law's home can be quite tenuous. Among Chhattisgarhi *satnami*'s, such widows, if they are still young (early twenties or younger) may either return to their families' home or become the wife (first or second) of a brother-in-law. Because Moti was already in her thirties at the time of Siddharam's death, neither of these options was even considered. According to Siddharam, both his brother and his mother, who was still alive at the time, strongly supported his wish for Moti to inherit his home and property. In turn, Moti assured Sitabai of her continued welcome and care as well.

During the traditional mourning period of a year, the two widows attended all the Ramnami gatherings they could, and sect members who lived nearby always sought to include them when traveling to any *samaj* function. At the end of the mourning period, Moti and Sitabai held a huge feast in honor of Siddharam at their home. It is estimated that nearly two hundred Ramnamis attended. The following year, they decided to do the same, and they have continued to do so every year since, each time feeding several hundred Ramnamis, who spend all night there chanting in honor of Siddharam.

Over the years, Moti and Sitabai have become very close, can nearly always be found together, and for many years spent a major part of their lives attending Ramnami, functions or journeying on pilgrimages to holy places both within Chhattisgarh and throughout much of northern India. Sitabai also took initiation as a Ramnami, and gradually had much of her body adorned with tattoos as well. Together, they offered financial support to various sect functions and to individuals as well, while living somewhat like renunciants themselves when at home. In this way, they continued to keep the memory of Siddharam alive and have garnered both respect and status within their community.

In the 1990s, nearly ten years after the death of Siddharam, Moti's long-surrendered desire to have a child suddenly became fulfilled. The husband of one of her younger relatives died, leaving the widow with several very young male children. Because of her poor financial situation and lack of land, she was incapable of raising them alone. Hearing of her plight, Moti immediately offered to help. To her surprise and tremendous joy, her cousin agreed, and she gave Moti one of her sons to raise as her own. Moti felt complete and as if Siddharam had been reborn and had returned to be with her and Sitabai. Although she and Sitabai continue to make *samaj* gatherings a regular part of their lives, they no longer live the pilgrim's existence that marked much of the decade following Siddharam's death. Because their son is still quite young, they limit themselves to those activities in their region where they feel comfortable taking the boy.

Moti has become one of the highly regarded elders in her region and in the *samaj,* and many young *satnami* women in her area seek her out for advice and blessings. Ramnamis speak of her with great respect, and most see her efforts in finding a woman who could bear Siddharam a child as an expression of great selflessness, devotion, and love. For Moti, her son and the *samaj* have now become the large family she so desired, and she continues to treat the younger members as her own children.

Ramjatan

I looked forward to my first visit to Kasturi, as I had been told that nearly the entire village is comprised of Ramnamis. As is so common in India, we arrived quite late, nearly eight hours after we had been expected. We later found out that a greeting party had waited much of that time for us, but, since it was now past nine o'clock at night, most had gone home. As we reached the outskirts of the village, we were spotted by a few sect members, who were sitting at the village well chanting and waiting to see if we would still arrive that night. Seeing us, they immediately came forward to greet us, led by Ramjatan. I had known about him for over a year but was only now getting the opportunity to meet him. After giving me a great and long bear hug and making sure our bags had been taken by the others with him, he grabbed my hand and said, "It is dark, so let me lead you." As it was new moon, my eyes were of little help in navigating the rocky path, but Ramjatan, my blind Ramnami host and one of the few *sadhus* in the sect, deftly maneuvered me around every curve, tree, and boulder until we reached our destination.

Nearly all Ramnamis live with their families. Whether yet unmarried, married, or widowed, the householder life is the one the *samaj* promotes for its members, while the ascetic life is strongly discouraged. Sect elders say the reason for this is that one of the major functions of their movement is the promotion of unity and togetherness within their community. While they view the life of the householder as supportive of this, they see the ascetic life as being one of independence, individuality, and aloneness, as summed up in the expression, "*Ramtā yogi, bahatā pānī*."[5] Said one *sadasya,* "If a Ramnami becomes a *sadhu,* then he will inevitably leave to wander and will not be around to help our community. He may help his own spiritual growth but will likely do little or nothing to help other members of the sect."

Although there is a small group of *sadhus* affiliated with the sect, they are primarily either Ramnami widowers who, after the death of their wives, have adopted the renunciant life-style or Chhattisgarhis who had become *sadhus* in the past, wandered or lived in other areas of the country and have now returned to the region to live out the latter part of their lives within the comfort and security that the Ramnami community provides. The few Ramnami widows who have become renunciants have continued to live with or near their families. Other than those just mentioned, it is extremely rare for non-widowed sect members to become *sadhus* after becoming Ramnamis. Nevertheless, this has happened on a few occasions, and Ramjatan is one of these.

Ramjatan was the sole child of a poor *satnami* couple in the small eastern Chhattisgarhi village of Dhana approximately fifty years ago. Like many villagers in North India, his parents were illiterate but had learned from wandering renunciants, *leela* troupes, and village elders a great many stories of gods, saints, and *sadhus* from the vast corpus of Hindu mythology and local folklore. From as far back as he can remember, Ramjatan would spend most evenings listening to the stories that have traditionally formed an important part of pastime and entertainment for Indian villagers. By the age of five or six, he began to work with his father during the day, either on their own small plot of land or as sharecroppers for one of the wealthier landowners in his village. He loved spending time with and listening to his father since the latter had become quite adept in reciting and embellishing the myths, to make each telling a bit more exciting, frightening, or funnier than the last. Ramjatan loved to memorize the scarier stories to tell his playmates whenever they had the opportunity to spend time together. In those days, very few poor children, especially *harijan* youth, attended school, and he was no exception. When he was not busy with farm work, he and his friends would find a barren field to be the stage for acting out some of their favorite stories. Ramjatan most enjoyed playing the role of one of the demons. He was attracted by the ability to frighten, and the excitement of being frightened. His interest in the many Hindu myths and tales he heard inspired him to learn to read by the time he was ten years old. Because of its popularity and availability, the *Mānas* was the text to which he was most drawn, and he enjoyed memorizing its stories and verses.

When Ramjatan was about fourteen, there was a small pox epidemic in the region that infected many young people, killing, blinding, or permanently scarring the majority of them. Although Ramjatan survived the disease, it robbed him of his sight. In Chhattisgarh, small pox was known as *"Mātā chechak,"* because it was believed to be caused by a goddess. When it became clear to his parents, and to him, that he was not going to regain his vision, they sought to console the young boy. They told him the goddess must have special plans for him and would surely protect him. However, that did little to lift him out of the deep depression in which he was rapidly sinking. No longer would he be able to work in the fields with his father, no longer able to run around, act, and play with his friends the way he had done for so long, and no longer able to read the *Mānas* and memorize its tales. He refused to leave his home and spent most of the daylight hours with his grandparents, for his mother worked as a servant and was seldom home during the day. Ramjatan saw himself as a burden, and even a failure to his parents and family. He realized that he would never be able to get married and have children for his parents to enjoy in their old age. Instead, they would always have to care for him. He thought of his life as no longer having any worth and often contemplated suicide. His grandfather saw that the only time Ramjatan seemed at all happy was when he listened to or told stories. As a result, the elder tried to keep the youth occupied as much as possible. Their days were passed telling stories to each other, and as Ramjatan gradually accepted his fate, he began to memorize as many new tales as possible. Even though, his boyhood friends visited from time to time, he felt ashamed and powerless in his condition; he no longer wanted to be around them. The time when most of their parents were beginning the search for wives for them, he knew that he would never have such a life. Moreover, he felt that he would never become a man, but always be little more than someone dependent on others. His world increasingly became isolated to his immediate family and the realm of myths into which he often sought to escape.

His grandfather, increasingly his primary caretaker, spent most of his waking hours trying to buoy Ramjatan's spirits. The elder liked to chant and play the harmonium, one of the few musical instruments found in most Indian villages. He taught the chants and harmonium to his grandson as well, and they became more ways for the boy to pass his days and help forget his blindness. On one hand, he became quite talented in singing and playing devotional songs, yet he continued to harbor a resentment against God for cursing him with such an affliction. He justified his anger by rationalizing to himself that although he had probably done some evil in the past to warrant his affliction, surely his parents had done nothing to be cursed with an only son who would not be able to care for them in their old age, provide them with a daughter-in-law and grandchildren, or continue their family name. He often felt he was a hypocrite chanting *Ramnam,* while feeling bitterness toward Ram. Eventually, he stopped his chanting, music, and storytelling altogether, finding little desire within himself to do anything at all. His misery and bitterness ate away at both his heart and body, and he longed for death. Although he says he had become an atheist, he even prayed to Mata Chechak to quickly take his life and end the pain that she had given him.

About six months after falling into this immobilizing depression, there was a Ramnami Bhajan Mela in a village nearby his home. A few weeks prior to the beginning of the festival, Ramjatan's grandfather told him about the upcoming *mela.* He also related to the youth wonderful stories about the *samaj,* and how its members enjoy chanting and reciting the *Mānas.* He ended by expressing his own desire to attend the festival and asked Ramjatan to accompany him. At first, the boy rejected his elder's invitation, saying he did not want to be around other people, especially festive ones, since there was nothing in his life to celebrate. The day before his grandfather was to depart, however, Ramjatan gave in and decided to join him. As they walked to the event some fifteen miles away, they joined a small band of Ramnamis from their own and one other village who were also going to the festival. Throughout the daylong jaunt, the villagers passed their time chanting and telling stories as they walked. At first, this made Ramjatan angry that the others all seemed so happy and excited about going. He wanted them to be sad like him. As the day wore on, however, he could not help but join in the chanting, and by the time of their arrival at the host village, he actually had to admit to himself that he had enjoyed the walk. The two spent the next three days listening to and participating in the chanting and storytelling.

Toward the end of the *mela,* Ramjatan was introduced to an elder Ramnami who would greatly transform him and the way he understood his life. Lakhanram had been a Ramnami for nearly twenty years, and he, too, had been blinded by small pox as a youth. Because his parents had been members of the sect, he found solace within the group quite early. Ramjatan was enthralled to meet him and to find someone who could empathize with his pain, as well as his bitterness. They spoke together the entire night, and into the next day. Ramjatan had endless questions regarding this elder's feelings about almost every aspect of life.

Lakhanram had grown up in the *samaj,* listening to and participating in *bhajan* sessions at his and other sect members's homes. As a child, he attended several yearly *mela*s and other sect activities with his parents. After contracting small pox and losing his sight, his parents continued to include him in as many activities as possible. By foot or by oxcart when available, they would journey together to nearby villages, wherever there happened to be a *samaj* function. He became so accustomed to visiting some of the closer villages that he was soon able to make the journey alone. In time, he was invited and traveled on his own to villages farther away to visit sect members and join in various *samaj* activities. He usually went with other Ramnamis from his village, but on occasion he attempted to go by himself. People who encountered him on the road would help lead him in the right direction, and sometimes they even accompanied him to his destination if it was nearby. Over the years, such movement became an increasingly important part of his life. Eventually, he spent as much time away from home as he did at home, sleeping wherever he happened to be when it was night. Because of his blindness and his itinerant life-style, people in the area he frequented began to refer to him as "Sur Sadhu."[6] North Indian villagers traditionally show a great deal of respect and deference to *sadhus*, so Lakhanram felt that to be called this was a sign of respect. When sect members from his district went on pilgrimages, he usually was invited to go along. By the time he was in his thirties, he had been to nearly every major pilgrimage place in North India.

Due to his mobility, knowledge of the region, lack of other commitments, and *sadhu*-type life-style, Lakhanram also began to act as an envoy, of sorts, for sect members, taking messages from one village to another of a pending gathering or some other news of the sect. Eventually, he came to be relied upon for this function within his district, and the *samaj* would turn to Sur Sadhu to disseminate sect news throughout his area. Whenever there would be a gathering, it was he who would travel between villages, informing sect members of the upcoming event, getting others to pass the word on, and, in turn, providing the hosts of the gathering with some idea of how many were expected to attend.

That night, Ramjatan realized that so many of the limitations he had believed to be inherent with blindness were, in fact, not necessarily so. He began to feel his faith, and even his hope was returning; he felt Ram Ji had sent Lakhanram to him to open his eyes, as it were, so that he could begin to see his life differently. For the first time since his illness, Ramjatan began to sense that he, too, might have a useful role and function in life, rather than simply a burden on his parents. This gave him an experience of happiness he had long forgotten, and he could not wait to tell his parents and family about Lakhanram. When the *mela* ended, Ramjatan and his grandfather convinced the elder *sadhu* to visit their village with them. Lakhanram accepted the invitation and spent nearly a week in Dhana. By the time he left, Ramjatan had firmly decided that he, too, wanted to become a Ramnami *sadhu*. His parents, anxious for their son to find something meaningful to him in life, happily agreed. One of the elders in his own village sponsored him, and within a few weeks he took initiation as a Ramnami, having *Ramnam* tattooed twice on his forehead. Fortunately for him, there were several Ramnami families in his village, so his grandfather often took him to one of their homes in the evening to chant and partake in the *satsang*. The emotional depression that had made his heart its home seemed almost nonexistent during the times he was with them.

However, as the excitement and comfort of Lakhanram's presence diminished with the passing of time, Ramjatan began to once again doubt his own abilities. As his fear of the unknown would overcome him, he found himself retreating into the familiarity of the depression he had known so well. Several months after meeting Lakhanram, he received word that the latter was going on a pilgrimage to Haridwar and wanted him to go along. Great distances and great worlds separated his village from the famous pilgrimage site more than 400 miles to the north, and the only emotion that matched Ramjatan's fear was the seductive excitement of the journey, and the opportunity to be with Sur Sadhu again. He remembered how much he used to enjoy being frightened, but this was real life. After days of riding the emotional gamut that occupied his heart, the lure and the excitement of the pilgrimage were too strong, and he ultimately decided to go.

The journey lasted about six weeks, and nearly one hundred sect members went along. They traveled mostly by train, and along the way, Ramjatan met many other travelers and pilgrims. Some were physically healthy, and some were not. Some were blind, had leprosy, or had been crippled by disease or injury. Yet, they all were going about their lives, seeking their own way to find fulfillment. The journey was filled with lessons and challenges for Ramjatan, and he returned to Dhana a very different person than when he had left. Most importantly, he came back seeing his blindness as but one characteristic of his being, rather than as its definition.

The following year, Ramjatan went again to the *samaj*'s annual *mela,* but this time as a Ramnami. Because he felt the other sect members treated him as one of them and did not exclude him in any way because of his blindness, he had a strong sense, for the first time in several years, that he had a reason to live. Since most of the *bhajan* was done at night, in the dark or with minimal light, external sight was not that important. In the realm of chanting and storytelling, the only vision necessary is within the imagination of the heart and mind of speaker and listener. Ramjatan hoped the festival would never end, for he felt so much at home with his new community, his new family.

His involvement with the *samaj* came to be the central focus of his life. Members seemed to enjoy his presence and participation, and this helped his growing self-confidence as someone more than simply an invalid, ever dependent on others. By the time he was in his early twenties, Ramjatan had his entire body covered in tattoos, and his clothing was essentially limited to *Ramnam*-covered cloth. As the number of sect members in his area increased, there was also an increase in *bhajan* gatherings. Ramjatan readily took on the role of envoy, notifying members in surrounding villages of any pending events. Like Lakhanram, Ramjatan adopted the life-style and personae of a Ramnami *sadhu.* Whenever he traveled far enough away as to not be able to return the same day, he always found lodging in the home of another Ramnami. Moreover, many members in distant villages began to look forward to his visits and usually encouraged him to stay for the night and participate in an evening chant. He came to be known in the area simply as "Sadhu" or "Dhanadiha Sadhu."[7]

The more he traveled the more he became known in the surrounding villages, and soon he was being invited for his *satsang,* chanting, storytelling, and accumulating knowledge of the *Mānas*. During the last two decades, he has increasingly come to be looked upon, not only as a *sadhu,* but also as a teacher, a mediator, and an organizer. In the early 1980s, he was chosen as a *sadasya* from his area and has been one ever since. In his own village, many sect members look up to him, invite him to any and all functions at their homes, and would not think of attending any festivals without him. When there is a dispute within a *satnami* family or between two families in his village or area, he is often called in to arbitrate. He has come to play an important role in the organizing of the annual Bhajan Mela. Not only does he visit the site with other *sadasya*s during the year to check on the progress of the preparations, but he also decides upon the pilgrimage routes within his district to the festival. Having one's village chosen as a stopping point along the route is considered a great honor, so Ramnamis from many of the villages along the course invite him to visit their village, usually with the hopes of having their's chosen. In this and other ways, Dhanadiha Sadhu has become a commanding and influential member of the sect.He has gained such respect there that several Ramnamis families consider him as their guru, even though any such formal relationship is inconsistent with sect philosophy and teachings.

During the struggle for power within the hierarchy of the sect that ensued during the late 1980s, the Ramnamis from his district looked to him for direction and blessings before supporting any side or candidate. Although he did not officially endorse any candidate or faction, he made his feelings clear that change was needed. Many felt that his views were an important factor leading to the removal, in the late 1990s, of the *adhyaksha* who had been in place for more than 25 years. The growing interest in the politics beyond the *samaj* also led to members seeking out his views and advice on the pros and cons of political participation. Some have even encouraged him to seek office in his own village as well as beyond it, emphasizing his fairness, intelligence, and leadership qualities. Ramjatan has consistently and flatly rejected all such suggestions, and usually resonded by reminding members of the practice of *Ramnam* as the only dependable vehicle for change. After one all night *bhajan* in his village, he addressed the question by saying,

> There is no greater leader than Ram,
> and there no greater source of joy than *Ramnam*.
>
> *RamRam sab se barda nayak*
> *Ramnam sab se ananda dayak*

Ramjatan has found a secure place for himself in the Ramnami community. He still spends much of his time listening to and telling stories from the

Mānas and other texts. These days when he travels, there are always several other sect members who accompany him. At any gathering he attends, his presence is almost always acknowledged with deference by other sect members. He is well regarded for both his knowledge and his disarming personality. He also has learned the practice of *takkar* quite well, and is considered one of the better *gyanis* in his district. Like many other Ramnami *gyanis*, he is often searching for new texts and other sources for stories and verses to include in his repertoire. Since he cannot read them himself, he is often found listening to someone reading to him from some scripture. Wherever he is, there will inevitably be *bhajan* and *satsang* in the evening. In the twenty-five years I have known him, I have seen his influence and popularity in his district steadily increase. Nevertheless, whenever we are together, his personal humbleness is readily apparent. His joy of chanting seems to be matched only by his love of stories. Often, when we are together, he says to me, "Hey, tell me a good story."

Sukhibai

There are few rules and restrictions that govern Ramnamis, because sect members prize the personal autonomy that comes with this approach. At the same time, however, because most Ramnamis find a great deal of comfort and security in the *samaj,* very few members will actually seek to thwart the few foundational guidelines and values that form the basis of the sect's beliefs and practices. Yet, Sukhibai has found even these minimal rules to be too confining for her to follow. Instead, she has opted to carve her own road, one that has proven to have its hills and valleys. With her body covered in Ram tattoos, often donning her *mukut* and *ordhni* whenever she ventures beyond her home or fields, she generally appears vigorous, and always determined, on the path she has chosen.

Born in the mid-1950s in a devout Ramnami family, Sukhibai was raised to the sound of *Ramnam*. Moreover, she says that the sect and its members are integral parts of almost every one of her childhood memories. As an only child, her parents doted on her a great deal and kept her with them everywhere they went. Because like many *harijan* girls her age, Sukhibai did not attend school, her parents felt free to take her with them every time they attended a sect function, whether it be a one-day event in a nearby village or a month-long pilgrimage to another state. She nearly always enjoyed the opportunity to spend time with the other Ramnami children, as well as to visit new places and meet new people. Also, from an early age she displayed a knack for memorizing *Mānas* verses and would often sit and try to participate with her parents as they chanted *Ramnam* in a group. In this way, the childhood events most significant to her were imbued with *Ramnam*.

Predictably, her parents betrothed her to a boy of similar upbringing, whose parents were also sect members. At the time, she was thirteen and he sixteen. Because both sets of parents attended many of the same sect functions, by the time the marriage took place two years later, Sukhibai and Bholeram had already spent much time together and become well-acquainted. In traditional Chhattisgarhi culture, betrothed youth do not associate with their spouses-to-be until the actual marriage takes place. However, the Ramnamis generally allow such fraternization provided the youths are never actually alone together. Thus, by the time of their marriage, Sukhibai and her husband had become close, and she had won over the affection of her in-laws-to-be as well. Since Bholeram was the oldest brother in the family, Sukhibai was the first daughter-in-law in the house. For many young Hindu girls, leaving the security of family and home to live in a new and unknown environment traditionally causes a great deal of fear and trepidation. However, Sukhibai was excited about getting married, for she had already established a relationship with her in-laws, one in which they had apparently accepted the fact that she was an intelligent and independent thinker. In reflecting on the time, she says, that she was confident that she would be treated well—and also that she would get her way when she really wanted it.

Even after their marriage, Sukhibai and Bholeram continued to be regular participants at all Ramnami gatherings in their vicinity, and both showed a substantial ability to memorize and understand verses from the *Mānas*. Both also began the process of becoming tattooed, she more intent on the adornment than he. By the time she became pregnant with their first son, Sukhibai already had extensive tattooing on her forehead and limbs. Her pregnancy did not seem to slow down her participation in sect functions, and she remembers chanting with the *samaj* the entire night on the eve of giving birth, both to their first son, as well as to their second son, the following year. In her life at this time, Sukhibai remembers feeling she had the ability to live pretty much as she chose within her immediate surrounding; the only real constraints she perceived were from the broader society and culture rather than from the more insulated family or sect. Events soon to unfold would threaten this freedom in her eyes, causing her to challenge Ramnami leaders in the direction they sought to move the *samaj*. Apparently, it was the very freedom she had felt and that she understood to be a direct result of the *samaj* life-style at the time that inspired her to want to prevent any changes in rules or practices that might alter the existing conditions of the sect, and consequently of her life in it.

The catalyst for many of these changes—the Arab oil embargo—was starting to take effect, and the sect was beginning to alter its approach to and view of tattooing. While Bholeram agreed with the diminished importance being given to tattoos, Sukhibai contested the change. Instead, she strongly supported a continuation of the practice, stressing that the economic hardship so many were experiencing was RamRam Swami's way of testing their devotion and commitment to *Ramnam*. Moreover, when her oldest boy was three years of age, she had *Ramnam* tattooed on both her sons' foreheads, in defiance of the decision made two years earlier to cease the tattooing of children.[8] Bholeram did not necessarily support her move, but he also knew that disagreeing with Sukhibai was seldom a pleasant, or successful, endeavor on his part. Many of the Ramnami *sadasya*s had also become well aware of her tenacity, so, openly at least, there was only mild criticism of her actions. The defiance she exhibited on the tattooing issue set the tenor of her approach to other issues that were to inevitably arise.

At first, it was Bholeram who got involved in the practice of *takkar,* but within a year or so Sukhibai also became an active participant. Together, they would read the *Mānas,* searching for and memorizing verses that could be used in chanting and in *takkar.* Within a few years, she came to be known as one of the best young *gyani*s in her area, and she relished "jousting" with older and more experienced sect members whenever she got the opportunity. Again, Sukhbai felt free, happy, and in control of her life. Her husband, her in-laws, her caste community, and her religious community, all seemed to allow her to live and function as she chose.

By the mid-1980s, Sukhibai found another rule change made during the 1970s to which she had growing objection: the liberalization of commensality practices with non-Ramnamis. She increasingly began to complain at sect gatherings that, in order to maintain a true vegetarian diet, Ramnamis should return to the old commensality practice of eating only with other members of the sect. Moreover, she felt that Ramnamis should not even eat with non-initiated family members, since many of them may not be vegetarian. At first, most Ramnamis gave little attention to her complaints. Although she was able to garner support from a small following, the majority felt that such strict rules would divide the membership and limit, rather than promote, the spread of *Ramnam.* However, Sukhibai again held fast to her beliefs, and after failing to get more than one *sadasya* to support her, she declared that she would only eat with those sect members who maintained the same strict practice. While most of her supporters declined to do the same, she, Bholeram, and five other members withdrew participating in communal meals in the sect. This was seen by the *sadasya*s and many other Ramnamis as a serious challenge to the unity of the *samaj,* since communal meals, especially at *bhajan* gatherings, had come to be a fundamental and unifying part of sect practice.

Many *sadasya*s, both individually and as a group, approached her and pleaded with her to relent, but she refused. They then went to Dhanibai, an elderly and respected *sadasya* who had joined with Sukhibai in the stringent commensal observance, and implored her not to participate in what they saw as a very divisive activity. She, too, refused their request. After much discussion, both private and public, the *sadasya*s ultimately decided to simply overlook the practice of Sukhibai and her group of followers and say nothing more to try to dissuade them. However, she and Bholeram lost respect in the eyes of many Ramnamis, who saw her actions as based more on ideology and self-promotion than on love of *Ramnam*.

Throughout the 1980s, Sukhibai gradually had her entire body adorned with *Ramnam* tattoos. There was concern that she might pressure her sons to do the same, but she did not. Bholeram also increased his tattoos, not nearly as extensively as Sukhibai. By the late 1980s, she also began to wear a small *mukut*. Prior to this, widows were the only females who would wear the sect hat, and even then only a small number of them did so. During the early years of the *samaj,* the wearing of *mukut* was traditionally confined to men. It was one of the only sect activities that acknowledged a gender difference. In the early 1950s, with the increase in the number of Ramnami widows, the practice was extended to them as well, although few have ever actually chosen to wear a *mukut*.

At the first Bhajan Mela where Sukhibai donned her hat, no one said anything to her, and many members thought it was just a passing whim of hers. They had come to expect the unexpected from her. However, Sukhibai began to show up with her *mukut* at every *samaj* activity, and it became clear she had incorporated it as a regular part of her *samaj* attire. By then, most Ramnamis had come to accept Sukhibai's obstinance and strong-willed personality, and few, if any, members challenged her in this regards. Unfortunately, this practice seemed to further alienate her from many who used to enjoy her company, and many of those who would previously invite her and Bholeram to their homes or villages for *bhajan* increasingly left the couple off their list of invitees. However, if she got word of a *bhajan* gathering anywhere nearby, she would go, whether or not she was invited, and she would nearly always be greeted warmly and special arrangements would be made for her to cook her own food.

Over the next several years, Sukhibai, Bholeram, and her small group of followers would continue to participate in sect activities, but could always be expected to separate themselves at the time of meals. In the late 1980s, after about five years of participation with Sukhibai, Dhanibai, who was now in her late seventies, became very ill, and thereby dependent on the assistance of other Ramnamis to be able to attend *samaj* functions. Subsequently, she dropped out of Sukhibai's group and resumed taking part in the communal meals. Various members suggested that her illness, as well as her loss of stature in the sect, were both the karmic results of her participation in the group. As of 2001, only one other sect member, an elder in their village, would eat with Sukhibai and Bholeram, who have continued to eschew dining with the rest of the sect.[9]

In various discussions with Bholeram over the years regarding Sukhibai's activities and challenging of Ramnami traditions, he readily acknowledges that she, and he, have caused tension, pain, and some division in the sect. He neither defends his own actions, nor criticizes what she has chosen to do. The last time we spoke about it, his closing comment was, "She is my wife, given to me by RamRam Swami. I just try to focus on *Ramnam* and not get caught up in the politics."

Sukhibai has provided a real challenge to the *samaj* in various ways. Much of the admiration and respect that she had earned through her early participation in sect activities, *takkars*, and so forth, has gradually lessened because of her seeming intractability and confrontational nature with regards to the activities mentioned above. Although she was once seen as a young and upcoming member of the sect, a candidate to eventually become a leading *sadasya,* she is now seen as unrepresentative of most other Ramnamis. Be it a consequence of age, all the conflict and confrontations she had with the *samaj,* or other factors, Sukhibai has become far more subdued and has lost much of the outgoing demeanor and charisma that used to be a regular part of her character. Where her village's *chandni* was once a lively spot in the Bhajan Mela, now it is far more quiet as fewer sect members chose it as a spot to sit and chant. Some sect members still do show her attention and some deference, but the respect she once enjoyed has largely been replaced with tolerance and acceptance. Recently, one of the sect members from her village speculated, "Sukhibai became more concerned with exterior things than with *Ramnam*. Devotion is not an easy path." Still, Sukhibai remains an important sect member in her village. Her path may eventually bring her once again in closer affinity with the rest of the *samaj,* or it may not. Either way, she will likely continue to tread a course largely of her own crafting.

Kamalabai

I had heard about her for several months before actually meeting her for the first time. Ramnamis would tell me about this new young devotee who seemed to have boundless energy, devotion, and commitment. This, at a time, when the *samaj* was obviously aging in its membership, and new initiates were few and far between. Thus, the first time I met Kamalabai, I was already interested to get to know more about her. Initially, I was struck by her extensive tattooing, a practice that is almost dead to the newer Ramnami initiates. Then, I was struck by her personality, a blend of coyness and strength, gentleness and intensity. In a seemingly timid manner, she almost always manages to get her way. This is because she simply does not accept "no" as an answer.

Now in her late thirties, Kamalabai has been a Ramnami for much of her life, having taken initiation at the age of sixteen. Her parents have been members of the sect since before she was born, so she and her brothers grew up spending a great deal of time around various sect members and activities, often listening to the drone of *Ramnam* or recitations from the *Mānas* evening after evening in their home. As a child, she would often don her mother's *ordhni* and father's *ghunghru* and parade around her home singing *Ramnam*. Kamalabai and her mother were always close. She was the oldest child, the only daughter, and the only one of four children who showed an interest in following their parents' spiritual avocation.

By the age of eight, Kamalabai had decided that she, too, wanted to become a Ramnami and, like several other sect members in her village, have her entire body tattooed with *Ramnam*. While her parents enjoyed her enthusiasm, they did not want her to join the sect and get tattoos until after she got married and had the approval of her husband. Her betrothal had taken place when she was six or seven to a twelve-year-old boy from a village twenty kilometers from her own. Because of her physical beauty and grace, her parents had been able to arrange her marriage with a good, relatively well-to-do family, by village standards. Her husband-to-be was an intelligent and promising student with a strong desire to get an education and a government job. Kamalabai's parents were thrilled with the match. They attempted to persuade her to also continue with her schooling, at least through the tenth grade, so that she and her husband-to-be would have more in common, he would appreciate her more, and they would have a better chance of being happy together. School never held her interest, however, and by the third grade she simply refused to attend any longer, preferring instead to help her mother at home. Her parents could do nothing to change her mind, for nearly all her life she has maintained a strong will-power and self-determination.

At the age of ten, Kamalabai told her parents that she had no intention to go through with her *gauna* (when the marriage is completed and the wife departs for her husband's home). Instead, she had resolved to become a Ramnami and remain with them as their single daughter as long as they were alive. Countless times her mother pleaded, "Go to school. Prepare yourself for married life. Your husband is a good boy. You will have healthy sons, and we will have grandchildren to enjoy in our old age." Kamalabai always refused to even consider the proposal and fought back with her characteristic stubbornness. "No, I don't want a husband, a house in a city. I don't want to get married and have children. I want to be a Ramnami like you and spend my days chanting *Ramnam*." Her mother prayed that this was the idle fantasy of a young girl that would pass before her husband came for her.

When she was fourteen, Kamalabai's parents decided it was time for her *gauna,* for by this time her husband had been admitted to a nearby college, and he wanted her to be there with him. As soon as the young girl came to know of her impending departure, she broke down in tears and begged her parents to let her remain with them. However, they were firm in their decision, believing that this was what was best for their daughter. Kamalabai immediately began a food fast, which she continued for the next eight days, until the day of the marriage. Throughout the entire ceremony, she remained resolute and refused to participate. Nevertheless, the ceremony was performed. Before her departure, she forewarned her mother that she would soon be back, for she knew it would not last.

Several months went by, but Kamalabai steadfastly refused to consummate the marriage by having sex with her husband. She told him she did not want to have children and get bound in a life that gave her no time for *Ramnam*. Frustrated after six months of enduring her obstinacy, her husband and his father finally returned Kamalabai to her parents' home, saying she was unfit to be a wife. Although this is not a frequent occurrence in the region, it is also not unique. Low-caste Chhattisgarhi females do not seem as utterly dependent on their husbands and in-laws and as separated from their parents as is often the case in other areas and communities in India. Thus, they are known to express themselves quite frankly to their husbands and in-laws, and to return to their parents' home if they are unhappy. Thus, Kamalabai's family was more hurt than disgraced. Her mother wept for days on end, wondering what to do with her daughter. She had refused education, refused married life, and now what was left for her? After months of praying that she would return to her husband, her parents finally accepted their daughter's determination and agreed to let her remain with them. They also agreed to her decision to become a Ramnami.

They approached a respected Ramnami elder in a nearby village, but he said she should not be initiated until she was at least sixteen, nearly a year away. Disheartened at another postponement, Kamalabai nevertheless did not waver in her desire. She continued to remain at home, caring for her younger siblings, helping her mother with her chores, and visiting other sect members who lived nearby. She had few friends her own age, since she had always preferred being with her mother and brothers to spending much time with the other children in her village. Moreover, by this time, nearly all the girls her age were married, moved to new villages, and involved with their own families.

Shortly after she turned sixteen, Kamalabai once again sought to be initiated, and during the Bhajan Mela the following year she finally had her wish fulfilled. At first, her parents balked at her desire to have more than one *"Ram-Ram"* tattoo, which they made sure was on her arm, and not on her forehead as she had wanted. In their hearts, they hoped she would eventually agree to another marriage attempt. Although the caste-Hindu culture in rural Chhattisgarh mirrors much of India in its prohibition against females having more than one marriage, such restrictions are not as strong in the *satnami* community. Here, it is not uncommon for females to have one or even several subsequent informal "marriages." In Chhattisgarh, there is a ritual, but not an actual marriage, by which either a female has a second marital union or a second wife is accepted and acknowledged as part of a family. Also, there does not seem to be much stigma attached to either of these types of union. It may be the second wife's first marriage, or she may have been previously widowed or divorced. Similarly, her new husband may be single, divorced, widowed, or currently married to a barren woman. In addition, in Chhattisgarh it is not unheard of for an angry wife to leave her husband, and move in to the home of some other man, only to return to her husband after some time, often at the latter's pleading.

For several years, Kamalabai continued to live with her parents, helping her mother manage the house and working with her father in the fields whenever called upon. She would accompany them to all the Ramnami functions in their vicinity. During this time, many of the *samaj* members and others in the area began referring to her as *"brahmcharini,"* a title of sorts given a female who has chosen a life of celibacy. Also during this time, she began to spend time with Balakram, a Ramnami boy several years her junior from a nearby village. On occasion, she would not return home at night but always assured her parents that she had spent the night chanting *Ramnam* with sect members nearby. Increasingly, her absence from her home would last for several days at a time, and often she could not satisfy her parents' questions regarding her whereabouts. Her parents saw her becoming intensely moody and unwilling to stay at home or be involved in family matters.

Kamalabai's parents worried that their daughter might have become possessed and approached several Ramnami elders for advice. A shaman from a nearby village was called in to diagnose and treat her condition, but his rituals and talismans did not seem to alter her moods or seemingly erratic behavior. Since she was not actually causing harm to anyone, elders from the sect and her caste community decided she should not be bothered for the time being, in hopes of some change.

Increasingly, she was spotted with Balakram in or near an abandoned house on the outskirts of her village. While her neighbors may have had their doubts about her, they remained friendly and on occasion they would give her an invitation to their homes for *bhajan*. By this time, she was attending nearly every Ramnami function she could, even if it meant walking for several days each way. She was also spending a great deal of time with Balakram, to whom she simply referred to as "brother."

At the age of twenty-one, Kamalabai decided to have her entire body adorned with *Ramnam* tattoos. She informed her parents of her decision and asked their blessings. At first her mother refused, then reluctantly agreed to support her daughter's wishes provided that the latter would endure the procedure over a long period. Kamalabai began the process by having her entire face covered with rows of *Ramnam,* which lace across her forehead and cheeks and wrap around to the back of her head. After a few months she had her arms decorated with *Ramnam,* from shoulder to wrist. By the end of the year, Kamalabai had nearly her entire body covered with tattoos. She inspired several other young Ramnamis in her area to do likewise. Balakram was in awe of her feat, but chose not to follow suit. At this time, he had only one *"RamRam"* tattoo on his forehead.

Shortly thereafter, Kamalabai was able to get permission from its owners and moved into the empty house at the edge of her village, telling her parents that she needed to be on her own. The people of the village had come to accept her peculiar life-style, although many of the women continued to suggest to her parents that another marriage for her might "straighten her out." More and more, she could be found in Balakram's village, nearly 75 percent of whose residents are Ramnamis, and where nightly *bhajan* is a regular occasion. More and more, Balakram was spotted at Kamalabai's new home, and eventually he moved into the house with her. Naturally, the relationship between the two became one of the favorite topics of gossip in the village, yet no one ever directly confronted her with the common suspicions. During this time, apparently at her urging, Balakram started getting more tattoos as well.

For nearly five years, the two of them lived together in the house and were visible at all the major Ramnami functions in the region. Not having any land to farm, they occasionally found menial work in their vicinity, and sect members would often provide them with food and other essentials. While some people continued to refer to her as a *brahmcharini,* her increasingly open displays of affection toward Balakram drastically diminished use of that title.[11] During this time she also began to wear a *mukut.* Possibly because of Sukhibai's regular breaking of the tradition that confined the *mukut's* use to males, hardly anyone seemed to mention Kamalabai's action. Her lifestyle clearly was of greater concern than her adornment.

Then, in early 1995, Kamalabai became pregnant. Within a few months, both she and Balakram returned to their respective parents' homes, and they remained apart throughout her pregnancy. A month or so after the birth, Kamalabai returned to live in the house she and Balakram had shared, and shortly thereafter he reappeared there as well. Although their families and many sect members urged them to get married, Kamalabai continued to refuse, and the two of them returned to their previous life-style together. She apparently expressed little or no motherly concern for the child, so, her parents have been raising the child, to whom Kamalabai would refer as "little sister."

While many Ramnamis privately expressed concern over the relationship, they stopped short of censure. This was especially so since many sect members felt that Kamalabai exhibited a sincere commitment to the *samaj* and devotion to *Ramnam.* Both the people of her village and the Ramnamis generally continued to accept, begrudgingly or otherwise, her chosen way of life. Because of their caste status and sectarian affiliation, most Ramnamis have had a great deal of experience and understanding of life on the periphery of society and outside the realm of social acceptance. Thus, the couple is to their community somewhat like the sect is to the society in which they exist. This similarity is not lost on many Ramnamis, who remain hesitant to openly criticize Kamalabai and Balakram, and instead refocus any questions about her by talking about her devotion.

In the late 1990s, Kamalabai and Balakram suddenly stopped attending any sect functions and soon disappeared from the region completely. For nearly six months, no one claimed to have any knowledge of their whereabouts. Eventually, however, there began to be rumors that the couple were living in Punjab and that she had recently given birth again. A few friends received letters disclosing more information about the couple: that they were working as day laborers whenever and wherever they could find employment, that their lives were easy in the new land, and that they had second thoughts about leaving Chhattisgarh. Kamalabai's mother seemed encouraged by this news, and she began to suggest that her daughter may soon return to Chhattisgarh. As of the spring of 2001, this had not come to pass, as those who knew her daughter well had predicted. Apparently, Kamalabai left her homeland hoping to find a life beyond the confines of village existence, and a few of her close friends think that any return at this point would mean a failure that she would find hard to accept.

Kamalabai's life thus far and her relationship to the Ramnami Samaj has been eventful and joyful, yet turbulent and troubled for her as well as her family, Balakram, and many members of the *samaj*. Although, like Sukhibai, she challenged sect traditions, as long as she remained in Chhattisgarh, she was able to find relatively peaceful co-existence, support, and freedom within her community. As a member of the *samaj,* she found an acceptance, if not legitimation, of her atypical lifestyle, and a community in which she could act out her rejection of established cultural norms. The sect afforded her the opportunity and support to live outside the traditional sociocultural parameters of the region. With her departure to a "foreign" land such as Punjab, her parents and friends feared that an uneducated, tattooed, *harijan* couple with no land or any real marketable skills would surely face the kinds of hardships and challenges that neither had faced in their relatively secure world in Chhattisgarh. While they hope that new home and new life can be the stimuli to bring the peace and freedom that she long seemed to seek, nevertheless, her parents and friends will continue to pray for her return to them and to the *samaj.*

Gauravram

Gauravram's involvement with the Ramnami Samaj has been since the outset fundamentally different from that of most other members. Unlike most Ramnamis, he is a college graduate, extremely literate, and well aware of many aspects of the world outside his region. At the same time, he shares with many of them a frustration with the caste Hindu culture in which they have long existed, and it was his search for a life outside of its confines that led him to the *samaj.*

Gauravram was born to a very poor family in western Chhattisgarh. When he was still an adolescent, his father became an alcoholic, frustrated by his poverty and low social standing. By the time the boy was ten years of age, his father had sold what little his family owned in order to support his addiction, and shortly thereafter he died from it. His wife, mother, and four children—three boys and a girl—were left essentially penniless. Even though Gauravram was but ten at the time, because he was the oldest male he became the man of the house, and it was left to him to find a way to support his family.

All his life Gauravram longed to become educated, live in a big city, and escape the oppression of poverty and untouchability that had plagued his family and contributed to the death of his father. He was a dedicated student, first in his class, and he felt assured he would succeed. He had begun working part-time in a rock quarry near his home when he was seven years old, but on the death of his father, his mother asked him to quit school so that he could work full time. Gauravram refused to end his education, and a compassionate employer raised the boy's wage and allowed him to work after school as well as on weekends in order to be able to support his family. For the next seven years he spent nearly every waking hour in school, studying, or carrying boulders. Thus, he managed both to fulfill his financial commitment to his family and to continue with his schooling.

When he graduated high school, Gauravram's grades and his status as an Untouchable made it possible for him to get some government assistance to attend college. By this time, he had also been able to work his way up to the position of a driver at the quarry and had secured employment for both his younger brothers. With the added income for his family, Gauravram was able to lessen the hours he had to work and could thereby spend more time on his education. For the next four years he attended the government college in Bilaspur, one of the larger towns in Chhattisgarh. Nearly every weekend and holiday, he would return to the quarry to work, and in this way he supplemented the government stipend he received for school.

The demands of his early years left Gauravram little time to spend playing with the other boys his age. Add to this a relatively introverted personality, and as a result, he almost always kept to himself and never developed any truly close friendships. Some neighbors thought of him as contemplative, others considered him melancholy. While at college, he studied engineering but also developed a deep interest in philosophy. Christian missionaries would come to the school, pass out their literature, and look for converts, especially among the low caste and disenfranchised. The upper caste and wealthier students generally paid them little attention. However, Gauravram's philosophical inclinations motivated him, on occasion, to get involved with various proselytizers in discussions about religion and spirituality. While the other students seemed primarily interested in more mundane matters, he found these interchanges to be both stimulating and challenging. They were among the only times when he enjoyed openly communicating with other individuals.

In 1985, Gauravram graduated from college but found it difficult to get a job, either with the government or with private companies. An educated Ramnami who was a close friend of his aunt heard about Gauravram's situation and put him in contact with a friend of his who was a caste-Hindu engineer from Raipur. The latter had become interested in the Ramnamis, had attended Bhajan Melas from time to time, and had befriended several sect members. The engineer was able to arrange employment for Gauravram, first with a private contractor, then with his own employer, the Madhya Pradesh Public Works Department. (It has long been extremely difficult for *harijans* to get good paying jobs in the region; many caste-Hindu businesses will simply not hire them, irrespective of their qualifications or abilities. While the government has a variety of quota-type laws to assure some access to government positions for Untouchables, the required red tape and inevitable bribes, known as *bakshish,* often make it impossible for *harijans* to actually get anything more than the lowest salaried position, if that.) Like Ramtaram, Gauravram became increasingly bitter in his dealings with most caste Hindus, and he blamed the caste-Hindu social structure for his father's death, his family's poverty, and his own work situation, which forced him to have to feign deference to any and all caste Hindus with whom he came into contact. Even though his employers, who were all caste Hindu, had often treated him with respect and even gone out of their way to help him, his negative experiences with caste Hindus nevertheless led him to paint all caste Hindus with the same brush of antagonism and resentment.

In 1987, Gauravram decided to become a Christian, hoping as do many Untouchables that this move would somehow improve his status with the society at large. The missionaries promised him they would help put his brothers through college if they too became Christian, but the two boys refused to do so. Gauravram's conversion did not bring about the changes he wished for, in fact, it made things worse. His caste-Hindu bosses viewed him as a traitor, most of his own caste community also felt betrayed, and even his mother saw his move as a forsaking of his family and culture.[11] As a result, his work assignment and pay were cut back a great deal, and as was the case with many of the new converts in the region, very little of the assistance promised him by the missionaries ever materialized. After two years, he minimized his association with the missionaries in the area and sought once again to find himself within his own community and religious culture.

It was in this condition that, in 1988, he first began to consider an affiliation with the Ramnami Samaj as a possible vehicle for finding his social and religious niche. His aunt encouraged him to attend the 1988 Bhajan Mela as it was being held in a village near his work. Although he went along, he felt out of place. He had spent his entire life up to that point getting educated and trying to move beyond the restrictions he had so acutely felt from his social and religious background, and here was a group of his own caste community, illiterate, still poor, and seemingly oblivious to the oppressive social situation in which he felt they lived. It angered him that they did not express the same bitterness to caste Hindus and the surrounding culture that he had long felt.

Once he met some of the *gyanis*, however, he was surprised to see their level of intellectual sophistication and their awareness of the world and society around them. Soon after that *mela,* he began to visit a village near his home in which several *gyanis* reside, for he found there a sympathetic ear to his concerns and aspirations.

During his many visits to the village, he became aware of the process of *takkar,* which intrigued him a great deal. It reminded him of a verse-based form of debate he used to participate in while in school (see section on *takkar).* Moreover, it had been one of the more enjoyable parts of his schooling for him. The more he learned about the practice of *takkar* the more he became interested in the sect and what it had to offer. Throughout the next year or so he became a frequent participant in various Ramnami functions and a regular guest at the homes of various *gyanis* in his area. At the 1990 Bhajan Mela, Gauravram approached one of the *gyanis* he had come to know and expressed an interest in becoming a member of the sect. At the same time, however, he made explicit his aversion to getting tattooed. On discovering that it was no longer a requirement, he went ahead and joined. Shortly after his initiation into the sect, his work load with the Public Works Department increased once again, and he was given an assignment near his home. Gauravram moved back in with his family about the same time his oldest brother left for college in Bilaspur.

For the first time since he was a child, Gauravram enjoyed being at home. He became an active participant in *bhajan* and in *takkars*, as they gave him a vehicle through which he was able to express his philosophical inclinations and debating talents. His educational background was a big help in his learning to *takkar.* He even began taking some verses from his Hindi New Testament and putting them in *doha* form to be used in *bhajan* and *takkar.* Sect members did not seem to mind this. Moreover, several seemed encouraged by his creativity and willingness to actively participate. For one of the only times in his life, Gauravram began to feel truly at ease around others and with himself. He even began wearing the local dress once again, rather than his near obsession with the wearing of western-style clothing.

Once back home, his mother immediately began to discuss the need to find a wife for him. Not at all desirous to become a husband and father at this time, he was able to stall his mother's search for a year or so. However, when he could no longer postpone the inevitable, he revealed to his mother that he had an interest in an educated *harijan* Christian girl from a nearby village with whom he had made friends several years before. His mother and uncle talked to the girl's parents, and the match was arranged. After the marriage, Gauravram once again began associating with the other Christians in the area. They increasingly began to warn him that continued affiliation with the Ramnamis would surely cause him eternal damnation. For the next several years, he tried to balance his relationship with both groups, although it became steadily more difficult.

Compelled by his wife, Gauravram ultimately ceased his relationship with the Ramnamis and became a Christian once again. In doing so, he terminated all but absolutely necessary contact with any sect members, with the exception of his aunt. Within a few years, he stopped visiting her as well. The Christian community in eastern Chhattisgarh sees itself in direct competition with any religious movement in the region that appeals to *harijans*. Missionaries often warn new converts of the likelihood of eternal damnation for those who continue to have close relationships with members of such religious groups, even if those members are immediate family. As a consequence, Gauravram and his wife moved out of his family home and the two of them moved in with her parents, who are also Christian.

During the early 1990s, the missionaries who led Christian services in his district convinced Gauravram to become a minister. For the next year, he was visited regularly by ministerial trainers, and he attended classes in a nearby town whenever possible. In 1996, he received ordination and began conducting weekly services in his home. Although he was able to convert dozens of *satnamis* rather quickly, especially with the free rice and other promises of assistance he gave them, by 2001, there were only about a dozen individuals who continued to acknowledge the affiliation and attend any of his prayer meetings.

The last personal contact I had with him was in early 1995. Since I had not seen him in a few years, I decided to visit him at his in-law's home. At first he appeared happy to see me, but noticing the two Ramnamis who had brought me there, he exhibited real discomfort as he hurried us away from his home out into the road. Although we spoke for about a half hour, it was clear that he was uncomfortable talking in the presence of others. He told me how the truth of Christianity had once again been revealed to him and that he had taken on himself the responsibility of saving his and his family's souls. When asked about his relationship with his mother and siblings, he changed the subject. He admitted that he felt alone again, much like he had felt as a teenager, yet he said that he believed our time on earth was for the purpose of finding salvation, not happiness.

As we spoke, his wife called to him in Hindi "reminding" him of all his chores. However, when he asked her to come outside and meet me, she switched to the local dialect, refused, and warned him of the dangers of talking with us. Although it seemed that he had more to say he slowly turned and walked away, saying only that he had much work to do. Our paths crossed again briefly during a visit I made to the bazaar near his village in early 2001, but he did not acknowledge my presence and simply passed by on his bicycle.

I remember speaking to Gauravram before he first became a Christian, and he wondered aloud if it would help or hinder his relationship with his community. One of his brothers said that he no longer visits his mother or any members of his birth family, although he does send her a little money on occasion. His relationship with members of his caste community has essentially ended, except for those few who converted to Christianity and attend the services he officiates. It is clear that Gauravram has chosen a course that has alienated him from many he once considered friends. Yet, most of his life has been spent following a lonely and private path. For him, the practice of *Ramnam* apparently went from being a vehicle to becoming an obstacle in his search for happiness. In the last meeting we had, he implied that he felt isolated from old friends and relationships, but he feels the need to pursue his chosen path. It appears that it is one path that does not fit in with the Ramnami lifestyle.

Conclusion
A Question of Values

One of the central themes of this study has been a rethinking of the formation and function of Hindu social and religious life, for whatever else can be said about India, it is, first and foremost, a land of multiple value systems. Collectively, these systems organize every aspect of life in a series of categories and levels, usually in the form of a set of continuums that stretch from their centers to their peripheries. Hindus have traditionally negotiated their places on these continuums through the rituals and practices they perform or do not perform, or through their associations with various religious teachers or movements.

As discussed earlier, the orthodox value system of a society is the value system of the religious and the political elite, and as a result, it has been the focus of most scholarly study. The orthodox system generally dominates the attention of anyone viewing a particular society, especially in its urban domains, for this system often sets the agenda for social, religious, and even scholarly dialogue. It is held up by the elite to represent the people's values. While it is important as a point of departure in understanding a society or a culture, it is typically not the system of the populace, or of the individual. Instead, it is the visible veneer that not only functions to give a sense of unity but often is used to obscure the levels and diversity lying beneath. Paul M. Harrison, in discussing the difficulties in attempting to use a narrow viewpoint to understand a whole tradition, observes "The study of noses, however hotly pursued, will never yield an accurate understanding of the entire face."[1]

Thus, even though the orthodox value system does not comprise the core set of personal values for most Hindus, it clearly sets the agenda for much of what occurs in India. In relating to the prevalent orthodox system, the low- caste religious groups prevalent in Chhattisgarh have used differing approaches. The Kabirpanthis, for example, have adopted the sanskritization of their religious beliefs and practices as their chosen path. With the sect's center in Varanasi, considered one of the holiest of cities to Hindus, the *panth* finds security in considering and presenting itself as another *nirgun* Vaishnav sect. In the process, it has adopted many ritual elements that had been flatly rejected by Kabir himself. The Kabirpanthi's outer trappings even include a *tulsi kanthi*—standard necklace for all Vaishnavs—and Vaishnav-style *tilak,* outer signs generally believed to denote both caste-Hindu status and religious purity. The *panth* actively solicits caste Hindus to bring into its fold, and in presenting itself, it emphasizes its caste-Hindu component as a form of religious and social certification. At the same time, many of the *satnami* members of the Dharamdas *sakha* in Chhattisgarh now claim *rajput (kshatriya)* status. Some *satnamis* in the sect have begun to list "Kabirha" as their caste name, as they seek to distance themselves, not only from both the Satnamis and the Ramnamis, but from *satnami* caste identity as well. As has traditionally been the case with many other Vaishnav groups, the Kabirpanthis have typically restrained themselves from active political involvement.

The Satnamis, on the other hand, have found in the political sphere a variety of tools they hope will aid them in accomplishing their goals of social and religious acceptance. Starting with their support for the Quit India movement in the early part of this century, they have aspired to use their close association with the Congress Party to elevate their status. As a part of this process, the sect had the name of their caste changed. They have de-emphasized their sectarian religious elements, and with the exception of their *sadhu* wing, wear no special dress and try to look as "generic" Hindu as possible. Some of the wealthier Satnamis have even built Ram and Krishna temples where the deities and rituals performed mirror those in caste Hindu temples in the region. Some have even hired *brahmans* as temple priests. Increasingly, in recent years, sect heads are beginning to deny the status of Satnamis as members of a separate sect at all, declaring instead that they are simply Vaishnav Hindus of the *satnami* caste. Nowadays, when Satnamis must list their religion on any government records, the majority simply put "Hindu."

There is division within the sect as to where in the caste hierarchy they should stake their claim. While some have pushed hard to become identified on the "touchable" side of the caste divide, others believe their greatest benefit can come from continuing official designation as Scheduled Caste *(harijan)*. The latter move formally keeps them qualified for the various affirmative action programs that the Central Government has instituted for Scheduled Tribes and Castes. In reality, however, many Satnamis, as well as most Kabirpanthis, see little or no ultimately worthwhile advantage in being designated "Scheduled Caste." There is a general acknowledgment that the only way any real benefits might come from this status would be if the politicians and administrators of Central Government programs meant to advance them could be depended on to follow through. The experience of *harijans* in Chhattisgarh, however, has taught them otherwise. One of the Satnamis school teachers expressed a universal feeling with respect to pledges of assistance by local politicians: "We receive great promises and assurances around election time, and then they disappear until the next election."

This attempt by Satnamis to become recognized as caste Hindu, while pursuing any benefits that may come from Scheduled Caste status, is a tight rope act that the sect cannot continue, or they may lose out both ways. Many Satnamis are understandably jealous of the situation of the various tribal groups in the region, who are given benefits as "Scheduled Tribes," yet are considered in the general culture as caste Hindus. Moreover, educated tribals in Chhattisgarh are pushing for tribal caste recognition as *rajputs*. With the newly appointed Chhattisgarh Chief Minister, Mr. Ajit Jogi, having tribal roots, it appears likely that this move for formal recognition will continue, at least within the state.

As a result of their religious and political efforts at elevating themselves in the eyes of the caste-Hindu society, many Kabirpanthis and the Satnamis resent the Ramnami Samaj's inaction in this regards. The two sects see most of their own sanskritizing efforts and attempts at social and religious elevation being ignored and even rejected by the Ramnamis. Because all three sects are essentially identified in Chhattisgarh as *satnami,* the laxity on the part of the Ramnamis is seen by the others as detrimental to their efforts toward attaining the status and recognition they are seeking. Kabirpanthis often refer to the Ramnamis as ignorant and dirty, because of the latter's disregard of many of the caste-Hindu rules dealing with purity and pollution. Satnamis frequently stress their own more ancient roots, calling the Ramnamis a younger, less sophisticated movement. Groups of Kabirpanthis and Satnamis regularly attend the Ramnamis' annual Bhajan Melas, ostensibly to participate in the religious activities. However, they can often be heard voicing the above criticisms of the Ramnamis while there.

By affiliating themselves so intimately and exclusively with the *Mānas* and *Ramnam,* the Ramnamis have chosen their own method of approaching and relating to the central value system. The sect has never sought caste-Hindu status, nor for the most part, even sought caste-Hindu validation. Instead, it has attempted to remain as autonomous as possible. Ramnamis do not frame their relationship with the brahmanical system using the latter's categories or parameters. They have opted to approach the orthodox set of values on their own terms, through the assimilation and expression of those values they cherish and the rejection of the remainder. However, this is only part of the dynamics of the relationship. In the way the Ramnamis utilize both the *Mānas* and *Ramnam,* they also defy brahmanical parameters set up around these elements of the current orthodox system. The *samaj* treats the *Mānas* both as *shruti* and *smriti,* but at the same time openly criticizes and freely alters it. It treats the physical text as sacred at one moment and as any other book the next. As for *Ramnam,* the Ramnamis wrap themselves in the sounds and forms of the name, literally from head to toe, and make it the absolute center of their religious and corporeal existence. At the same time, they wear it, and tattoo it all over their bodies, even on their feet and buttocks. Such actions by anyone, but especially by Untouchables, are seen as defiling to the name and a form of heresy. Thus, the Ramnamis provide a powerful challenge to caste Hindus who resent what they do, yet claim to accept the prevalent view of the omnipotence of the name as a purifier and a redeemer. As one sect member commented somewhat bitterly, "The *brahmans* are hypocrites. They say they believe *Ramnam* is all-powerful and all-purifying, like the Ganges River. Yet, they will never accept us as being purified, no matter how much we chant the name or how much we bathe in the Ganges."

Lutgendorf's research on *Mānas* recitation, as it exists in Varanasi and some of the other North Indian cities, does a thorough job of presenting the quintessential brahmanized version of *Mānas* worship. Here, the priest has taken over nearly all authority for "proper" ritualistic recitation of the text, and it has become enveloped in rituals and restrictions. Once one enters rural India, however, it becomes apparent that such a metamorphosis in the use of the *Mānas* has not taken place and its associated preistly proscriptions have not occurred in any appreciable way. Amidst the social and religious transformations occuring in India today, there is a process of decentralization of religious authority underway as well. Moreover, a socioreligious environment has been created in which most sets of values are being rethought and revamped.

The Ramnamis have participated in just such a rethinking process, by questioning traditional beliefs, practices, values, philosophical concepts, as well as authority. Most of India's Untouchables have lived in a world in which they have had little power or autonomy over their own lives. They have traditionally had to acquiesce to the whim and will of the more powerful caste Hindu social and religious leaders. A headstrong or willful Untouchable was a dangerous one, a threat to the established order. A docile, submissive, obedient one was useful and beneficial. The Ramnami Samaj has given many *harijans* an opportunity for the first time to take charge of their own spiritual lives, to lead rather than to follow. Moreover, it is their connection with the *Mānas* and *Ramnam* that has given them this opportunity.

Members of the sect clearly live in a world of multiple, and often competing, value systems. These include the more regional Ramnami, Chhattisgarhi, *satnami,* Satnami, and Kabirpanthi systems, as well as regional and transregional caste Hindu orthodox values. Because the latter have imposed the greatest number of restrictions on *harijans,* these have been the values least adhered to by the Ramnamis. An example of this can be seen in the variety of caste Hindu prohibitions covering public interactions of adults of different sexes, including shows of physical affection, such as holding hands, hugging, kissing, even with respect to married couples. In many regions, further limitations have also been imposed on close one-to one female interactions with nonrelated males, such as intimate conversations, joking, and so forth. Ramnamis have, for the most part, ignored all these restrictions. Thus, *samaj* members, both male and female, typically hug each other upon meeting and also on departing. Nonrelated couples sit together, joke together, touch, hug, and exhibit affection much like one finds in the more physically expressive cultures of Southern Europe or Polynesia. Although this is partly due to the nature of traditional *satnami* culture in the region, it seems to be predominately affected by the Ramnami acceptance and support of as well as respect given to individuality and personal freedom of expression. As mentioned earlier, the sect exhibits, in much of its thinking, a reticence in proscribing its membership in any activity but those that are widely held to be in direct conflict with the practice of *Ramnam*. While this attitude has had some problematic side effects, most sect members feel that the kind of openness the *samaj* accepts and even promotes allows for a freedom that is well worth any price they have had to pay.

This is not to say that Ramnamis reject all caste Hindu values. Many of them have simply learned to navigate their paths in and out of the various value systems, utilizing or rejecting aspects as the occasion arises. The means of relating to a situation is influenced by the value system in which they are functioning at the time. Thus, access to a greater number of systems allows more freedom and creativity of action. While some might call this hypocrisy, it can also be understood as the contextualization of values and beliefs, and this is actually a rather common practice wherever multiple value systems coexist, be they religious, social, or political. The functional reality of this was made expressly clear to me one full moon night in Chhattisgarh.

I had arrived at Ramtaram's village the day before an impending eclipse and heard mention of the event on several occasions. Having inquired of my host and his family what they did on the occasion of an eclipse, Ramtaram and the other members of the household told me of the prevalent Chhattisgarhi practice of fasting before and during an eclipse, not watching the eclipse itself, and then bathing in a natural body of water afterwards. Everyone present readily agreed that this was the proper thing to do.

I was away from the village during most of the full moon day but returned just as the sun was setting. The women of the house were preparing dinner as usual, so I thought to myself that it was likely going to be set aside until after the completion of the eclipse, about ten o'clock that night. The astrological event began just before eight that night, and shortly thereafter, I ventured outside to see what activity, if any, was taking place, and if anyone was actually out watching it. The village paths were empty, except for a few animals and an old man contemplating the smoke from a cow dung fire he had lit. Soon, a few of the children from my house came out to see what I was doing, and they were soon followed by Ramtaram himself. He began to tell me the story of Ketu, the demon who devours the moon during the eclipse, glancing all the while at the diminishing globe. Before long a group of nearly ten of us were having a conversation while observing the ensuing eclipse. Eventually, the oldest son of the family emerged from the house, and to my surprise informed us that it was time for dinner!

As we sat for the evening meal I remarked that the eclipse was still in progress and questioned why Ramtaram had decided not to wait to eat—I thought perhaps the family chose to eat at their regular time so as not to upset my schedule. My host quite proudly remarked, "Oh, I don't bother with such restrictive customs. For one who chants *Ramnam,* no other observance is necessary." His wife grinned as she added, "Especially if it might interrupt his dinner." Her comment actually helped me to understand how many Ramnamis view pan-Indian as well as local religious customs: they may be performed or adhered to if it is convenient. If not, then one can use one's identity as a Ramnami to justify ignoring a ritual or practice and still not be shunned for it.

With the twentieth century's move toward urbanization, Westernization, secularization, and mass education, caste Hindu adherence to brahmanical restrictions has relaxed somewhat and certain aspects of caste relations have changed. The values that exist in education, secularization, and Westernization have also made fashionable an overt rejection of the orthodox value system and a replacement of them with these newer sets of values. Among the urban educated, this often leads to a wholesale adoption of Western secular values. Many urban high caste who have spiritual inclinations may join non-brahmanical movements, such as the Radhasoami sect, which rejects brahmanical superiority and most caste restrictions. Others who seek religious meaning outside the narrow confines of brahmanical orthodoxy, but still within the Hindu tradition, find it in various *bhakti* movements which downplay the role of the *brahman.* Having already rejected the traditional value system, they are free to accept pre-brahmanized *bhakti* values (i.e., non-*brahman* mediated rituals, personal reading of the *Mānas* or other texts, caste-free association and *satsang* within, and sometimes without, their own sect). The Ramnamis often find audience from among this group of educated Hindus during their *melas,* or whenever they are "performing" in urban areas of Chhattisgarh. While none of these educated caste Hindus have "officially" joined the sect, many attend the Ramnamis' yearly *bhajans* and actively participate in the chanting.

On the one hand, the Chhattisgarhi Kabirpanthis and the Satnamis have sought, through the processes of sanskritization and politicization, to transform their social status and bridge the chasm of untouchability. However, while they have been successful in elevating themselves in the eyes of certain other Untouchable groups in the region, they have done little or nothing to alter their status in the eyes of most caste Hindus in Chhattisgarh. Moreover, they have alienated many. For the Ramnamis, on the other hand, *Ramnam,* and not sanskritization, has been the vehicle for transforming their relationship with the society in which they live. They have attached themselves firmly to what is now an integral part of the North Indian central value system and have so identified themselves with *Ramnam* that they have, in turn, become identified with it. If one mentions *"Ramnam"* in Chhattisgarh, an image of the Ramnamis usually comes to mind.

Ramnam and the Ram story have given the Ramnamis a belief and a value system. The sect's involvement with these has transformed their perception of their own relationship with the world around them. More importantly, their involvement with *Ramnam* and the *Mānas* has transformed their opinion of themselves, both individually and collectively. For the most part they seem confident in their relationship with Ram, and this has been for them a source of strength, both in the sense of communal solidarity and spiritual purposefulness. With respect to their view of their own status on the spiritual hierarchy, most deny that they are waiting to be reborn into a higher caste in order to be able to progress on the spiritual path, for they have *Ramnam*. When asked if he thought that his practice of *Ramnam* in this life would allow him to be born into a higher life next time, an old Ramnami mused, "Maybe it was the *Ramnam* I did in my past life that let me become a Ramnami this time."

Appendix I

Categories of Hindu Scripture: *Shruti* and *Smriti*

There is no single category in the Hindu tradition equivalent to the concept of "scripture" as found in Western religions. In the development of the brahmanical tradition, compilations of sacred words in the form of texts have typically come to be placed into two categories, *shruti,* "that which was heard," and *smriti,* "that which was remembered." *Shruti*[1] is said to designate the corpus of Vedic texts—Samhitas, Brahmanas, Aranyakas, and Upanishads—which are said to be eternal reverberations emanating forth from the Transcendent and directly cognized by seers at the beginning of each cycle of creation. Three characteristics are traditionally held to distinguish this class of texts. First, *shruti* constitutes a circumscribed, bounded category of texts—that is, the Vedic texts. Second, these texts, although transmitted by sages who "saw" and "heard" them, are generally held to be eternal and uncreated, not composed by any human or divine agent. Third, study of the Vedic Samhitas has focused on meticulous preservation of the purity of the Vedic sounds, or *mantras,* which are held to be intrinsically powerful and efficacious,[2] and thus precedence has usually been given to memorization and recitation of the texts over understanding and interpreting their meaning.[3]

The class of *smriti* texts, on the other hand, may be defined in terms of three characteristics that are in distinct opposition to those of *shruti.* First, *smriti* constitutes a fluid, dynamic, open-ended category of texts, which includes the Dharma-Shastras, Epics, Puranas, and an array of other texts that may be included in this class at different times or by different groups. Second, in contrast to *shruti,* these texts are believed to have been composed by personal authors, either human or divine, and hence are "that which was remembered" rather than "that which was heard." Third, study of *smriti* texts involves not only rote recitation of verses, but also an understanding and interpretation of their content and meaning.

While the characteristics delineated above have long defined the brahmanical view of *shruti* and *smriti,* the listed attributes fail to reveal the modifications of these categories that have taken place over the last thousand years. Sectarian devotional movements have been largely responsible for the increasing permeability and reinterpretation of these categories. They have precipitated the greatest number of additions to the class of *smriti,* and at the same time they have inspired the elevation of multiple sectarian works to a *shruti*-like status in the eyes of their own followers, and sometimes even in the eyes of the broader Hindu community as well. This advancement of status and use is precisely what has transpired with respect to Tulsidas's *Rāmcaritmānas* (see chap. 3).

Unfortunately, Indologists have traditionally concentrated on brahmanical Sanskritic texts when considering the concept of scripture in India, often neglecting to consider fully the depth of influence that sectarian movements and their writings have had on the evolution of the concept. In recent years, however, several scholars have suggested the need for an expanded understanding of *shruti* and *smriti* that would encompass more fully the dynamic role the sacred word has played in the Hindu tradition, particularly in post-Vedic times. In reflecting on the brahmanical categories and the various uses of scripture in Hindu life, J. A. B. van Buitenen notes: "While the distinction between *Shruti* and *Smriti* is a useful one, in practice the Hindu acquires his knowledge of religion almost exclusively through *Smriti*."[4]

Thomas Coburn, on the other hand, questions the applicability of the traditional categorization and has suggested that *shruti* and *smriti,* instead of constituting fixed categories of texts, may refer rather to "two different kinds of relationship that can be had with verbal material in the Hindu tradition."[5] As Coburn's observation implies, despite the apparently secure status of the Vedas themselves as *shruti,* the distinctions between the categories of *shruti* and *smriti,* as delineated above, do not represent an absolute classification of particular texts. Rather, they form part of a theoretical framework by means of which a variety of texts may be classified according to their status and function within a particular community. A text ultimately attains its sacred status as scripture—and more specifically as *shruti* or *smriti*—only in relationship to a particular religious community, for it is the community that determines whether a text is "sacred or holy, powerful or portentous, possessed of an exalted authority, and in some fashion transcendent of, and hence distinct from, all other speech and writing."[6]

Historically, several procedural strategies have been adopted to effect a change in the position of sectarian texts with respect to the categories of *shruti* and *smriti.* Those processes, which have played an important role in the evolution of the *Ramkatha* in India since its inception include brahmanization and vedacization.[7] Both will be discussed below with respect to their influence in the evolving character and conceptions of the Ram story.

Mantra and *Nam* in Early Epic and Vedic Literature

Since Rig Vedic times there has been a strong belief in India regarding the power of words and sounds. To the Hindu, speech *(vach)* is not simply a composition of arbitrary sounds meant to convey information and exchange knowledge; it is a means of contacting the divine. Moreover, it is the means by which creation came into being. Due to its creative power, *vach* became personified as a goddess of learning, wisdom, and inspiration. In various Vedic works, the goddess Vac is presented as being intimately connected with the creative process. She is a link between gods and men. In the *Śatapatha Brāhmaṇa* (VII.5.2.52), for example, she is said to be an instrument in the process of creation, causing the subtle to become manifest. In later Vedic literature, speech and *mantra* are identified with Brahman, each spoken word being one of Vac's manifestations.[8]

In the earliest formulations of Vedic thought, the gods were seen to be the possessors of power, and the hymns were meant to propitiate them in hope of gaining their assistance. Within the *Ṛg Veda* itself, however, one can perceive a shift in the recognition of power "away from the gods and into the elements of ritual technique."[9] The primary center of power attainable by humans came to be viewed as residing in the rituals and *mantras*. Although the concept of *mantra* is central to the development of Vedic thought, the term is actually rarely found in the text, appearing primarily in the later portions, Books I and X. Its emergence coincides with the increasing emphasis on ritualistic concerns.[10]

In early Vedic times, *mantras* were "hymns and prose formulae," which were recited or chanted during the performance of rituals and connected with supernatural power.[11] Edward Conze suggests that *mantras* were something spoken as "a way of wooing a deity."[12] *Mantras* were necessary for performing rituals, and various beliefs surrounding the *mantras* gradually evolved. Eventually, they came to be viewed as having inherent power in themselves. Moreover, they came to be ascribed with such potency that whoever had the knowledge to repeat them properly and reverently could wield divine power on his own. Increasingly, *mantras* were viewed as the most important part of rituals. Some could even be recited as substitutes for certain rituals or religious duties. An example can be seen in *Ṛg Veda* (10.9.1–3), where *mantrasnana* (lit. *mantra*-bathing) is said to be a valid alternative to actual bathing for someone who is ill or otherwise unable to fulfill the daily ritual.

It is difficult to say when the name of a deity first gained importance as a *mantra,* although it seems to have been a gradual development, beginning as early as the *Ṛg Veda.* According to Jan Gonda, in Vedic usage the verb *man-* carries the sense of "evoking, calling up" and that it is often associated with the noun *"nama,"* (Hindi: *nam*) literally "name."[13] The uses of *nam*—used here specifically in reference to the name of a deity—can be found in several places in the Vedas, such as *Ṛg Veda* 1.24.1 "of which god do we now invoke the beloved name?"[14] The belief in the efficacy of *nam* is widespread throughout the Vedic literature, and Gonda suggests the possibility of an ancient origin to this concept because of its presence in the *Avesta,* where Ahura Mazdah tells Zarathustra that whoever recites divine names continuously will be safe from any attacks.[15] In several places the *Ṛg Veda* elevates the status of *nam.* For example, *Ṛg Veda* 7.100.3 says that Vishnu's name inspires respect due to its inherent power, and 10.63.2

maintains that all the names of the gods deserve veneration, praise, and worship.[16] Other Vedic Samhita verses contain multiple names of a particular deity, possibly due to the belief that each epithet helps to manifest a different power of the deity. Thus, rather than the repetition of one name, repeating a variety of names and epithets will invoke more power. According to Gonda:

> The alteration of names and frequent epithets in the same stanza is already in the Ṛgveda far from rare, oft recurring epithets appropriated to a definite god being preferred to a repeated mention of his name.[17]

Although the concept of *nam* is important in these early texts, the perspective with which it is viewed is different from what is expressed in later devotional schools. References to its use are generally limited to specific ritual contexts. The goals of its use continue to lie within the realm of the material world rather than spiritual. The various ways in which names are utilized, for both good and evil, for supplication but also for commanding the gods to be present or to act, suggest a closer affinity with later tantric concepts of *mantra* than with the use of *nam* in the devotional schools that emerged much later. In Vedic literature, the power is inherent in the name as *mantra,* and the attitude of the reciter toward the deity being propitiated, or even coerced, into action appears to be of secondary importance.

Any use of *nam* among the brahmanical authorities must have been minimal, for although it had a place in certain Vedic rituals, it is never elaborated upon as a practice in any pre-Puranic Hindu texts. No additions made to either of the epics prior to second or third century C.E. reveal the use of *nam* as a form of *sadhana,* or religious practice. We know nothing as to whether the practice was a part of the popular religion of the time, for it is only with the advent of Mahayana Buddhist texts that the use of *nam* outside of a Vedic ritual context makes itself known.[18] Its appearance in Mahayana Buddhism in the first centuries C.E. suggests that it began evolving as a practice within that tradition quite early.

Ram and *Ramnam* in the Puranas

According to Gonda, the Puranas were originally the texts of the lower castes.[19] Their stories may be contemporaneous with or even predate the Vedic Samhitas and were a source for legends to which the latter allude. The diversity of material found in the Puranas suggests the presence of a vast array of myths, religious beliefs, and sentiments in the periphery. Ludo Rocher points out that not only did the Puranas start out as oral works, but they also have remained that way for ages. He argues that extant versions of the texts "represent only an infinitesimal part of the versions that have existed over the centuries, in different parts of India." He urges that we should consider the Puranas

> purely as an oral tradition, as a tradition that is solely carried forward by individual storytellers, and which is, therefore, authorless and anonymous, as a tradition only parts of which have accidently been committed to writing.[20]

Over a period of time many of these stories coalesced into textual form. Like other Indian texts, however, they have continued to be influenced by both the vast oral traditions that gave birth to them and the continuous efforts of the religious elite to brahmanize them so that they express orthodox beliefs and values.

A number of scholars have wondered about the lack of a Ram-focused Purana. Sir Charles Eliot suggests this shows "that his worship did not possess precisely those features of priestly sectarianism which mark the Puranas."[21] While not having its own Purana, the *Ramkatha* is mentioned in a variety of Puranas, occasionally appearing in a more elaborate form. Each Purana has presented the story in a slightly different way, at times altering details.[22] In most of these Ram is an *avatar* of Vishnu, and several have sections that refer to the worship of Ram or the practice of *Ramnam*. Some of these sections are of the *stotra* type, and Gonda suggests that many of these may actually predate the texts in which they exist.[23] These *stotras* generally end with a *phalashruti,* a statement describing the rewards that result from the hymn's repetition.

The version of the Ram story contained in the *Padma Purāna,* for example, agrees more closely with the Kalidasa's *Raghuvaṃśa* (fourth-fifth century) than with Valmiki's telling. Ram is also praised as the highest Brahman, and the *mantra "Oṃ Rāmāya namah"* is called the *"taraka mantra,"* which Shiva repeats into the ear of all those beings who die in Varanasi, thereby guaranteeing them liberation, or, at minimum, a human rebirth. The Purana also mentions worshippers of Ram, whom it calls "Ramadasa." The *stotra* verses in the final book of this text are collectively known as the *Rāmarakśāstotra.* There are actually several versions of this hymn, three of which are supposedly from the *Padma Purāṇa* and another that is contained within the *Ānanda Rāmāyaṇa.*[24] The hymn is attributed to Budha Kaushika and was included in a collection of Sanskrit texts taken to Java sometime between the seventh and ninth centuries. Like many *stotras*, it has a distinctly tantric character, its recitation often coupled with breathing practices, visualizations, and the wearing of talismans. It is chanted by Ram devotees as a form of protection from physical and psychic attacks. One of the most popular verses from the *stotra,* presented as a teaching by Shiva to Parvati, is frequently recited by North Indian Ram *bhaktas* today. It expresses the supremacy of *Ramnam* over all other names:

> Beautiful-faced one, I delight in the handsome Rāma by uttering
> "Rāma, Rāma, Rāma."
> Rāma's name is equal to one thousand names (of Vishnu).[25]

The type of worship that is expressed in the Puranic literature is nearly always formed-based *(sagun),* often providing dazzling descriptions of the physical form of the deity being supplicated. The same is true with respect to Ram. The *Yoga Sūtra* and the Tantric literature are the first texts to give strong indication of the presence of *nirgun bhakti,* although the practice does not gain textual legitimacy until centuries later. These texts focus on the name and its power, rather than on forms. The subsequent writings addressing Ram *bhakti* continue to develop in this direction, as we shall see.

By the end of the first millennium C.E. the *Ramkatha,* perhaps in full, in part, or in summary, came to be included in most of the Puranas. In addition to these, there were numerous secular texts and several Jain and Buddhist renderings. The story had even traveled outside India as well, showing up in Tibet, Cambodia, and Java.

The Influence of the Tantric Tradition

The Tantric tradition has endowed the practice of Hinduism with a variety of important contributions. Often reformulations or borrowings from Vedic and other sources, tantric elements have become such an established part of Hinduism that the popular, contemporary manifestations of the latter are often more tantric than Vedic. Several key aspects of Tantra are of specific interest in the study of the Ram tradition. The analysis herein will be confined to two of these, namely, *jap* and *beej* (seed) *mantras*.

Like most of the non-brahmanical religious movements in India, Tantrism owes its beginnings to the synthesis of a variety of sources. Archaeological and textual evidence both point to the origins of the Tantric tradition outside the brahmanical and even Aryan religion.[26] Vedic, non-Vedic, ascetic, and shamanistic influences are all apparent in this somewhat enigmatic system. Tantrism appears to have become well established in India by the sixth or seventh century C.E., finding its way into all the major religious systems of the subcontinent.[27] While parts of Tantra show strong Vedic influence, there is also an emphatic and often ritualistic rejection of fundamental aspects of the brahmanical value system. J. N. Farquhar maintains that a major reason for the differences between the two is that Tantra has its roots in the periphery, where the value systems were very different. In the process of brahmanization, however, much of Tantra's earlier form was kept in order to benefit the Hindu orthodoxy's competition with Buddhism and Jainism for the souls of the populace, most of whom existed outside the caste system.[28]

The use of *mantras* is of fundamental importance in the Tantric tradition, and a special status is attributed to *beej mantras*. Vedic literature contains some use of *beej mantras*, such as *"hoom,"* *"phat,"* and *"oṃ,"* the latter being ascribed the greatest status. The *Chāndogya Upaniṣad* (1.3.4) calls *om* imperishable and even gives guidelines for its use. In the *Kaha Upaniṣad* (1.2.15–6), *om* is said to be the vehicle to attain Brahman, and it is equated with Brahman in the *Taittirīya Upaniṣad* (1.8.1–2). The *Māndūkya Upaniṣad* (1.28) identifies *"oṃ"* with *atman,* that which resides in the hearts of all beings.[29]

With the rise of the Tantric tradition, there was an increase in the number of *beej mantras*, their uses, and their credited powers. For use of these new *mantras*, Tantric schools "established quasi-scientific methods about how to combine these syllables either with one another or with meaningful words in order to unfold their dormant powers."[30]

Beej mantras have been called "gibberish" or "meaningless chatter," since they have no standard definition. To the Tantric practitioner, however, the lack of conventional meaning enhances their power and the possibility of their use in meditation. They do not require comprehension, and they activate the consciousness.[31] The early use of *beej mantras* was often connected with Vedic *mantras*, the former increasing the power of the latter. Eventually, *beej mantras* came to have a life of their own, as does *om* in the later Vedic literature. Moreover, they came to be of central importance. The Tantric schools appropriated the *Yoga Sūtra* concept of the *beej*'s association with Ishvar (Lord) and developed the concept that each deity has its own *beej mantra*. Further, these *mantras* are shown to have a power and status beyond that attributed to them in the *Yoga Sūtra*. Paul Eduardo Muller-Ortega suggests that the use of *beej mantras* grew in prominence as a result of multiple factors in the developing tradition.

> Suffice it to say that a complex process of development culminates in a consolidation and simplification of the tantric *sādhanā* to such a great extent that it becomes possible . . . to announce that all that is necessary for the attainment of liberation is the proper reception of a single *bīja-mantra*.[32]

Two types of *beej mantra* exist in Tantra, those associated with a particular deity and those residing in the various *chakras* or energy centers of the body. The former generally have a lengthened medial vowel, while the latter have a shortened one. Abhinavagupta praises *beej mantras* and refers to them as self-illuminating. He elaborates a theoretical structure legitimating their superior status.[33] Each *beej* is said to be so intimately connected to a deity as to be the actual *svaroop* of the deity. To gain the *siddhi,* or perfection, of a *mantra* is to gain the power of the deity whose form it is.

One of the primary means for achieving a *mantra*'s *siddhi* is through the use of *jap,* or continual repetition of the *mantra*. In the Vedic literature, the term "*jap*" simply refers to the recitation of a prayer. By the time of the Tantric tradition, however, the practice had evolved a great deal and came to constitute a fundamental element of the Tantric *sadhana* for the gaining of insight and power. Two senses of the term *"jap"* are found in Tantra. The first is simply mantra repetition aloud, while the second is *tushnim jap,* or silent repetition. This latter practice takes on importance during the Tantric tradition and continues to be important in the ascetic schools in Hinduism. Here, fundamental to the process of doing *jap* is the belief that the deity is identical with the *mantra* being repeated.[34] This becomes an important belief in the development of the practice of *Ramnam.*

Initially, *beej mantras* were used by all those initiated into tantric practices. Over a period of time, the brahmanization of Tantra increased, and caste restrictions on the uses of *beej mantras* were instituted. Various texts set up conditions under which the practice of *jap* should be done, and elaborate preparatory rites evolved.[35] Many of these required knowledge of Vedic *mantras*, available only to the high caste. Some schools established requirements for initiates that severely limited admission by low caste, although low-caste women continued to be used as sexual partners for various rituals.

The Tantric texts also contain supplication *mantras* similar to those found in the Puranas. In the tantric forms, *"om"* is replaced with the *beej mantra* specific to the particular deity being addressed. The *beej* of a deity usually has an alliterative connection with the name of the deity. Thus, we find *"Klīṃ Kīṛṣṇāya namah," "Hrāṃ Hanumate namah,"*[36] and *"Rāṃ Rāmāya namah."* The addition of *beej* mantras is essential since they "express the special power of a deity or a degree of 'holiness' and are correlated with the very essence of that god or state."[37] This tantric form of *mantra* became important for the sects devoted to the respective deities, and such *mantras* often became the sect's central *mantra.* This is one of the many bridges linking devotional Hinduism with tantric practice.[38]

The developments in the Tantric schools provided Hinduism in general, and the Ram tradition in particular, with new avenues of expression and interpretation. Ram *bhaktas* possessed a powerful alternative way to practice Ram *bhakti,* apart from the brahmanized rituals that had already had their effect on many sectarian schools, especially in the case of Krishna. In a land increasingly influenced by the brahmanical value system, low-caste Ram devotees had in Ram's name both a powerful and effective devotional *mantra* as well as tantric vehicle with which to animate their own religious lives.

Another important concept began to emerge in this period as well, that of *nirgun bhakti.* While other sects were focusing on the anthropomorphic representations of their deities and their earthly and heavenly *lilas*, most texts dealing with Ram, beginning with the Vaishnav Upanishads, place a great deal of emphasis on the repetition of his name and suggest the existence of *nirgun bhakti* as a part of the Ram tradition. The practice of *Ramnam* is given a place of central importance in these texts, above that of image worship. *Ramnam* was eventually adopted by the majority of North Indian *nirgun bhakti* practitioners, including Sikhs, Shaivites, and Sufis. These Ram-focused texts prepared the way for

Tulsidas to present his Ram story to North India, which eventually came to dominate the religious life of the masses of all castes.

Ram and Ramnam in the Vaishnav Upanishads

Like nearly all the post-Vedic literature of India surveyed above, the sectarian Upanishads are difficult to date because of the multiple layers of material apparent in them. Further, they have gone through the process of sectarian brahmanization, with the result that most extant forms promote a sectarian brahmanical value system. The earliest of the Vaishnav Upanishads[39] are probably the two *Nṛsimha-tāpanīya Upaniṣads*, *Pūrva* and *Uttara*.[40] Together they were the chief scriptures for the Narsimha sect, which dates well before the seventh century.[41]

The *Nṛsimha-pūrva-tāpanīya Upaniṣad* opens with verses from the *Ṛg Veda,* then presents and glorifies the Narsimha *mantra,* which it calls *"mantrarāja."* It also gives four auxiliary, or *anga, mantras* said to be connected with the main *mantra. Om* is the first of these *anga mantras* and is given an important place throughout the text. Some of the literary styles used are patterned after various Brahmanas and Upanishads. The focus of the text is the greatness of Narsimha and his *mantras*.[42] The *Nṛsimha-uttara-tāpanīya Upaniṣad,* while praising the Narsimha *mantras*, also presents a sectarian theology, in which Narsimha is simultaneously equated with *om,* Atman, and Brahman:

> Indeed, the God Nṛsimha is the Ātman, is the Brahman. One who knows this, is "without desires, free from desires . . . for he is the Brahman and is merged in the Brahman."[43]

The *mantra* most emphasized in the *Nṛsimha-uttara-tāpanīya Upaniṣad* is *om,* rather than the Narsimha *mantra.* In the last *khandas* of the text, the two *mantras* are shown to have a relationship like that of Brahman and Ātman.[44] The popularity of these Upanishads, at least in style, is obvious in their use as models for subsequent sectarian Upanishads, especially those devoted to Ram.

The three Vaishnav Upanishads that concentrate on Ram and *Ramnam* are the *Rāma-pūrva-tāpinīya Upaniṣad,* the *Rāma-uttara-tāpinīya Upaniṣad,* and the *Rāma-rahasya Upaniṣad.* The former two are, in title, form, and execution, composed along the lines of the Narsimha Upanishads.[45] The *Rāma-pūrva-tāpinīya Upaniṣad* begins with various folk etymologies of the name "Rama," such as he "who rules *(rā-jate)* over the kingdom of the earth *(ma-hi),*" and "because the Yogins delight *(ra-mante)* in him," as reasons why "he was called *Rāma* by the wise ones in the world."[46] The second section of the text focuses on the Ram *mantra, "Rāṃ Rāmāya namah,"* and continues its etymological "analysis" of the name and the *mantra.* The *beej* is said to contain the whole animate world, Ram and Sita being the source of all existence. Ram is both Brahman and Atman, and since the *mantra* encompasses both it should be constantly repeated:

The formula is the glorifier,
And Rāma the glorified;
The two thus united surely bring
Reward to all who use it.

Just as a person bearing a name, turns
Towards the one who calls by that name,
So also the formula, budding from the germ,
Turns towards him who employs it.[47]

After numerous verses praising Ram, Sita, and the other major figures associated with him in the *Ramkatha,* the *Rāma-pūrva-tāpinīya Upaniṣad* (58–74) goes on to enumerate directions for the construction of a Ram *yantra* and the writing of various *beej* and other *mantras*.[48] The last section of the text exhorts the worship of Ram and promises,

He who worships him, enjoys fulfillment of desires
And, like He, rises to the highest place.
One, who this holy song, joyfully and piously
Recites, spotless he attains liberation,
—Recites, spotless he attains liberation.[49]

The *Rāma-uttara-tāpinīya Upaniṣad* may have been an entirely separate work that was later given its present name in order to attach an *Uttara* text to the *Rāma-pūrva-tāpinīya Upaniṣad* and thus correspond to the model of the texts. The main body of the work is made up of borrowed passages from various Upanishads, modified to make them express devotion to Ram and to *Ramnam.* The *Rāma-uttara-tāpinīya Upaniṣad* connects *Ramnam* with the *taraka mantra* and details the fruits derived from the practice. It tells of Shiva's constant repetition of *Ramnam* for thousands of ages, as a result of which Ram grants him the boon that

If you will whisper my formula
In the right ear of even a dying man,
Whoever he may be,
He shall be liberated, O Śiva![50]

The *mantra "oṃ"* is also given special status, but it does not overshadow the main *mantra* of the text, as it does in the *Nṛsimha-uttara-tāpanīya Upaniṣad.* The *Rāma-uttara-tāpinīya Upaniṣad* also provides *mantras* of supplication for Sita, Ram's three brothers, and Hanuman. The last section contains forty-seven *mantras* glorifying Ram and identifying him with the supreme Brahman, the Vedas, *om,* all the *avatars* and main deities, Death, the elements, indeed almost everything. The text concludes with a verse promising immortality to those who repeat these *mantras* at all times.[51]

Little is known of the *Rāma-rahasya Upaniṣad*. Paul Deussen omits it altogether from his discussion and translations of the sectarian Upanishads. J. N. Farquhar includes it in a list of 123 Upanishads, but says nothing about it. Maurice Winternitz only mentions it in a footnote, saying it is of a similar time period to the other Upanishads devoted to Ram. Nevertheless, its approach and content are sufficiently different from these texts to justify its mention here.

Most of the text is uttered by Hanuman, as he replies to the questions about true knowledge posed by various sages. He begins by affirming that Ram is the supreme Brahman as well as the vehicle for liberation.[52] Ram is then equated with many of the major deities, and *jap* of his six-syllable *mantra (Rām Rāmāya namah)* is encouraged. In one of the only sections put in the words of Ram (1.13), he tells Vibhishan that the repetition of *Ramnam* will remove the *karma* accrued from the killing of one's father, mother, guru, or a *brahman.*

In what is clearly a tantric technique, the text then details the combining of various *beej mantras* with names associated with Ram to form *mantras* of varying lengths, each having a different function. *Mantras* with a variety of syllables, from one to twenty-four, are thereby created. The results are *mantras*, such as *"Oṃ Rāmāya huṃ phat svāhā"* and *"Oṃ srīṃ Rām Daśarathāya Sītā vallabhāya sarvābhista dayā namah."*[53] Of all such *mantras*, the two- and six-syllable *mantras* are said to be the most powerful. Finally, the monosyllabic "Rām" is said to be the real signifier of Brahman, while the two-syllable "Rā-ma" is the bestower of liberation.

It is clear from these texts that by the time of their authorship, the practice of Ram *bhakti* and *Ramnam* had become sufficiently popular to warrant a series of such writings. While their source is yet unknown, their contents indicate tantric and ascetic influences. At the same time, the use of Vedic verses, especially in the *Rāma-uttara-tāpinīya Upaniṣad* suggest brahmanical influence, if not in their origins, then surely in their subsequent forms.

One final text deserves mention here, the *Agastya Saṃhitā,* another important document in tracing the development of Ram *bhakti*. Hans Bakker, in his exhaustive research on Ayodhya, uses internal and external evidence to pinpoint twelfth-century Varanasi as the date and location of the origin of the text.[54] As in the sectarian Upanishads, Vedantic philosophy had a major influence on the *Agastya Saṃhitā*. While an early teaching in the text emphasizes the importance of chanting and worship in Kali Yug, there is also a discussion of yoga and meditation.[55] Vishnu is shown to have two forms, *nirgun,* as in the Upanishadic concept of Brahman, and *sagun,* the highest personal deity who incarnates as the various *avatars*. Ram is then identified with both of these aspects, and his worship is said to be superior to any other. His name, "Rā-ma," contains all the syllables of the *devanagari* alphabet and thus has within it the power of all the *mantras* and all the deities. Further, he is the soul that resides in the heart of all beings.[56]

Nevertheless, while the value system expressed in the text is both devotional and sectarian, it is clearly orthodox as well. Everyone is urged to follow the priestly ordained socioreligious hierarchial system, known as *varnashrama-dharma*. Thus, only by worshipping Ram within the limitations of one's caste, stage of life, and so forth, *can* one achieve liberation.[57] The *mantra* used for worship is the same as that found in the previously mentioned texts—*Rām Rāmaya namah*—and all Ram devotees, irrespective of their caste and status in life, are urged to repeat it. Shiva was given this *mantra* by Brahma, and by means of it he is able to grant liberation to his devotees. Subsequently, Shiva used it to liberate all those who die in Varanasi. Hans Bakker and Charlotte Vaudeville both feel that the Ram *mantra* is a part of a very old tradition, much before its actual appearance in texts. They suggest that it may have even been in use within Shaivite circles prior to its appropriation by Vaishnavs.[58]

Appendix II

One of the most startling, and telling, examples of the brahmanization of the Valmiki *Rāmāyaṇa* can be found in its final book, known as *Uttarakāṇḍa,* which J. L. Brockington and various other Sanskritists believe was added long after the writing of the core story attributed to Valmiki. In it there is an incident involving a low-caste ascetic, and it provides an amazing example of the brahmanical effort to degrade and deter direct low caste participation in the religious life. The episode, contained in *sarga*s 73 through 76, aptly illustrates the type of brahmanization that has taken place, which occurs not only in Valmiki but in many subsequent texts, especially with respect to epic and Puranic literature. The story begins with the premature death of a *brahman* boy and his father's lamentations. These include blaming Ram and his rule of the kingdom for the possibility that such a death could occur. The father declares, "Assuredly the young inhabitants of other countries need not fear death!"[1]

Subsequent to the death, an assembly of *brahman*s and sages is convened to discuss the situation. In it, the heavenly sage, Narad, gives a discourse on the practice of asceticism during the four *yug*s, or ages of the universe. In Krita Yug, he adds, only *brahman*s practiced austerities (*tapasya*); during the next *yug,* Treta, members of the *kshatriya* caste were also permitted to engage in the practice. Narad then laments that in Dwarpara Yuga, "untruth and evil increased," and members of the *vaishya* caste also began to do austerities. Narad assured the assembly, however, that throughout these three *yug*s, the performance of such religious practices remained forbidden for *shudra*s. It is only during Kali Yug, the most defiled of times, that the low caste are permitted to do *tapasya.* The implication given here and asserted more directly in subsequent texts is that the practice of religious austerities by the low caste is not only a sign of unrighteousness, but helps induce it.

It is then revealed to Ram that a *shudra* is, in fact, performing austerities, and this "practice of unrighteousness, must be stopped," for "the monarch who does not mete out immediate punishment, goes to hell, of this there is no doubt."[2] Deeply concerned, Ram sets out to search his kingdom. Ultimately, he encounters Shambuka, a *shudra* ascetic doing *tapasya.* As soon as Ram ascertained the ascetic's caste, he instantly beheads Shambuka.

Witnessing Ram's deed, the gods rejoice, declaring, "By thy grace, this Shudra will not be able to attain heaven!" They then proceed to grant Ram a boon, which he uses to bring the *brahman*'s son back to life.[3] After the murder of Shambuka, Ram visits the hermitage of the renowned sage, Agastya, who says, "The Gods tell me that thou hast come here after slaying the Shudra and, by this act of justice thou hast restored the son of a brahmin to life!"[4] The sage then praises Ram's divinity.

The insertion of this episode seems to be an obvious brahmanical maneuver, meant to give several distinct messages. Foremost among these is the point that all religious practice, even asceticism done alone in the jungle, is firmly under the authority of the brahmanical hierarchy. Attempts by the low caste to engage in religious practice, even as ascetics, portend misfortune, and thus are legitimately to be dealt with by the authorities in a very severe manner. The duty of the low caste is to serve the higher castes, and the whole kingdom is benefited by their doing only this. When we contemplate the role that the epics and Puranas have played and continue to play in the life of the Hindu, it becomes evident that such brahmanized additions provide the rationale for suppression of and violence against the low caste that have been an integral part of the history of India. The tale also presents justice entirely in terms of brahmanical law and benefit, and it warns all those in authority of the consequences of not requiring adherence to such laws by all their subjects. Finally, the implication is made that a definite sign of righteousness in a kingdom is the prosperity of *brahmans*.

It is interesting, as well as significant, to note that there are several tales in the Puranas of humans doing *tapasya* to attain the level of the gods. In most of these stories, the gods feel extremely threatened by these actions, often sending obstacles to divert and even prevent the practices. It is this same feeling of threat to their power that is exhibited by the brahmanical orthodoxy in the addition of such stories as that of Shambuka into brahmanized texts. This fear can be seen as an impetus for a variety of restrictions and practices that the religious elite have instituted throughout Indian history.

Episodes such as the Shambuka story are used both to validate the degraded status allotted the low caste and to elevate in importance the role of the *brahman* and his rituals in the life of Ram, the Ram story, and the existing society. They counteract the few positive portrayals of low caste that do exist in the core text, by showing each to be responsible for great anguish and suffering. They characterize Ram as a dutiful deity, serving the "gods on earth," an appellation the *brahman* writers of many texts assign to themselves.

Notes

Introduction

1. Cited in Mark Juergensmeyer, *Religion as Social Vision* (Berkeley: University of California Press, 1982), p. 1.
2. During the last two decades, several works have sought to address this deficiency. Notable among these are: Frank Whaling, *The Rise in the Religious Significance of Rāma* (Delhi: Motilal Banarsidass, 1980); J. L. Brockington, *Righteous Rāma* (Delhi: Oxford University Press, 1985), and Philip Lutgendorf, *The Life of a Text: Tulsidas' Ramcaritmanas in Performance* (Berkeley: University of California Press, 1991).
3. Romila Thapar, "Epic and History: Tradition, Dissent and Politics in India," *Past and Present* 125 (Nov. 1989): 25.
4. See "Definition of Terms" below for an explanation of sanskritization and brahmanization as used herein.
5. J. N. Farquhar, *An Outline of the Religious Literature of India* (Delhi: Motilal Banarsidass, 1967), p. 47.
6. William A. Graham, *Beyond the Written Word: Oral Aspects of Scripture in the History of Religion* (Cambridge: Cambridge University Press, 1987), p. 47.
7. Edward Shils, *Center and Periphery* (Chicago: University of Chicago Press, 1972), p. 3.
8. Ibid., pp. 3–5.
9. Ibid., p. 6.
10. I first encountered this term in J. L. Brockington, *Righteous Rama*. It has been used by several scholars of India, referring to the process by which various non-Vedic texts have been modified and interpolated to more closely reflect and present brahmanical values. Brockington describes this process with respect to the evolution of the Vālmīki *Rāmāyaṇa*. In later sectarian works, such as the *Bhāgavata Purāṇa*, brahmanization is also quite apparent.
11. M. N. Srinivas, *Social Change in Modern India* (Berkeley: University of California press, 1971), p. 6.
12. My definition of the process of vedacization was inspired by two articles that address the concept. They are (1) Sheldon Pollock, "From Discourse of Ritual to Discourse of Power in Sanskrit Culture," and (2) Philip Lutgendorf, "The Power of Sacred Story: Rāmāyaṇa Recitation in Contemporary North India," in *Ritual and Power*, ed. Barbara A. Holdrege, *Journal of Ritual Studies* 4, no. 2 (Summer 1990): Special Issue. Lutgendorf's article examines the elevation of the *Mānas* to the status of *shruti* by the *brahmans* of Varanasi.

13. Ramnamis often refer to all caste Hindus as simply *"Hindu log"* (Hindu people), thus distancing themselves from caste Hinduism. At other times, however, and depending upon the circumstance, the same Ramnamis may refer to themselves as Hindu.
14. For a further look at the diversity of the Ram tradition, see *"Many Rāmāyaṇas": The Diversity of a Narrative Tradition in South Asia,* ed. Paula Richman (Berkeley: University of California Press, 1991).
15. *"Ramnam"* generally refers both to the name "Ram" as well as to the practice of its repetition. I will utilize both definitions in this paper.
16. Throughout this book, I will use the terms *"harijan"* and "Untouchable" interchangeably. While Mark Juergensmeyer in *Religion as Social Vision* (p. 14) writes that the Untouchables in the Punjab dislike the name *"harijan"* and consider it patronizing, Ramnamis often use the term when referring to their general social designation in relation to caste-Hindu society.

Chapter 1: Providing the Context

1. From the time of British land demarcation in the nineteenth century until 1956, Chhattisgarh was a part of the Central Provinces, and from then until statehood a part of Madhya Pradesh. Thus, many aspects of life for the people there, including the Ramnamis, have been influenced by the religion and politics of those larger geopolitical entities. One can only watch for and speculate as to the effects statehood will have on Chhattisgarh and on the Ramnamis.
2. This is an official designation for those castes considered "depressed" and includes all the Untouchable subcastes.
3. R. S. Khare, *The Untouchable as Himself* (New York: Cambridge University Press, 1984), p. 1.
4. R. V. Russell and Hira Lal, *Tribes and Castes of the Central Provinces,* vol. 2 (Delhi: Cosmo Publications, 1975), p. 403.
5. Makhan Jha, "Ratanpur: Some Aspect of a Sacred City in Chhattisgarh," in *Chhattisgarh: An Area Study,* ed. Ajit Kumar Danda (Calcutta: Anthropological Survey of India, 1977), pp. 39–42.
6. Lawrence A. Babb, *The Divine Hierarchy: Popular Hinduism in Central India* (New York: Columbia University Press, 1975), pp. 3–7.
7. For more on the religious life of the region see chapter 3, "Religion and the Low Caste in Central India."
8. Paul Stoller and Cheryl Olkes, *In Sorcery's Shadow* (Chicago: University of Chicago Press, 1987), pp. x–xi.
9. *"Sadhu"* literally means "hermit, mendicant, or ascetic." The term has a variety of connotations, the broadest referring to all religious renunciants, the narrowest referring only to Vaishnav renunciants, both monastery dwellers and wanderers. In this study, I will use both "monk" and "ascetic" as alternate translations of the broader sense of the term.
10. That which is referred to as standard or "proper" Hindi today is a standardized form based primarily on several dialects spoken in urban areas of western Uttar Pradesh. There are dozens of languages that, while considered dialects of Hindi, actually have no more in common with standard Hindi than other distinct languages of North India, such as Punjabi, Gujarati, Bihari, and so forth.

11. This is much more the case with the sect of Shaivite ascetics known as *naga sannyasis* than with Vaishnav ascetics, most of whom avoid all intoxicants.
12. There were and are many practical and ideological reasons for this, although explanation and analysis are not within the scope of this study.
13. Hussein Fahim, *Indigenous Anthropology in Non-Western Countries* (Durham: Carolina Academic Press, 1982). The work focuses closely on the issues of indigenous and non-indigenous anthropology. The various articles in the text provide the reader with some important discussion of the benefits and drawbacks that result from proximity as well as distance in anthropological research.
14. M. N. Srinivas, *The Remembered Village* (Berkeley: University of California Press, 1976), p. 319.
15. Although Shaivite *sannyasis,* or "*swamis,*" are almost exclusively from high-caste families, the Shaivite *naga* (naked) *sannyasis* are often from lower-caste backgrounds. Through close associations and friendships within the Ramananda order and various other ascetics over the years, I nevertheless have come to believe that a significant percentage of all Hindu renunciants, especially with wandering mendicants, are likely from low-caste backgrounds. Not surprisingly, the heads of most of the various monasteries, especially the more financially endowed ones, seem to come from high-caste backgrounds.
16. This is the script used in writing Sanskrit and several other Indian languages.
17. The caption in the magazine mistakenly identified the sect as "Namdhari," and it gave no clue as to where it was located.
18. For the purpose of this study, I will use *"satnami"* (previously *"chamar"*) when referring to the subcaste to which most Ramnamis belong. "Satnami," on the other hand, will be used in reference to the religious sect, from which the subcaste name was adopted. Chapter 4 contains a discussion of the history of the sect and attempts an explanation of the differentiation between the sect and the caste.
19. At various times, there have been many questions I have wanted to ask but chose not to, out of respect for privacy and cultural taboos. Also, some experiences and information revealed to me privately have been purposely omitted from this study. The latter has been done out of respect for certain individuals and does not alter the validity of the material presented.
20. All names of specific Ramnamis and specific villages discussed in this work are pseudonyms. All initiated Ramnamis have adopted "Ramnami" as their surname.
21. Hussein Fahim, ed., *Indigenous Anthropology in Non-Western Countries,* p. xv.

Chapter 2: Historical Development of the Ram Tradition

An earlier version of some of this material has been published in a chapter entitled, "Personalizing the *Rāmāyaṇa:* Ramnamis and their Use of the *Rāmcaritmānas,*" in *Many Rāmāyaṇas: The Diversity of a Narrative Tradition in South Asia* (Berkeley: University of California Press, 1991). Anyone interested in vernacular renditions of the Ram story in South Asia will likely find great value in this volume.

1. In Appendix I, there is a more extensive discussion of the origins and development of *mantra* and *Ramnam,* from Vedic to medieval times.
2. A. K. Ramanujan, "Three Hundred Ramayanas: Five Examples and Three Thoughts on Translation," in *Many Rāmāyaṇas: The Diversity of a Narrative Tradition in South Asia.* Ramanujan prefers the term "tellings" to "versions" or "variants," since he feels the

latter imply an invariant form of the text. However in this analysis, I utilize the terms "tellings," "renderings," and "versions" as seems fit.

3. George A. Grierson, "Indian Epic Poetry" (a review of Hermann Jacobi's *Das Ramayana*), *Indian Antiquary* 23 (Feb. 1894): 55.
4. According to J. L. Brockington in *Righteous Rama* (p. 317), the oldest of the manuscripts utilized in the compilation of the Sanskrit Critical Edition of the Valmiki *Rāmāyaṇa* is dated early in the eleventh century, and subsequent manuscripts contain added passages. Consequently, he argues for the possibility of textual interpolation up until as recent as the twelfth century. Judging from the degree of brahmanization that the text experienced during the first millennium after the creation of its core, Brockington's theory does not seem farfetched.
5. Brockington, *Righteous Rama,* pp. 206–13, 307–27. J. N. Farquhar acknowledges at least three stages in the development of both epics. In her "Epic and History," Romila Thapar supports Brockington's basic speculations. His construction of the various stages has been put to substantial use in this chapter, in an effort to sort out the evolution of the story as it relates to my central theses.
6. However, prior to these texts, the Puranas also added to the development of the Ram tradition. Their influence with respect to Ram *bhakti* and *Ramnam* is addressed in Appendix I.
7. Two translations of the text have been used for this thesis: (1) *Adhyātma Rāmayāṇa* (Mylapore, Madras: Sri Ramakrishna Math, 1985); trans. Swami Tapasyananda; and (2) *Adhyātma Rāmayāṇa,* trans. Rai Bahadur Lala Baijnath (Allahabad: Panini Office, 1913). The first is useful because it contains the Sanskrit text and can thus be compared, and the second because it contains Book VII, absent in Tapasyananda's translation.
8. In contemporary India, the vast majority of those who study or even read the Valmiki version are scholars. It actually has little place in the religious life of the populace, except in reference.
9. Baijnath, *Adhyātma Rāmayāṇa,* p. i; Tapasyananda, *Adhyātma Rāmayāṇa,* p. v.; Brockington, *Righteous Rama,* p. 111.
10. Brockington, *Righteous Rama,* p. 112. As with other Indian texts, additions made to the original make dating difficult. Current estimates seem to be based on late material.
11. Tapasyananda, *Adhyātma Rāmayāṇa,* p. viii.
12. In all probability, additions have been made to the first six books as well, although no comprehensive study of this has yet been undertaken.
13. Maurice Winternitz, *A History of Indian Literature,* trans. S. Ketkar, vol. I.(New Delhi: Oriental Books Reprint Corp., 1972) pp. 578–9.
14. *AdhR* (I.1.1–2); Tapasyananda, *Adhyātma Rāmayāṇa,* p. 1.
15. Ibid., pp. 214–5.
16. *AdhR* (I.1.32–34); Tapasyananda, *Adhyātma Rāmayāṇa,* p. 6.
17. *AdhR* (I.1.43); Tapasyananda, p. 7.
18. *AdhR* (III.7.1–4); Tapasyananda, p. 148.
19. *AdhR* (III.5.59–60); Tapasyananda, pp. 142–3.
20. Tulsidas identifies him as the uncle of Ravana, but no relationship is given here.
21. *AdhR* (II.6.1–28); Tapasyananda, *Adhyātma Rāmayāṇa,* pp. 143–6.
22. The term *"dvij"* is translated by both Baijnath and Tapasyananda as *"brahman,"* but there seems to be nothing in the context that requires this over its literal meaning, "twice-born."

23. *AdhR* (VI.64–87); Tapasyananda, *Adhyātma Rāmayāṇa,* pp. 87–9.
24. *AdhR* (III.6.78); Tapasyananda, p. 88.
25. In Tulsidas's *Mānas,* for example, there are several such statements.
26. *AdhR* (II.5.59–64); Tapasyananda, *Adhyātma Rāmayāṇa,* pp. 79–80.
27. *AdhR* (III.10.21–2); Tapasyananda, p. 168.
28. *AdhR* (III.9.51–2); Tapasyananda, p. 165.
29. Tapasyananda, *Adhyātma Rāmayāṇa,* p. viii.
30. *AdhR* (VII.6.3–5); Baijnath, *Adhyātma Rāmayāṇa,* p. 213.
31. *AdhR* (VII.4.28–9; VII.6.34); Baijnath, pp. 200, 214.
32. *AdhR* (VII.4.24–7); Baijnath, p. 200.
33. *AdhR* (VII.4.41–63); Baijnath, p. 201.
34. *AdhR* (VII.8.9–72; VII.10) cf. *Vāl.* (VII.103–11); Baijnath, pp. 220–7.

Chapter 3: Ramnam and the Ram Story in Hindi

1. The term *"sant"* (*"sat,"* meaning both "existence" and "truth") is often inaccurately translated as "saint." It originally meant any existing being and subsequently came to refer to a good or a holy person. When used in reference to medieval times, it generally refers to those who followed and preached the path of *nirgun bhakti.* In contemporary times, *"sant"* carries the meaning of "ascetic" or "mendicant" and is often used to refer to *sadhus*, *sannyasis*, or members of other ascetic groups.
2. There is no consensus on the dates of Kabir. Those given by historians range from 1348 to 1440 for his birth and 1448 to 1518 for his death.
3. Karine Schomer and W. H. McLeod, eds., *The Sants: Studies in a Devotional Tradition in India* (Delhi: Motilal Banarsidass, 1987), pp. 2–6.
4. Most scholars exclude Tulsidas from the list of North Indian *sants*, using the *sagun*-orientation found in his writings as their primary justification. In reality, however, the Maharastrian Varkari *sants* are no less *sagun* in their devotion to Vithoba, yet they are readily included as *sants*.
5. Charlotte Vaudeville, "*Sant Mat:* Santism as the Universal Path to Sanctity." In *The Sants: Studies in a Devotional Tradition of India,* ed. Karine Shomer and W. H. McLeod, (Delhi: Motilal Banarsidass, 1987), p. 115.
6. Ibid. p. 50.
7. Kabir, *Bījak* (*Śabda* 11); Sukhdeo Singh and Linda Hess, trans. *Selections from the Bījak of Kabir* (Varanasi: Kabir Bani Prakashan Kendra, 1977), p. 8.
8. Charlotte Vaudeville, *Kabīr,* Vol 1. (Oxford: Oxford University Press, 1974), p. 329.
9. Kabir, *Bījak* (*Ramaini* 76); Ahmad Shah, trans. *The Bijak of Kabir* (Delhi: Asian Publication Service, 1977), p. 89.
10. *Bījak* (*Kahara* 5); Shah, *The Bijak of Kabir,* p. 163.
11. *Bījak* (*Śabda* 40); Shah, *The Bijak of Kabir,* p. 114.
12. Ainslie T. Embree, *The Hindu Tradition* (New York: The Modern Library, 1966), p. 249.
13. In Hindi-speaking North India the *Rāmcaritmānas* is referred to in several ways, including "Tulsi *Rāmāyaṇ,*" "Hindi *Rāmāyaṇ,*" *"Rāmāyaṇ,"* and *"Mānas."* The latter is by far the most common and is the one that will be primarily used in this study. Valmiki's text, on the other hand, is known primarily as "Valmiki *Rāmāyaṇ*" and occasionally "Sanskrit *Rāmāyaṇ*."
14. George A. Grierson, "Notes on Tul'sī Dās," in *Indian Antiquary* 22 (April, 1893): 89. He also gives 1532 as the year of Tulsidas's birth, but most scholars prefer the later date.
15. Events of the last several decades, such as the serialization of the Ram story on

television, the destruction of the Babri Masjid by a Hindu mob in 1992, and the subsequent rise of the Bharatiya Janta Party, has made this even more so.

16. Philip Lutgendorf, *The Life of a Text: Tulsidas' Ramcaritmanas in Performance* (Ph.D. diss., University of Chicago, 1986), p. 24. The subsequently published version of this study, *Life of a Text: Tulsidas' Ramcaritmanas in Performance* (Berkeley: University of Califormnia Press, 1991), does not contain this quote.
17. Tulsidas, *Vinay Patrikā (ViPa)* (227.2–3.). Edition used is by Gita Press, Gorakhpur (n.d.). The numbering of *Mānas* verses can be somewhat confusing, as a consequence of the variety of different meters used by Tulsidas, and also because of a lack of unanimity by academic scholars, both Indian and Western, with respect to methods of numbering. I have thus decided to follow the system utilized by Lutgendorf in his *The Life of a Text,* in which two-line *doha*s are numbered in order throughout a chapter, and four-line *caupai*s are numbered by line relative to the *doha* that follows them. Verses in *chand* meter are marked *"ch."*
18. Tulsidas, *Rāmcaritmānas (RC)* (I.5). The edition used is that of Gita Press, Gorakhpur (n.d.).
19. These include: *Bhaktamāl* by Nabhadas, 1624; *Gautam Candrikā* by Krishnadatta Miśra, 1624; *Mūl Gosāīṅ Caritra* by Benimadhavdas, 1630; *Bhaktiras Bodhini* by Priyadas, 1713; *Tulsī Caritra* by Dasanidas, ca. 1770; and *Gosāīṅ Caritra* by Bhavanidas, ca. 1770.
20. Frederic S. Growse, trans. *The Rāmāyaṇa of Tulsi Dās* (Allahabad: Ram Narain Lal Beni Prasad, n.d.), p. iv. Nabhadas's stanza is given, both the Hindi original and an English translation.
21. Growse, *Rāmāyaṇa,* pp. v–ix; Priyadas's full commentary, in Hindi and in English are given.
22. Edmour J. Babineau, *Love of God and Social Duty in the Ramcaritmanas* (Delhi: Motilal Banarsidass, 1979), p. 11.
23. Ibid., p. 12.
24. W. D. P. Hill, *The Holy Lake of the Acts of Rama* [English translation of the *Rāmcaritmānas*] (Calcutta: Oxford University Press, 1971), pp. xiii–xvi.; F. R. Allchin, *The Petition to Rām* [English translation of the *Vinay Patrikā*] (London: George Allen and Unwin Ltd., 1966), pp. 31–5.
25. Tulsidas, *Kavitāvalī,* trans., F .R. Allchin (New York: A. S. Barnes and Co., 1964), pp. 33–62.
26. This obviously suggests that, in the eyes of the *brahman* priests, the appropriation of the Ram story by the orthodoxy had been complete.
27. *RC* (2.125.4, ch 1).
28. *RC* (2.128.4; 2.130.1).
29. Babineau, *Love of God,* pp. 23–37.
30. Ibid., pp. 34–46.
31. *RC* (1.1–7).
32. Friedhelm Hardy, *Viraha Bhakti: The Early History of Kṛṣṇa Devotion in South India* (Delhi: Oxford University Press, 1983), p. 15.
33. *Vinay Patrikā* (67).
34. *RC* (5.60).
35. *RC* (6.112.7).
36. *Eka Rāma Dasaratha ke betā*
    Eka Rāma ghaṭa ghaṭa meṅ baithā
    Eka Rāma saba ke pyrārā

Eka Rāma saba se nyārā
This verse is often recited by Ramanandi *sadhus* to explain their theological view of Ram.

37. *RC* (7.71.1–4).
38. William J. Dwyer, *Bhakti in Kabir* (Patna. India: Associated Book Agency, 1981), p. 126.
39. *RC* (1.23–26).
40. *RC* (1.18–21).
41. *RC* (1.18–20; I.23).
42. *RC* (1.22.1).
43. *RC* (1.26.1).
44. Gandhiji, *Rāmnām* (Ahmedabad: Navjivan Prakashan Mandir, 1949), pp. 13, 32, 35–6.
45. Literally, "Oh, God, oh, God."
46. Lutgendorf, *The Life of a Text,* p. 724.

Chapter 4: Religion and the Low Caste in Central India

Kabīr Granthāvalī (*sākhī* 21.4); trans. in Charlotte Vaudeville, "*Sant Mat:* Santism as the Universal Path to Sanctity," in *The Sants: Studies in a Devotional Tradition of India,* ed. Karine Schomer and W. H. McLeod (Delhi: Motilal Banarsidass, 1987), p. 24.

1. G. H. Westcott, *Kabir and the Kabir Panth* (Delhi: Munshiram Manoharlal Publishers, 1986), pp. 61–2. Bloodline successorship can be found in religious sects throughout the world and can be traced to the successor method of both clans and monarchies.
2. David Lorenzen, "The Kabir-panth and Social Protest," in *The Sants: Studies in a Devotional Tradition of India,* ed. Karine Schomer and W. H. McLeod (Delhi: Motilal Banarsidass, 1987), pp. 291–92.
3. Ibid., p. 290.
4. Ibid., p. 295.
5. Lorenzen has done a great deal of research on the *panth,* both in Banaras and in Chhattisgarh. He contends that although the Chhattisgarh branch is generally comprised of more lower castes than the one in Uttar Pradesh, many are still caste Hindu. My own research among set members in Chhattisgarh has indicated that an overwhelming percentage of them are from *satnami* background, particularly in the rural areas. However, my information on the *sakha* has been gathered primarily from members of the Kawardha faction, as well as from the smaller monastery at Kharasiya.
6. Saurabh Dube, *Untouchable Pasts: Religion, Identity, and Power among a Central Indian Community, 1780–1950* (Albany: State University of New York Press, 1998), p. 42.
7. H. L. Shukla, *Chhattīsgarh Rediscovered: Vedantic Approaches to Folklore* (New Delhi: Aryan Books International, 1995), p. 12.
8. Westcott, *Kabir and the Kabir Panth,* p. 62. Any premature death of a *mahant,* however, would result in the immediate establishment of his son as the new *mahant.*
9. Lorenzen, "Kabir-panth and Social Protest," p. 24.
10. Westcott, *Kabir and the Kabir Panth,* pp. 59–63.
11. Lorenzen, "Kabir-panth and Social Protest," p. 301.
12. Westcott, *Kabir and the Kabir Panth,* pp. 8–9, 73n.
13. R. V. Russell and Hira Lal, *Tribes and Castes of the Central Provinces of India,* I:241.
14. "*Rāmnāmī log Rāmnām kā prayog nahīn kar dete, ve usko kharāb kar dete*" She also confessed that, privately, she chants *Ramnam,* but that she would never do it in public

because of its close connection in the eyes of Chhattisgarhis with the Ramnamis. Conversation took place in January 1982.

15. For an in-depth study of the origin and development of the Satnamis, see Dube, *Untouchable Pasts*, p. 42.
16. Ahmad Shah, *The Bijak of Kabir* (Delhi: Asian Publication Service, 1977), p. 32.
17. P. D. Barthwal, *Traditions of Indian Mysticism Based upon Nirguna School of Hindi Poetry* (New Delhi: Heritage Publishers, 1978), p. 209–11.
18. Dube, *Untouchable Pasts,* pp. 37–8.
19. George W. Briggs, *The Chamārs* (Calcutta: Association Press, 1920), p. 219.
20. Briggs (p. 220) says they had a reputation for esoteric doctrines and "uncleanliness in morals."
21. Quoted in Stephens Fuchs, *Rebellious Prophets:A Study of Messianic Movements in Indian Religions* (Bombay: Asia Publishing House, 1965), p. 98.
22. Some accounts say he was born to a *rajput* (*kshatriya*) family in Saradha village, Barabanki District, while others say he was a *thakur* (*vaishya*).
23. Barthwal, *Traditions of Indian Mysticisms,* p. 264; Briggs, *Chamārs,* p. 220.
24. Karine Schomer, "Introduction: The Sant Tradition in Perspective," in *The Sants: Studies in a Devotional Tradition of India,* ed. Karine Schomer and W. H. McLeod (Delhi: Motilal Banarsidass, 1987), p. 6.
25. Dube, *Untouchable Pasts,* p. 39.
26. Briggs, *Chamārs,* p. 221.
27. N. N. Bhattacharya, *History of the Tantric Religion,* pp. 306, 311; Barthwal, *Traditions of Indian Mysticism,* p. 264.
28. Briggs, *Chamārs* p. 222. There is a also text named *Gyān Prakāś* that is connected with the Kabirpanth, and it may be that this is the text to which Briggs makes reference.
29. M. A. Sherring, *Hindu Tribes and Castes* (Delhi: Cosmo Publications, 1974),1:111.
30. Fuchs, *Rebellious Prophets,* p. 100. He theorizes that while in Sarangarh, Ghasidas likely encountered the teachings of Jagjivandas and the Satnamis.
31. Russell and Hiralal, *Tribes and Castes,* II:307–14. They give a more detailed and slightly different account of Ghasidas's life. Many current Satnamis are unfamiliar with several aspects of his account.
32. Russell and Hiralal, *Tribes and Castes,* II:390–91) According to Russell and Hiralal, meat eating was commonplace among the Kanaujia *brahmans*, the largest *jati* of the caste in the Central Provinces at the time he wrote.
33. In Ghasidas's day, brass was probably the cheapest of the metals used for most utensils. Since Independence, the use of aluminum has greatly increased as the metal of choice by the poor. It has only been in the last decade that it has come to be accepted by some of the orthodox Hindus as "clean" and therefore permissible to use for cooking and eating.
34. In Chhattisgarh, rural people seldom use the term *"jati"* when referring to subscaste. *"Samaj"* (lit. community) is the term most often heard and is used to refer to sect as well as subscaste. In this work, "community" will be used for both.
35. James Preston, "Creation of the Sacred Image," in *Gods of Flesh, Gods of Stone: The Embodiment of Divinity in India,* ed. Joanne P. Waghorne and Norman Cutler (Chambersburg, PA: Anima Publications, 1984), p. 14. Preston discusses an ancient practice in neighboring Orissa, where a pole is used in the worship of a female form of Narsimha, called "Narsimhā" This may have been the inspiration for the Satnami

practice. Preston also sees the possibility of the Orissan pole as a forerunner of the wooden deities at the Jagannath Temple in Puri, Orissa.

36. Briggs, *Chamārs,* p. 223.
37. Lawrence Babb, "The Satnamis—Political Involvement of a Religious Movement," in *Untouchables in Contemporary India,* ed. J. M. Mahar (Tucson: University of Arizona Press, 1972), p. 145.
38. Russell and Hiralal, *Tribes and Castes,* I:406.
39. Ibid., p. 144. Many of the more educated Satnamis with whom I have spoken reject this, saying Ghasidas did not stipulate such a lineage tradition, but it was his oldest son who claimed that it was the best way to honor his father's memory.
40. Babb, "The Satnamis," p. 146.
41. J. F. K. Hewitt, "Raipur Settlement Report, 1869," *Madhya Pradesh District Gazetteer,* p. 47.
42. M. A. Sherring, *Hindu Tribes and Castes,* 2:87, as quoted in H. L. Shukla, p. 23. The priesthood mentioned is in likely reference to those found in the Kabirpanth and/or the Satnami sect.
43. Saurabh Dube, *Caste and Sect in Village Life: Satnamis of Chhattisgarh 1900–1950* (Simla: Indian Institute of Advanced Study, 1993), pp. 7–20.
44. At first, only sect members used the caste name *"satnami."* Over time, however, most of the Chhattisgarhi *chamars*, even those with no affiliation with the sect, adopted the *"satnami"* as their caste designation.
45. H. L. Shukla, *Social History of Chhattisgarh* (Delhi: Agam Kala Prakashan, 1985), p. 27.
46. Sect members refer to themselves as "Ramnamis"; Satnamis who are not personally familiar with them often call them "Ramramiya Satnamis"; urban-caste Hindus often refer to them as "Ramramiya *harijans*."
47. Narayandas Ramnami, personal interview, 1985.
48. Among Chhattisgarhi villagers in general, use of the term *"Mānas"* for Tulsidas's telling of the Ram story is not as popular as it is in Uttar Pradesh. Instead, most villagers simply refer to the text as the *"Rāmāyaṇ,"* for few know any other version. In order to prevent any confusion for the reader as to which rendering of the Ram story is being referred, I will continue to use the name *Mānas* for the rendering currently attributed to Tulsidas.
49. Ramnamis use this title as a term of respect for their more literate members.
50. This is still a common practice in certain rural areas throughout North India.
51. One's *ishtadev* is that form of God chosen as the object of worship. For a more detailed description of the concept and function of *ishtadev,* see Milton Singer, ed. *Krishna: Myths, Rites, and Attitudes* (Honolulu: East-West Center Press, 1966), pp. 113–18, 156–61.
52. The statement attributed to the *sadhu* is *"Chatī meñ Rāmnam aegā,"* which can mean either that *Ramnam* will appear "in the heart," or "on the chest."
53. See section in chapter 5, entitled *"Ankit, Mukut, Ordhni,"* for a detailed description and discussion of the Ramnamis' ritual dress and their use of tattoos.
54. Babb, *The Divine Hierarchy*. Lawrence Babb discusses in greater detail the various village deities propitiated in Chhattisgarh.
55. *"Satsang"* generally refers to a gathering of people who participate in or listen to a religious discussion.

56. See section on "Ordhni" in chapter 5.
57. Both myth and ritual can be used to justify violence and persecution, because they have the ability to interpret such acts in a metaphorical or cosmic context and thus diminish personal responsibility in participation. For this reason, the brahmanization of texts, such as in the case of the Shambuka episode in the Valmiki *Rāmāyaṇa* (see appendix II), can have not only religious and social implications, but also serious economic and political ramifications.
58. From Indian independence until the sect became an official organization in 1960, the grant of police protection had been halted.
59. See section on "Bhajan Mela" in chapter 5.
60. Briggs, *Chamārs,* p. 219. I include this paragraph since it is the earliest and one of the only written references to the sect made prior to Indian independence. I asked sect members about Briggs' mention of them carrying a flute, and they said that some *chamars* in the region are flute-makers and sellers by profession, and the author may have come into contact with such Ramnamis.
61. V. K. Sethi, *Kabir:The Weaver of God's Name* (Beas: Radha Soami Satsang Beas, 1984), p. 59. Many Ramnamis integrate verses from Kabir into their chanting and also acknowledge him as a source of inspiration.
62. *"Roti-beti"* (lit. food-daughter) is a term often used by village Hindus as one way of defining the parameters of relationship between groups. In essence, any two groups whose members are freely permitted to eat with one another can also come together in marriage alliances.
63. See section on "Bhajan Mela" in chapter 5 for a discussion of Ramnami-officiated marriages.
64. See section on "Bhajan Mela" in chapter 5 for more discussion on their duties.

Chapter 5. The Ramnami Samaj

1. The term *"panchayat"* is used in a variety of social and political organizational levels in rural society. I will be using it specifically in reference to traditional subcaste organizations. For further information on caste councils in India, see J. H. Hutton, *Caste in India* (Bombay: Oxford University Press, 1951), pp. 92–110. Oscar Lewis discusses the function of caste *panchayats* in *Village Life in Northern India* (New York: Random House, 1965), pp. 26–31.
2. See "Bhajan Mela" section below for more on this.
3. Priyabala Shah, *Tilaka: Hindu Marks on the Forehead* (Ahmedabad: The New Order Book Co., 1985), p. 72.
4. Ibid., p. 69.
5. Ibid., pp. 67–68.
6. In *The Gazetteer of India* 9 (1973):120, it is suggested that the tattooing of females became popular during Mughal times as a means of identifying Hindu women as such and thereby discouraging their abduction by Muslims.
7. Russell, *Tribes and Castes,* 2:500.
8. Ibid., pp. 335, 500.
9. Shyam Parmar, *Folklore of Madhya Pradesh* (New Delhi: National Book Trust of India, 1972), p. 154.
10. Russell, *Tribes and Castes,* 3:123–27. The practice still exists among some Gonds.
11. Ibid., 2:386.
12. Ibid., 3:165.

13. The *devarin* does not like to reveal the exact substances she uses to make her ink, seeing it as a sort of trade secret. Parmar, *Folklore* (p. 155) says that most tattoos are made with vegetable dye.
14. The complete original verse is:
Dadau tasya tatah prītah svanāmākopaśobhitam |
Agulīyamabhigyānam rājaputryāh parantapah | | *Vāl.* (IV.44.12)
In the original, the verse refers to Ram giving his signet ring to Hanuman for Sita.
15. See chapter 7 for an in-depth discussion of this practice in the context of *"takkar."*
16. Hanuman is said to be the eleventh incarnation of Shiva.
17. These are not peculiar to the region and can be seen throughout North India.
18. Most Ramnamis, however, make no mention of Hanuman, and he has no role whatsoever in the sect's devotional practices.
19. See chapter 3 for more on the consequences of the embargo on the sect and the people of Chhattisgarh.
20. Some Ramnamis also have tattoos on their eyelids, in their ears, and on their tongue.
21. Russell, *Tribes and Castes,* 4:346.
22. According to one of the elders, the Ramnamis' wearing of peacock feathers was another justification caste Hindus used for their attacks on the sect.
23. For the Ramnamis, this means someone who has the talent to make the ink properly and to write the name in straight lines on cloth or on the body.
24. Although the only parameters for the number is that it be uneven, it has generally been between eleven and fifteen. During the last few years, however, the deciding committee has consisted of twenty-five members.
25. On average over the last decade, hosting villages have cleared and prepared approximately 80 to 100 acres for festival use.
26. The presence of a *kalash* (lit. water-pot, dome ornament) on the peak of a Hindu temple is said to indicate the presence of the deity within, functioning in some ways similar to a cross on a church.
27. During the last 20 or so years, the price of the *mela* has ranged from $4,000 to more than $16,000, influenced both by inflation, as well as by the devaluation of the *rupee* with respect to the U.S. dollar.
28. *Arti* is a traditional Hindu ritual, which involves making clockwise circles with an oil lamp in front of the object being venerated. In rural Chhattisgarh, this is done with a steel or brass tray on which a camphor flame, some rice, a coconut, and money are placed.
29. As mentioned above, vegetarianism is already a rule of the sect, but here the families must also vow to be vegetarians. This is the council's way of emphasizing the importance to them of this practice.
30. It is primarily for this reason that the number of *sadasya*s choosing the *mela* site has been increased to twenty-five.
31. There are only about one dozen *sadhu* members of the sect, as it is not encouraged or emphasized as a life-style. Currently, two of the most influential Ramnami *sadhus* are blind, yet they easily travel throughout the region, keeping villagers in touch with the news of the sect.
32. A variety of factors influences the number of participants at each village on the procession route, including village size, remoteness, proximity to the actual *mela* site, and so forth. On the last day of procession in 1989, the average number of Ramnamis and devotees present at each of the four villages was approximately five hun-

dred, according to those in attendance. At the village on the route I followed, there were at least this many, if not more.

33. Traditionally, Hindu rituals involving circular movement, such as *parikram* and *arti,* are always in a clockwise manner. Specifically for this reason, the Ramnamis have ritually decided to do these counterclockwise.

Chapter 6: Ramnamis' Contemporary Use of the *Mānas* and *Ramnam*

An earlier draft of portions of this chapter appears in my "Personalizing the *Rāmāyaṇa,*" in *Many Ramanayaṇas* (Berkeley: University of California Press, 1991).

1. For a more detailed explanation of *shruti* and *smriti,* see appendix I.
2. See definitions in the introduction.
3. Lutgendorf, "The Power of Sacred Story" (1990), p. 29.
4. As previously mentioned, texts of the *smriti* category are open-ended, that is, subject to additions, interpolations, and so forth.
5. In the preliminary pages of many of the current Hindi editions of the *Mānas,* there is a section titled "Praśnāvalī," which contains techniques for using specific *Mānas dohas* and *chaupais* to answer questions about one's future. In addition, Ramanandi *sadhus* often prescribe the reading of certain passages or the recitation of certain verses to rid one of various difficulties or to help bring about certain events.
6. Over the last three decades, I have attended a variety of ritual functions, such as weddings, initiations, and purifications, in which *brahman* priests chanted from the *Mānas* as an integral part of the ritual. One marriage, that of a district magistrate's daughter, took place only after the wedding site had been "purified" by a twenty-four hour *akhanda path,* or continuous recitation, of the entire *Mānas* by three priests.
7. Lutgendorf, "The Power of Sacred Story" (1990), pp. 19–22.
8. The *arti* ritual to the text as performed by most Chhattisgarhi women is quite similar, if not the same, as they might do in the region to a deity in a temple. Offerings made during the ritual are placed on a steel or brass plate and consist of a husked coconut, a mound of uncooked grains of rice, several flowers, burning incense sticks (usually three in number), and a lit oil lamp. Some women burn small cubes of camphor in place of the oil lamp.
9. There is a division of feeling among sect members in this regard. Some are strongly against such practices, saying that *Ramnam* and the *Mānas* should only be used for spiritual, and not material, goals.
10. Many current Ramnamis have become sufficiently conversant in the language of the *Mānas* so as to be able to understand the original without a translation.
11. It should be noted that individual chanting of *Ramnam* has never been a fundamental part of Ramnami practice. The sect maintains that if one is going to chant *Ramnam,* it should be done in the company of others so everyone present can partake of its benefits.
12. Some sect members are not even aware that non-*Mānas* verses are being chanted, believing that all verses being used have come solely from the text.
13. Owing to the predominance of the *doha* (two lines, 24 beats) and the *chaupai* (four lines of 4 parts, 64 beats) in the *Mānas,* these two verse forms have set the metrical parameters of the Ramnamis' chanting style and thus have also determined which verses can be incorporated into *bhajans*. For examples of these verses see pp. 250–

56, 265f below. For a detailed explanation of the structure of *Mānas* verses see Lutgendorf, *The Life of a Text,* pp. 13–18.

14. These two are connected to the Kabirpanth.
15. Of recent origin, this text is filled with devotional verses primarily focused on *sagun* Krishna. Nevertheless, several Ramnamis find it a useful source of chanting and *Takkar* verses.
16. This is a small text of recent origin that has devotional verses dedicated to both Ram and Krishna.
17. This is a text of devotional songs *(kirtans)* dedicated to a variety of deities. A few Ramnamis have taken some of the chants and rewritten them in *doha* and *chaupai* meter, in order that they may be used in *bhajan.*
18. For Hindus, Hanuman is obviously more than just a monkey deity. He is said to be the eleventh incarnation of Shiva and the epitome of devotion. For the Ramnamis, however, the status of any being, human or divine, lies in his or her relationship of subservience and devotion to *nirgun* Ram.
19. Officially, the *Mānas* is no longer viewed as *ishtadev* and many Ramnamis openly criticize it. For some of the older sect members, however, a continuing relationship of reverence is apparent in their treatment of the physical text.
20. In the section entitled *"Takkar"* below, there are examples of such verse changes.
21. *Vipra dhenu sura santa hita līnha manuja avatāra|* RC (I.192).
22. To accomplish this change, the Ramnamis simply replace *"Vipra dhenu"* with *"Rāmanām denā."*
23. *Mana krama bacana kapaṭa taji jo kara bhūsura sev|*
Mohi sameta Biranci Śiva basa tākeṇ saba dev| | RC (III.33).
24. *"Seva"* can mean "service," "worship," or "devotion."
25. *Citavata panth raheuñ din rāīt|*
Aba prabhu dekhi jurdānī chātī| |
Nātha sakala sādhana maiñ hīnā|
Kīnhī krpā jāni jana dīnā| | RC (III.7.2)
26. *Aba mohi bhā barosa Hanumantā|*
Binu Hari kṛpā milahi nahiñ santā| | RC (V.7.2)
27. *Kī tumha Hari dāsanha mahañ koī|*
Moreñ hrdaya prīti ati hoī| |
Kī tumha Rāmu dīna anurāgī|
Ayahu mohi karana bardmāgī| | RC (V.6.4)
28. *Nātha Dasānana kara maiñ brātā|*
Nisicara bas janama surtrt| | RC (V.45.4)
29. *Dhanya dhanya taiñ dhanya Bibhīṣana|*
Bhayahu tāta nisīcara kula bhūṣana| | RC (VI.64.4)
30. *Ko tumha śyāmala gaura sarīra|*
Chatrī rūpa phirahu bana bīra| | RC (III.0.4).
31. The verse was modified to:
Ko tumha videśī [śyāmala] gaura sarīra|
Sādhu [chatrī] rūpa phirahu bana bīra| |
32. *Citavat panth raheuñ din rātī|*
Ab prabhu dekhi jurdāni chātī| | RC (III.7.2)
33. *Nāri bibasa nara sakala gosāī|*
Nācahiñ naa markaṭa kī nāī| RC (VII.98.1)

34. *Sunahu Rām kara sahaja subhāū |*
Jana abhimāna na rākhahiñ kāū | |
Sansṛta mūla sūlaprada nānā |
Sakala soka dāyaka abhimānā | | RC (VII.73.3)
35. The original verse is:
Timi Raghupati nija dāsa kara harihiñ māna hita lāgi |
Tulsīdāsa aise prabhuhi kasa na bhajahu bhrama tyāgi | | RC (VII.74A)
In the chanting of the verse, the words *"timi Raghupati"* (In that way, Ram) and *"Tulsīdāsa"* were changed to *"Rāmnām swāmī"* (the Lord of *Rāmnām*) and *"Rāmnāmī bhāī"* (brother Ramnami), respectively.
36. Until the mid-1980s, the term *"vidvan,"* traditionally used in Northern India to refer to a Sanskrit scholar, was used by the Ramnamis in reference to any sect member who studies the *Mānas* and/or other texts and actively takes part in philosophical dialogues and *takkar.* However, during the last decade or so the term *"gyani"* has come to be the preferred designation for those sect members who are active *takkar* participants. This is to emphasize that their primary focus is wisdom and not intellectual knowledge, as is implied in the term *"vidvan." "Gyani"* is also used in the Sikh tradition in reference to those who represent the Sikh orthodoxy.
37. Not all verses are selected strictly on the basis of their philosophical viewpoint. Many verses are learned simply as a matter of course, such as those that are frequently repeated during *bhajan,* and thus are not necessarily in complete harmony with a particular Ramnami's personal philosophy. A sect member may also memorize certain commonly repeated verses without understanding them, solely out of a desire to join in whenever they are recited.
38. I sat in on one late night village *bhajan* and *takkar* session that involved verses drawn solely from the *Viśrām Sāgar.* Seven of the eleven participants were erudite *gyanis,* and their collective "debate" set the direction of the *bhajan* for over five hours.
39. I have noticed that most of the *gyani* females are either older sect members who have learned a great deal of the *Mānas* by heart, or the wives of younger *gyanis,* with whom they study the various texts and verses used in *takkar.*
40. A few *gyanis* have taken verses in a different meter and recast them into *doha* or *chaupai* format, thereby rendering them usable in *bhajan.*
41. Shivanandan Ram Ramnami, Sur Sadhu Bharadvaj Ramnami, and Śriram Lahare, *Ram Rasik Gītā* (Raipur: Śriram Lahare, 1979).
42. Ibid., p. 7.
43. Although the festival had an attendance in the vicinity of seventy-five thousand people, less than 10 percent were initiated Ramnamis. Nearly half the participants of the yearly event consist of Ramnamis, members of their families, and non-initiated devotees. The other half are generally curious spectators, both villagers and those from nearby urban areas, most of whom attend irrespective of the type of *mela* taking place.
44. *Kahahiñ beda itihāsa purānā |*
Vidhi prapañcu guna avaguna sānā | | RC (I.6.2)
45. *Jara cetana juna doṣamaya bisva kīnha kartāra |*
Santa hansa guna gahahiñ paya parihari bāri bikāra | | RC (I.6)
In India, enlightened saints, with their ability to distinguish the self from the non-self and good from evil, are often compared to swans (*hamsas*), who when given a

mixture of milk and water are said to have the ability to separate out the milk, leaving behind the water.

46. *Graha bhoṣaja jala pavana paṭa pāi kujoga sujoga |*
Hohiñ kubastu jubastu jaga lakhahiñ sulacchana loga | | RC (1.7A)
Asa bibeka jaba dei Vidhātā |
Taba taji doṣa gunahiñ manu rāta | | RC (1.6.1)
47. The modified *chaupai* was:
Rāmrām nāmamaya [Sīyarāmmaya] saba jaga jānī |
Karauñ pranāma jori juga pānī | | RC (1.8.1)
48. *Sira saroja nija karanhi utārī |*
Pūjeū amita bāra Tripurārī | | RC (VI.24.2)
49. *Umā kahuñ maiñ anubhava apanā |*
Sata Rāmnām [Hari] bhajanu jagata saba sapanā | | RC (IV.38.2)
50. *Buddhi hīna tanu jānikai sumeraoñ Rāmnām apār [Pavana Kumār] |*
Bala buddhi vidyā dehu mohi harahu kaleś vikār | Hanuman Cālīsā (verse 2)
51. *Binu satasanga na Hari katha tehi binu mohi na bhāg |*
Moha gaeñ binu Rāma pada hoi na dṛḍha anurāg | | RC (7.61)
52. Ellison Banks Findly, "*Mantra kaviśasta:* Speech as Performative in The *Ṛgveda,*" in *Mantra,* ed. Harvey P. Alper (Albany: State University of New York Press, 1989) pp. 32–4; see also Franciscus B. J. Kuiper, "The Ancient India Verbal Contest," *Indo-Iranian Journal* 4, no. 4:217- 81.
53. Ibid., p. 36.
54. Ibid., p.32.

Chapter 7: The Ramnami Life

1. Betrothal does not necessarily mean an imminent marriage, especially when the couple are so young. Typically, the actual marriage does not take place until sometime shortly after the bride-to-be reaches puberty.
2. These are: Prayag, Haridwar, Nasik, and Ujjain.
3. *Maiñ samāj meñ nete kām vāste nahīñ āyā |*
Maiñ nām aur satsang vāste hī āyā |
4. The last time we spoke was about a year prior to his death, and his words revealed an acceptance of his physical condition and subsequent fate. He spoke with great love and concern for Moti and how he wanted to do whatever possible to make sure that she would never have to want for material necessities, and that she would be able to devote her life to the *samaj* and to *Ramnam.*
5. "A wandering yogi is like flowing water," that is, a renunciant does not have a home or remain in any one place.
6. Surdas was a famous medieval Hindu poet/saint who was blind. As a consequence, it is common for blind males in North India to be referred to as "Surdas." "Sur Sadhu" is but a variation due to Ramjatan's life-style.
7. One traditional way of addressing people in Chhattisgarh is to identify them with their village by adding "*iha*" or "*adiha*" as a suffix on their village's name. Thus, "Dhanadiha" refers to someone from the village of Dhana.
8. Refer to pp. 86–87.
9. Privately, Bholeram has eaten with many other sect members, but there is an unspoken acknowledgment that no one will disclose this fact to Sukhibai.
10. It is not uncommon, nor is it looked down upon, for female Ramnamis to show

physical expressions of affection to male sect members, spouse or not. It is also not uncommon to see various male and female sect members sitting alone, touching, holding hands, and so forth, spouse or not. Thus, Kamalabai's open show of affection to Balakram was, for a long time, perceived and accepted in this light.

11. Most missionaries in India attempt to get new converts to reject not only previous beliefs and practices, but also much of their cultural ways, including diet and dress, saying that these are a part of Hindu culture and must be given up along with the religion itself.

Conclusion: A Question of Values

1. Paul M. Harrison, "Buddhānusmṛti in the Pratyutpanna-buddha-saṃmukhāvasthita-samādhi-sūtra," *Journal of Indian Philosophy* 6 (1978) 35.

Appendix 1

1. Since there are no universally accepted demarcations of the categories *"shruti"* and "*smriti,*" I have chosen to present first traditional Western academic definitions, which essentially reflect orthodox-Hindu beliefs, followed by reference to several supplementary views expressed by current Indological scholars.
2. This "intrinsic" power and efficacy is said to be activated through recitation by *shrotriyas* (masters of *shruti*). The belief in the inherent power of sounds is subsequently reflected both in the Tantric schools' conception of *beej* (seed) *mantras* and the devotional schools' belief in the power of the Name of God.
3. Wendy Donniger, Brian K. Smith, and others point out that knowledge and understanding of the Vedas were considered by some to be of great importance. However, this was not a crucial point for the ritual use of the text, which, functionally speaking, was its primary raison d'être. Barbara A. Holdrege presents an extensive discussion of conceptions of Veda and their application in the modes of preservation and memorization of the Vedic Samhitas in her *Veda and Torah: Transcending the Textuality of Scripture.* Albany: State University of New York Press, 1996.
4. J. A. B. van Buitenen, "Hindu Sacred Literature," in *Encyclopedia Britannica, III, Macropaedia,* 1970, pp. 932–933.
5. Thomas B. Coburn, "'Scripture' in India: Toward a Typology of the Word in Hindu Life," *Journal of the American Academy of Religion* 52, no. 3 (Sept. 1984): 448. Coburn presents an illuminating discussion of various approaches to the understanding of *shruti* and *smriti,* and encourages a rethinking of traditional categorizations.
6. Graham, *Beyond the Written Word,* p. 5.
7. See a discussion of these terms in the introduction, pp. 8–10.
8. Howard Coward, *Sacred Word and Sacred Text* (Maryknoll, New York: Orbis Books, 1988), pp. 112–3.
9. Harvey Alper, ed., *Mantra* (Albany: State University of New York Press, 1989), p. 23.
10. Ibid., pp. 15–6.
11. Farquhar, *An Outline of the Religious Literature of India,* p. 25.
12. Edward Conze, *Buddhism* (Oxford University Press, 1953) p. 183.
13. Jan Gonda, "The Indian Mantra," *Oriens* (1963): 250. This is a well-researched study of the concept of name in the Vedic literature. However, several of the verses to which he refers in his attempt to show the use of *nam* do not seem to have the significance he attaches to them.

14. Other references to *nam* in the *Ṛg Veda* include 4.39.4; 5.22.3; 5.52.3; 6.18.8; 8.10.12; 8.11.5; 8.47.3.; and 10.64.1.
15. Jan Gonda, *Notes on Names and the Name of God in Ancient India* (Amsterdam: North-Holland Publishing Co., 1970), pp. 48, 76.
16. Ibid., pp. 15, 8.
17. Ibid., p. 69.
18. The earliest Mahayana Buddhist texts in which the name of a deity is given importance are the *Sukhāvatī Vyūha Sūtras* and the *Saddharma Puṇḍarīka.*
19. Gonda, "The Indian Mantra," p. 260.
20. Ludo Rocher, *The Purāṇas,* vol. II, no. 3 of *A History of Indian Literature,* ed. Jan Gonda. (Wiesbaden: Otto Harrassowitz, 1986), pp. 98–9.
21. Cited by Rocher, *The Purāṇas,* p. 34.
22. Camille Bulcke, *Rāmkathā: Utpatti aur Vikās* (Prayag: Hindi Parishad Prakashan, 1950). On p. 744–6, he provides a list of twenty-one Puranas in which portions of the Ram story are presented. Among the earliest are the *Viṣṇu, Brahmāṇda, Harivaṃśa, Vāyu, Nṛsimha, Matsya,* and *Kūrma Purāṇas.*
23. Gonda, *Medieval Religious Literature* (1977), pp. 232–4. A *stotra* is a type of eulogistic hymn generally written in a standardized pattern and often imbedded in various Puranas, Upapuranas, and Mahatmyas.
24. Gudrun Buhnemann, *Budha-Kauśika's Rāmarakṣāstotra* (Vienna: Gerold and Co., 1983), pp. 14–5. This is a useful text for understanding both the *stotra* and its liturgical and tantric uses.
25. *Rāma rāmeti rāmeti rame rāme manorame* |
Sahasranāma tattulya rāmanāma varānane | |
Buhnemann, *Budha-Kausikas,* p. 33.
26. Bhattacharya, *The History of the Tantric Religion,* pp. 158–64.
27. Andre Padoux, "Tantrism," *Encyclopedia of World Religions* Vol. 14, pp. 273–5.
28. Farquhar, *An Outline of Religious Literature,* p. 204.
29. A. M. Esnoul, "Om" in *Encyclopedia of Religion* Vol. 11, ed. by Mircea Eliade (New York: Macmillan Publishing Co., 1987), p. 69.
30. Agehananda Bharati, *The Tantric Tradition* (Westport, CT: Greenwood Press, 1977), p. 109.
31. Paul Eduardo Muller-Ortega, *The Triadic Heart of Śiva* (Albany: State University of New York Press, 1989), p. 173.
32. Ibid., p. 162.
33. Ibid., p. 174.
34. Sanjukta Gupta, Teun Goudriaan, and Dirk Jan Hoens, *Hindu Tantrism* (Leiden: E. J. Brill, 1979), p. 126–27.
35. Ibid., p. 107.
36. Because Hanuman has become an important deity for Vaishnav practitioners of Tantra, there are many *beej mantras* associated with him, such as *"hrām," "hrīm," "hrūm,"* and so forth.
37. Gonda, *The Indian Mantra* (1963), p. 280.
38. When performing *jap* both of *beej mantras* and of supplication *mantras* of a deity, the practitioner is traditionally supposed to conceive of the deity contained within the *mantra.* The early practitioners who were also Ram devotees no doubt drew on the similarities between the *beej mantra "rāṃ"* and the name "Ram" in the development of their theology and practice. Here the deity's name, used in devotional prayers, is

essentially the same as his *beej mantra,* used in tantric *jap.* No other Hindu deity's name has as close an aural connection with its *beej mantra.* Both name and *beej* are said to contain the power of Ram. This fact likely provided a rationale for early Ram devotees to elevate the status of *Ramnam* as being superior to other names.

39. Sources cited for these texts are (1) in Sanskrit: Pandit Mahadeva Sastri, *The Vaiśṇava Upaniṣad-s* (Adyar: The Adyar Library and Research Centre, 1979); and (2) in English: Paul Deussen, *Sixty Upaniṣads of the Veda* (Delhi: Motilal Banarsidass, 1980); and T. R. Sharma, *Studies in the Sectarian Upanisads* (Delhi: Indological Book House, 1972).
40. Deussen, *Sixty Upanisads* (p. 809) translates the title, *Nṛsihatāpanīya Upaniṣad,* as "the esoteric doctrine concerning the ascetic surrender to Nṛsimha."
41. Farquhar, *An Outline of Religious Literature,* p. 188. This sect was, and continues to be more predominant in the south than in the north.
42. Deussen, *Sixty Upanisads of the Veda,* p. 809–33.
43. *NutUp* (5.1); Deussen, *Sixty Upanisads of the Veda,* pp. 846–7.
44. *NutUp* (7.1–15, 8.1–5); Deussen, Ibid., pp. 849–54.
45. Deussen, Ibid., p. 859.
46. *RptUp* (1.1–6); Deussen, Ibid., p. 863.
47. *RptUp* (1.20–21); Deussen, Ibid., pp. 865–6.
48. Similar but less complicated instructions are given in the *NptUp* for the construction of a Narsimha *yantra.*
49. *RptUp* (5.10); Deussen, *Sixty Upanisads of the Veda,* p. 877.
50. *RutUp* (3.16); Deussen, Ibid., p. 885. See also T. R. Sharma, *Studies in Sectarian Upanisads,* p. 27.
51. *RutUp* (5.1–47); Deussen, Ibid., pp. 886–88.
52. *RrUp* (1.6); T. R. Sharma, *Studies in Sectarian Upanisads,* p. 29.
53. N. S. Subrahmanian, trans. *Encyclopedia of the Upanisads* (New Delhi: Sterling Publishers Pvt., Ltd, 1985), pp. 345–47.
54. Hans Bakker, *Ayodhya* (Groningen: Egbert Forsten, 1986), p. 70.
55. Ibid., p. 70.
56. Ibid., p. 71–72.
57. Ibid., p. 74–75.
58. Ibid., p. 75n.

Appendix II

1. Hari Prasad Shastri, trans, *The Ramayana of Valmiki,* vol. 3 (London: Shantisasan, 1962), p. 579.
2. Ibid., p. 581–82.
3. Ibid., p. 583–84.
4. Ibid., p. 584–85.

Glossary

The definitions given herein are those used in the specific context of this study. When traditional scholarly transliteration of terms used herein use diacritics, or otherwise vary, these are presented in parentheses following the term.

adhyaksha (adhyakṣa). Literally "chairman"; the title given to the organizational head of the Ramnami Samaj.

adivasi (adivāsī). Member of a tribal group.

ankit. Literally "mark, inscription"; the name Ramnamis use in reference to their tattoos.

ashram (āśram). A hermitage, monastery, or other religious abode.

avatar (avatār). Incarnation of a deity, usually Vishnu.

bhajan. Prayer; devotional chanting.

bhakta. A devotee.

bhakti. Devotion.

beej (bīja). Mantra a one syllable *mantra* believed to possess great power.

brahman (brāhmaṇ). A member of the priestly caste.

brahmacharini (brahmcārinī). A celibate female; usually refers to an ascetic.

chakra (cakra). An invisible energy center in the spine.

chamar (camār). Largest of the Untouchable castes; originally said to be a caste of leather workers.

chandala (caṇḍāla). In ancient times, the lowest caste. In contemporary times, a derogatory term.

chaupai (caupāī). Four-line, sixty-four-beat verse in Hindi poetry.

devanagari (devanāgarī). The script in which both Sanskrit and Hindi are written.

doha (dohā). Two-line, twenty-four-beat verse in Hindi poetry.

ghuṅghru (ghuṅghrū). A set of ankle bells.

gopi (gopī). Krishna's female lovers in Brindaban.

gyan (gyān). Spiritual wisdom.

gyani (gyānī). Literally "an exponent of wisdom"; Ramnamis who actively participate in *takkar.*

harijan. A member of an Untouchable caste.

harijan ward. A village mandated by Madhya Pradesh Government to have a *harijan sarpanch,* or headman.

iṣṭadev (iṣṭadev). One's chosen deity.

jap (japa). Continual repetition of a *mantra.*

jati (jāti). A subscaste.

kand (kāṇḍ), or

khand (khaṇḍ). A chapter or section of a text.

kanthi (kaṇṭhī). A necklace, usually made of wooden or seed beads.

katha (kathā). The oral recitation or narration of a devotional scripture or story.

kshepak (kṣepak). A commentary or elaboration inserted into an existing story or text.

kshatriya (kṣatriya). A member of the warrior caste.

kushilava (kuśīlava). An ancient storyteller; probably low caste.

leela (līlā). God's divine play; an enactment of a religious tale.

magadha (māgadha). An ancient bard from Magadha area of eastern India.

mahant. Head of a religious sect, of the branch of a sect, or of a temple.

maya (māyā). Delusion; God's delusive power.

mela (melā). A religious festival.

moksha (mokṣa). Liberation.

mukut (mukuṭ). Literally"crown"; the term Ramnamis use in reference to their peacock feather hat.

nam (nām). Literally "name"; used in reference to the name of a deity.

nirgun (nirguṇ). The formless aspect of God.

nirvan (nirvāṇ). Liberation from the cycle of rebirths.

nishad (niṣād). An indigenous group of boatmen/fishermen; subsequently relegated to the status of Untouchable.

ordhni (orḍhnī). Literally "covering"; a Ramnami shawl on which *Ramnam* is written.

pandit (paṇḍit). A learned person, usually a *brahman;* used by Ramnamis and others in Chhattisgarh to refer to anyone who is considered to be knowledgeable about religion or philosophy.

panth. Religious sect; used herein in reference to the Kabrpanth.

phalashruti (phalaśruti). A statement describing the rewards that result from the repetition of a hymn, scripture, etc.

prashad (prasād). Literally "gift, blessing"; food offered to a deity.

puja (pūjā). Any form of religious worship.

Ramkatha (Rāmkathā). The Ram story.

Ramnam (Rāmnām). The name "Ram"; repetition of the name.

sadasya. Literally "member"; the name used by Ramnamis for members of the sect's ruling council.

sadhana (sādhanā). Spiritual practice.

sadhu (sādhu). A religious mendicant; usually used in reference to a member of a Vaishnav sect.

sagun (saguṇ). The aspect of God having form.

sakha (sākhā). A branch of a sect.

samaj (samāj). Literally "group, community"; used in Chhattisgarh to refer both to a religious sect and also to a subscaste.

samarthak. Literally "conclusive"; a verse used by Ramnami *gyanis* to "win" or complete a *takkar.*

sannyas (samnyās). A class of ascetics, usually of high-caste origin.

sanchalak (sañcālak). Literally "director"; the assistant to the *adhyaksha* in the Ramnami Samaj. Functionally, he has the most influence in the actual running of the sect.

samsar (saṃsār). This world, a world of suffering.
sangh. Organized group of Buddhist monks.
sarpanch (sarpañc). A village headman.
satnami (satnāmī). The official name for what used to be the *chamar* caste in Madhya Pradesh and Chhattisgarh.
satsang (satsang). A gathering of devotees for religious discussion or chanting.
siddhi. The attainment of the power of a *mantra.*
smriti (smṛti). Literally "that which was remembered"; a secondary class of Hindu scripture.
shravak (śrāvak). A Buddhist ascetic.
shruti (śruti). Literally "that which was heard"; a primary class of scripture, originally limited to Vedic scriptures.
stambh. A post or pole; used as a religious symbol by various sects.
stotra. A hymn of praise and supplication; a class of literature.
shudra (śūdra). A member of the servant caste; lowest "touchable" caste.
shushumna (suṣumnā). Invisible energy channel along the spine, in which the *chakras* are located.
suta (sūta). An ancient class of bards.
svarup (svarūp). The actual form of a deity.
takkar (ṭakkar). Literally "collision, quarrel"; a form of philosophical dialogue or debate practiced by Ramnamis during *bhajan.*
tapasya. Austerities.
tarak (tārak) mantra. *Mantra* said to guarantee liberation, or at least a better human birth, if heard at the time of death; *Ramnam.*
vach (vāc). Speech; the goddess of speech.
vaishya (vaiśya). A member of the merchant/business caste.
varna (varṇa). Caste.
vipra. Literally "inspired"; an epithet for a *brahman* priest.
yagya (yajña). Brahmanical fire sacrifice.
yantra. A ritual diagram, often used as an object of meditation; also called "mandala."
yogini (yoginī). A female ascetic.

Bibliography

Texts in Indian Languages

Primary

Adhyātma Rāmāyaṇa. see Baijnath, Rai Bahadur LaLa, trans.Tapasyananda.
Agastya Saṃhitā. see Bakker.
*Chāndogya Upaniṣ*ad. see Swāhānanda.
Manusmti (Dharma Śāstra). see Kumār.
Rāmāyaṇa. Vālmīki. see also Goldman; Pollack; Shastri.
Rāmcaritmānas. Tulsīdās. Gorakhpur: Gita Press. see also Atkins; Growse; Hill.
Sukhāvatī–vyūha Sūtra. see Cowell.
Vaiṣṇava Upaniṣad-s. Edited by Pandit Mahadeva Sastri. Adyar: The Adyar Library and Research Centre, 1979.
Vinay Patrikā. Tulsīdās. Gorakhppur: Gita Press.
Viśrām Sāgar. Raghunāthdās. Lucknow: Navalkiśor Book Depot, 1987.

Secondary

Agarwal, Satya Prakash. *Tulsī Rāmāyaṇ . . . Jagmagal-Parāyaṇ*. Columbia, MD: Urmila Agarwal, 1997.
Bulcke, Camille. *Rām kathā: Utpatti aur Vikās*. Prayāg, Allahabad: HindīPariṣad Prakāśan, 1950.
Gandhiji (M. K.) *Rāmnām*. Ahmedabad: Navjivan Prakashan Mandir, 1949.
Upadhyay, Kaśhinath. *Nām-bhakti: GoswāmīTulsīdās*. Beas: Rādhāswāmī Satsang, 1989.

English Texts

Allchin, F. R. *The Petition to Rām*. London: George Allen and Unwin Ltd., 1966.
Alper, Harvey, ed. *Mantra*. Albany: State University of New York Press, 1989.
Altekar, G. S. *Studies on Vālmīki's Rāmāyaṇa*. Poona: Bhandarkar Oriental Research Institute, 1987.
Apte, Usha M. *Vedic Hindu and Tribal Marriage: A Study in Culture Change*. Hyderabad, India: Aware, 1982.
Arya, Sharada. *Religion and Philosophy of the Padma-Purāṇa*. Delhi: Nag Publishers, 1988.
Atkins, Reverend A. G., trans. *The Ramayana of Tulsidas*. 2 Vols. New Delhi: The Hindustan Times, 1954.
Austin, John L. *How to do Things With Words*. Cambridge: Harvard University Press, 1962.
Avalon, Arthur (John Woodroffe). *The Serpent Power*. 1918. Reprint, Madras: Ganesh and Co., 1964.
Babb, Lawrence. *The Divine Hierarchy: Popular Hinduism in Central India*. New York: Columbia University Press, 1975.

———. "The Satnamis—Political Involvement of a Religious Movement." In *Untouchables in Contemporary India.* Edited by J. M. Mahar. Tuscon: University of Arizona Press, 1972.

Babineau, Edmour J. *Love of God and Social Duty in the Ramcaritmanas*. Delhi: Motilal Banarsidass, 1979.

Baijnath, Rai Bahadur Lala, trans. *Adhyatma Ramayana.* Allahabad: Panini Office, 1913.

Bakker, Hans. *Ayodhya.* Groningen: Egbert Forsten, 1986.

Banerjee, Nikunja Vihari. *Studies in the Dharmaśāstra of Manu.* Delhi: Munshiram Manoharlal Publishers Pvt. Ltd, 1987.

Barnes, J. A. "Social Science in India: Colonial Import, Indigenous Product, or Universal Truth?" In *Indigenous Anthropology in Non-Western Countries.* Edited by Hussein Fahim. Durham: Carolina Academic Press, 1982.

Barthwal, P. D. *Traditions of Indian Mysticism Based upon Nirguna School of Hindi Poetry.* New Delhi: Heritage Publishers, 1978.

Basham, A. L. *The Wonder That Was India.* New York: Taplinger, 1968.

Basu, Patricia L. "A Study of the Hindu Concept of Vak: The Power of the Word in an Oral Society." Ph.D. diss., Princeton University, 1978.

Becker Howard S., and Blanche Geer. "Participant Observation and Interviewing: A Comparison." In *Qualitative Methodology: Firsthand involvement with the Social World.* Edited by W. J. Filstead. Chicago: Markham Publishing Co., 1970.

Bharati, Agehananda. *The Tantric Tradition.* Westport, CT: Greenwood Press, 1977.

Bhattacharya, Jogendra Nath. *Hindu Castes and Sects.* 1896. Reprint, Calcutta: Editions India, 1968.

Bhattacharya, N. N. *History of the Tantric Religion.* New Delhi: Manohar Publications, 1987.

Bhattacharyya, P. K. *Historical Geography of Madhya Pradesh from Early Records.* Delhi: Motilal Banarsidass, 1977.

Briggs, George W. *The Chamrās.* Calcutta: Association Press, 1920.

Brockington, J. L. *Righteous Rama: The Evolution of an Epic.* Delhi: Oxford University Press, 1985.

Buck, Harry M. "Lord Rāma and the Faces of God in India." *Journal of the American Academy of Religion.* Vol. 36, No. 3 (Sept. 1968): 229–41.

Buhnemann, Gudrun. *Budha-Kauśika's Rāmarakṣāstotra.* Vienna: Gerold and Co., 1983.

Bulcke, Camille. "About Vālm īki." *Journal of the Oriental Institute.* Vol. 8, No. 2 (Dec. 1958): 121–31.

———. *Rāmkathā: Utpatti aur Vikās.* Prayag: Hindi Parishad Prakashan, 1950.

Bulmer, Martin, ed. *Social Research Ethics.* New York: Holmes and Meier Publishers, Inc., 1982.

Burghart, Richard. "Theoretical Approaches in the Anthropology of South Asia." In *Indian Religion.* Edited by R. Burghart and Audrey Cantlie. New York: St. Martin Press, 1985.

Cavan, Sherri. Review of *Investigative Social Research: Individual and Team Field Research.* Vol. 29 of *Library of Social Research,* by Jack Douglas. Beverly Hills: Sage Publications, 1976. In *American Journal of Sociology.* 83, No. 1 (July 1977): 809–11.

Coburn, Thomas. "`Scripture' in India: Towards a Typology of the Word in Hindu Life." *Journal of the American Academy of Religion* Vol.52, No. 3 (Sept. 1984): 435–59.

Cohn, Bernard. "Notes on the History of the Study of Indian Society and Culture." In *Structure and Change in Indian Society.* Edited Milton Singer and Bernard Cohn; 3–28. NY: Wenner-Gren Foundation for Anthropological Research, 1968.

Conze, Edward. *Buddhism*. Oxford University Press, 1953.
Coomaraswamy, Ananda K. *Elements of Buddhist Iconography*. Delhi: Munshiram Manoharlal Publishers, 1979.
Coward, Howard. *Sacred Word and Sacred Text*. Maryknoll, NY: Orbis Books, 1988.
Cowell, E. B. et al, trans. *Buddhist Mahayana Texts*. Delhi: Motilal Banarsidass, 1968.
Cuiseneir, Jean. "Indigenous Anthropology and Cultural Heritage." In *Indigenous Anthropology in Non-Western Countries*. Edited by Hussein Fahim. Durham: Carolina Academic Press, 1982.
Danda, Ajit Kumar, ed. *Chhattisgarh: An Area Study*. Calcutta: Anthropological Survey of India, 1977.
Dasgupta, Shashibhusan. *Aspects of Indian Religious Thought*. Calcutta: A.R. Mukherjee, 1957.
Denny, Frederick M. and Rodney Taylor, eds. *The Holy Book in Comparative Perspective*. Columbia, SC: University of South Carolina Press, 1985.
Deussen, Paul. *Sixty Upanisads of the Veda*. Parts 1–2. Translated by V. M. Bedekar and G. B. Palsule. Delhi: Motilal Banarsidass, 1980.
Dube, Saurabh. *Caste and Sect in Village Life: Satnamis of Chhattisgarh 1900–1950*. Simla: Indian Institute of Advanced Study, 1993.
———. "Myths, Symbols, and Community: Satnampanth of Chhattisgarh." In *Subaltern Studies VII: Writings on South Asian History and Society*. Edited by Partha Chatterjee and Gyan Pandey. Delhi:Oxford University Press, 1992.
———. *Untouchable Pasts: Religion, Identity, and Power among a Central Indian Community, 1780–1950*. Albany, NY: State University of New York Press, 1998.
Dumont, Louis. *Homo Hierarchicus*. Chicago: University of Chicago Press, 1970.
———. *Religion, Politics and History in India*. Paris: Mouton, 1970.
Dumont, L., and David Pocock. "For a Sociology of India," *Contributions to Indian Sociology* 1 (1957): 7–22.
Dutt, Nripendra Kumar. *The Aryanization of India*.1925. Reprint, Calcutta: Firma K. L. Mukhopadhyay, 1970.
Dwyer, William J. *Bhakti in Kabir*. Patna. India: Associated Book Agency, 1981.
Eck, Diana L. *Banaras: City of Light*. New York: Alfred A. Knopf, 1982.
Eliot, Sir Charles. *Hinduism and Buddhism: An Historical Sketch*. Vols. I-III. 1921. Reprint, London: Rutledge and Kegan Paul, 1957.
Embree, Ainslie. *Charles Grant and British Rule in India*. New York: Columbia University Press, 1962.
———. *The Hindu Tradition*. New York, Modern Library, 1966.
Esnoul, A. M. "OM" *Encyclopedia of Religion*. Vol. 11. Edited by Mircea Eliade. New York: Macmillan Publishing Co., 1987.
Fahim, Hussein, ed. *Indigenous Anthropology in Non-Western Countries*. Durham: Carolina Academic Press, 1982.
Farquhar, J. N. *An Outline of the Religious Literature of India*. 1920. Reprint, Delhi: Motilal Banarsidass, 1967.
Fernandes, Walter. *The Emerging Dalit Identity: The Re-Assertion of the Subalterns*. New Delhi: Indian Social Institute, 1996.
———. *Caste and Conversion Movements in India*. New Delhi: Indian Social Institute, 1981.
Filstead, William J. *Qualitative Methodology*. Chicago: Markham Publishing Co., 1970.
Findly, Ellison Banks. "Mantra Kaviśasta: Speech as Performative in the Rgveda." In *Mantra*. Edited by Harvey P. Alper. Albany: State University of New York, 1989.

Fuchs, Stephen. *At the Bottom of Indian Society*. Delhi: Munshiram Manoharlal, 1981.

———. *Rebellious Prophets: A Study of Messianic Movements in Indian Religions.* Bombay: Asia Publishing House, 1965.

Gandhi, Mohandas. *The Story of My Experiments with Truth*. Ahmedabad: Navajivan Publishing House, 1927.

Gangadharan, N. *Ligapurāṇa: A Study*. Delhi: Ajanta Publications, 1980.

Gans, Herbert J. *The Urban Villagers: Group and Clan in the Life of Italian-Americans*. New York: Free Press, 1962.

Geertz, Clifford. *Works and Lives: the Anthropologist as Author*. Stanford: Stanford University Press, 1988.

Ghurye, G. S. "The Teaching of Sociology, Social Psychology and Social Anthropology." In *The Teaching of Social Sciences in India*. Delhi: Universal Book & Stationery Co., 1968.

Goldman, Robert P., trans. *The Rāmāyaṇa of Vālmīki: An Epic of Ancient India*. Vol. I: *Bālakāṇḍa*. Princeton: Princeton University Press, 1984.

Gonda, Jan. "The Śatarudriya." In *Sanskrit and Indian Studies, Essays in Honour of David H. H. Ingalls*. Edited by M. Nagatomi, Vol. 16. Leiden, E. J. Brill, 1963. 75–91. Dordrecht: D. Reidel Publishing Co., 1980.

———. *Medieval Religious Literature in Sanskrit*. Vol.II,1 of *A History of Indian Literature*. Edited by Jan Gonda. Wiesbaden: Otto Harrassowitz, 1977.

———. *Notes on Names and the Name of God in Ancient India*. London: North-Holland Publishing Co., 1970.

———. "The Indian Mantra," In *Oriens*. 1963.

———. *Stylistic Repetition in the Veda*. Amsterdam: N. V. Noord-Hollan dische Uitgevers Maatschappij, 1959.

———. *Some Observations on the Relations Between "Gods" and "Powers" in the Veda, a Propos of the Phrase Sūnuḥ Sahasa*. The Hague: Mouton and Co., 1957.

———. *Aspects of Early Viṣṇuism*. Utrecht: Oosthoek's Uitgevers Mij, 1954.

Gopal, Madan. *Tulasi Das: A Literary Biography*. New Delhi: The Bookabode, 1977.

Gould, Harold. *The Hindu Caste System*. Delhi: Chanakya Publications, 1987.

———. "Two Decades of Fieldwork in India—Some Reflections." In *Encounter and Experience*. Edited by Andre Beteille and T. N. Madan. Honolulu: University of Hawaii Press, 1974.

Graham, William A. *Beyond the Written Word: Oral Aspects of Scripture in the History of Religion*. Cambridge: Cambridge University Press, 1987.

———. "On the Adbhuta-Ramayana." *Bulletin of the School of Oriental Studies*. Vol. 4: 11–27. London: School of Oriental Studies, 1926.

———. "Notes on Tulas ī Dās." In *Indian Antiquary* 22 (April, 1893).

———. "Tulas ī Dāsa, Poet and Religious Reformer." *Royal Asiatic Society of Great Britain and Ireland*. 35 (1903): 447.

Grierson, George A. "Indian Epic Poetry." *Indian Antiquary* 23 (Feb. 1894): 55.

———. "Notes on Tuls ī Dās." *Indian Antiquary* 22 (Apr. 1893): 89.

Growse, Frederic. S., trans. *The Rāmāyaṇna of Tulsi Dās*. Allahabad: Ram Narain Lal Beni Prasad, n.d.

Guha, Ranajit. "On Some Aspects of the Historiography of Colonial India." In *Subaltern Studies I*. Edited by R. Guha (Delhi: Oxford University Press, 1984.

Gupta, Samjukta, et al. *Hindu Tantrism*. Leiden: E. J. Brill, 1979.

Guruge, Ananda. *The Society of the Ramayana*. Ceylon: Saman Press, 1960. Hardiman, David. *The Coming of the Devi: Adivasi assertion in Western India*. Delhi: Oxford University Press, 1987.

Hardy, Friedhelm. *Viraha Bhakti:The Early History of Kṛṣṇa Devotion in South India*. Delhi: Oxford University Press, 1983.

Harrison, Paul M. "Buddhānusmti in the Pratyutpanna-buddha-samukhāvasthita-samādhi-sūtra." *Journal of Indian Philosophy* 6 (1978): 35–57.

Heesterman, J. C. *The Inner Conflict of Tradition*. Chicago: University of Chicago Press, 1985.

Herman, Phyllis Kaplan. "Ideal Kinship and the Feminine Power: A Study of the Depiction of *Rāmrāya* in the Vālmīki *Rāmāyaṇa*." Ph.D. Diss., University of California, Los Angeles, 1979.

Hewitt, J. F. K. "Raipur Settlement Report, 1869," *Madhya Pradesh District Gazetteer*.

Hill, W. D. P., trans. *The Holy Lakes of the Acts of Rama*. London: Oxford University Press, 1952.

Holdrege, Barbara A., ed. *Ritual and Power. Journal of Ritual Studies* 4, No. 2 (Summer 1990): Special Issue.

———. "Veda and Torah: Ontological Conceptions of Scripture in the Brahmanical and Judaic Traditions." Ph.D. dss., Harvard University, 1987.

Hopkins, Thomas J. *The Hindu Religious Tradition*. Encino, CA: Dickenson Publishing Co., 1971.

Hua, Tripitaka Master. *A General Explanation of The Buddha Speaks of Amitabha Sutra*. San Francisco: Buddhist Text Translation Society, 1974.

Hurvitz, Leon, trans. *Scripture of the Lotus Blossom of the Fine Dharma*. New York: Columbia University Press, 1976.

Hutton, J. H. *Caste in India*. Bombay: Oxford University Press, 1951.

Inden, Ronald. "Orientalist Constructions of India." *Modern Asian Studies,* 20, No. 3 (1986): 401–446.

Indian Council of Social Science Research. *A Survey of Research in Sociology and Social Anthropology*. Vol. I. Bombay: Popular Prakashan, 1974.

Indian Institute of Advanced Study. *Sikhism and Indian Society. Transactions of the Indian Institute of Advanced Study*. Vol. IV. Simla: Rashtrapati Nivas, 1967.

Jackson, A. V. Williams. *History of India*. 9 Vols. London: Grolier Society, 1906–7.

Jacobi, Herman. *Das Ramayana*.

Jha, Makhan. "Ratanpur: Some Aspects of a Sacred City in Chhattisgarh." In *Chhattisgarh: An Area Study*. Edited by Ajit Kumar Danda, 39–42. Calcutta: Anthropological Survey of India, 1977.

Jhavery, Mohanlal Bhagwandas. *Comparative and Critical Study of Mantrasastra*. Ahmedabad: Sarabhai Manilal Nawab, 1944.

Jogdand, Prahlad Gangaram. *Dalit Movement in Maharashtra*. New Delhi: Kanak Publications, 1991.

Joshi, Barbara R., ed. *Untouchable! Voices of the Dalit Liberation Movement*. New Delhi: Selectbook Service Syndicate, 1986.

Juergensmeyer, Mark. "The Radhasoami Revival of the Sant Tradition." In *The Sants: Studies in a Devotional Tradition of India*. Edited by Karine Shomer and W. H. McLeod. Delhi: Motilal Banarsidass, 1987.

———. *Religion as Social Vision*. Berkeley: University of California Press, 1982.

Kadetotad, N. K. *Religion and Society Among the Harijans*. Dharwar: Karnatak University, 1977.

Kapferer, Bruce, ed. *Transaction and Meaning: Directions in the Anthropology of Exchange and Symbolic Behavior*. Philadelphia: Institute for the Study of Human Issues, 1976.

Khare, R. S. *The Untouchable as Himself*. New York: Cambridge University Press, 1984.

Keith, Arthur. *Buddhist Philosophy in India and Ceylon.* 4th edition, The Chowkhamba Sanskrit Studies, 26. 1923. Reprint, Varanasi: Chowkhamba, 1963.

Khan, Benjamin. *The Concept of Dharma in Valmiki Ramayana.* Delhi: Munshi Ram Manohar Lal, 1965.

Kishwar, Madhu. "In Defence of Our Dharma." *Manushi* 60: (1990): 2–15.

Koentjaranin grat. "Anthropology in Developing Countries." In *Indigenous Anthropology in Non-Western Countries.* Edited by Hussein Fahim. Durham: Carolina Academic Press, 1982.

Kolenda, Pualine. *Caste, Cult and Hierarchy: Essays on the Culture of India.* Meerut, India: Folklore Institute, 1981.

Kuiper, Franciscus B. J. 'The Ancient India Verbal Contest." *Indo-Iranian* Journal 4, No. 4: 217–81.

Kumar, Nita. *Friends, Brothers, and Informants: Fieldwork Memoirs of Banaras.* Berkeley: University of California Press, 1992.

Kumar, Ṣahdev. *The Vision of Kabir.* Ontario, Canada: Alpha and Omega Books, 1984.

Kumar, Surendra, trans. *Manusmṛti (Dharma Śstra).* Delhi: Āṛsa Sāhitya Pracār Trust, 1981.

Lala, Chhagan lal. *Bhakti in the Religions of the World.* Delhi: B. R. Publishing Co., 1986.

Lamb, Ramdas. "Asceticism and Devotion: The Many Faces of Rām *Bhakti* in the Rāmānanda Sampradāy." *Journal of Vaiṣṇava Studies.* 2, No. 4 (Fall 1994).

———. "Transforming Power of the Name: *Rāmnām* from Tuls īdās to the Rāmnāmīs." *Journal of Vaiṣmava Studies.* 2, No. 2 (Spring 1994).

———. "Personalizing the *Rāmāyaṇa:* Rāmnāmīs and their use of the *Rāmcaritmānas.*" *Many Rāmāmāyaṇas: The Diversity of a Narrative Tradition in South Asia.* Berkeley: University of California Press, 1991.

Lewis, Oscar. *Village Life in Northern India.* New York: Random House, 1965.

Levi-Strauss, Claude. *Introduction a l'oeuvre de Marcel Mauss.* London: Routledge and Kegan Paul, 1987.

Lizot, Jacques. *Tales of the Yanomami.* Translated by Ernest Simon. New York: Cambridge University Press, 1985.

Lobo, Lancy. "Dalit Religious Movements and Dalit Identity." *The Emerging Dalit Identity.* New Delhi: Indian Social Institute, 1996.

Lorenzen, David N. "The Kabir-panth and Social Protest." In *The Sants: Studies in a Devotional Tradition of India.* Edited by Karine Shomer and W. H. McLeod. Delhi: Motilal Banarsidass, 1987.

———. "The Kabir Panth: Heretics to Hindus." In *Religious Change and Cultural Domination.* Edited by David N. Lorenzen. Mexico: El Colegio de Mexico, 1981.

Lutgendorf, Philip. *The Life of a Text: Tulsidas' Ramcaritmanas in Performance.* Berkeley: University of Califormnia Press, 1991.

——— "The Power of Sacred Story: Rāmāyaṇa Recitation in Contemporary North India." In *Ritual and Power.* Edited by Barbara A. Holdrege. *Journal of Ritual Studies* 4, No. 2 (Summer 1990).

———. "The Quest for the Legendary Tulsidas." *Journal of Vaisnava Studies* 1:2 (Winter, 1993).

———. "Video Games: The Television Ramayan and the Ramlila Tradition." Unpublished paper.

Macfie, J. M. *The Ramayan of Tulsidas.* Edinburgh: T. and T. Clark, 1930.

Macnicol, Nicol. *Indian Theism: From the Vedic to the Muhammadan Period.* Delhi: Munshiram Manohar lal, 1915.

Madan, T. N. "Anthropology as the Mutual Interpretation of Cultures: Indian Perspectives." In *Indigenous Anthropology in Non-Western Countries*. Durham: Carolina Academic Press, 1982.

———. "For a Sociology of India." *CIS*. No. 9 (Dec.1966): pp.9–16.

Mahar, J. M., ed. *Untouchables in Contemporary India*. Tucson: University of Arizona Press, 1972.

Malinowski, Bronislaw. *Magic, Science and Religion*. New York: Anchor Books, 1954.

Marriott, McKim. "Caste Systems." *Encyclopaedia Britannica*. 982–991.

———. "Hindu Transactions: Diversity Without Dualism." In *Transaction and Meaning: Directions in the Anthropology of Exchange and Symbolic Behavior*. Edited by Bruce Kapferer. Philadelphia: Institute for the Study of Human Issues, 1976.

Mayer, Adrian C. *Caste and Kinship in Central India*. Berkeley: University of California Press, 1960.

Moffat, Michael. *An Untouchable Community in South India: Structure and Consensus*. Princeton: Princeton University Press, 1979.

Monier-Williams, M. *Buddhism*. 1889. Reprint, Varanasi: Chowkhamba Sanskrit Series Office, 1964.

———. *Religious Thought and Life in India*. 1883. Reprint, 1883. Reprint, New Delhi: Oriental Books Reprint Corporation, 1974.

———. *Sanskrit-English Dictionary*.1899, Reprint, London: Oxford University Press, 1974.

Morgan, Kenneth. *The Religion of the Hindus*. New York: The Ronald Press Co., 1953.

Muller-Ortega, Paul Eduardo. *The Triadic Heart of Śiva*. Albany: State University of New York Press, 1989.

Nagatomi, M. et al., eds. *Sanskrit and Indian Studies: Essays in Honour of Daniel H. H. Ingalls*. Dordrecht, Holland: D. Reidel Publishing Co., 1980.

Nakamura, Hajime. *Indian Buddhism:A Survey with Biographical Notes*. Tokyo: Kufs Publications, 1980.

Nakane, Chie. "Fieldwork in India—A Japanese Experience." In *Encounter and Experience*. Edited by Andre Beteille and T. N. Madan. University of Hawaii Press, 1974.

Nath, Kanailal. *Historicity of Ramayana and its Relation with Kalinga*. Calcutta: Firma KLM Private Limited, 1986.

O'Flaherty, Wendy Doniger. *Other Peoples's Myths*. New York: Macmillan, 1988.

———. *The Rig Veda*. Middlesex: Penguin Books Ltd., 1983.

Ogbu, John. *The Next Generation:An Ethnography of Education in an Urban Neighborhood*. New York: Academic Press, 1974.

Omvedt, Gail. *Dalit Visions:The Anti-caste Movement and the Construction of Indian Identity*. New Delhi: Orient Longman Ltd., 1995.

Padoux, Andre. "Tantrism," *Encyclopedia of World Religions*. Vol. 14. Edited by Mircea Eliade. New York: Macmillan Publishing Co., 1987.

Pande, Susmita. *Birth of Bhakti in Indian Religions and Art*. Delhi: Books and Books, 1982.

Pandey, Gyanendra. "The Colonial Construction of Communalism: British Writings on Banaras in the Nineteenth Century." In *Subaltern Studies VI*. Edited by Ranajit Guha. Delhi: Oxford University Press, 1989.

Parganiha, B. L. "The Satnami Movement." *Journal of Social Reform*. 10, No. 1 (March, 1967).

Parmar, Shyam. *Folklore of Madhya Pradesh*. New Delhi: National Book Trust, 1972.

Parvathamma, C. *Scheduled Castes at the Cross Roads*. New Delhi: Ashish Publishing Co., 1989.

———. "The Remembered Village: Brahmanical Odyssey." *Contributions to Indian Sociology* [NS], 12, No. 1 (1978): 91–6.

Pathak, R. C., ed. *Bhargava's Standard Illustrated Dictionary of the Hindi Language.* 1946. Reprint, Varanasi: Bhargava Book Depot, 1977.

Patwardhan, M. V. *Manusmti:The Ideal Democratic Republic of Manu.* Delhi: Motilal Banarsidass, 1968.

Pollack, Sheldon. "From Discourse of Ritual to Discourse of Power in Sanskrit Culture." In *Ritual and Power.* Edited by Barbara A. Holdrege. *Journal of Ritual Studies* 4, No. 2 (Summer 1990).

———. "The "Revelation" of "Tradition": *Śruti, Smti,* and the Sanskrit Discourse of Power." *Lex et Litterae [Festschrift Botto].*

Pollock, Sheldon, trans. *The Rāmāyaṇa of Vālmīki: An Epic of Ancient India.* Vol. II: *Ayodhyakānda.* Princeton: Princeton University Press, 1984.

Preston, James. "Creation of the Sacred Image." In *Gods of Flesh, Gods of Stone: The Embodiment of Divinity in India.* Edited by Joanne P. Waghorne and Norman Cutler. Chambersburg, PA: Anima Publications, 1984.

Punch, Maurice. *The Politics and Ethics of Fieldwork.* Beverly Hills: Sage Publications, 1986.

Raghunāthdās. *Viśrām Sāgar* (Hindi). With Commentary by Kauśal Kiśor Ś īrvāstav. Lucknow: Navalkiśor Book Depot, 1987.

Ramanujan, A. K. "Three Hundred Ramayanas: Five Examples and Three Thoughts on Translation." *Many Rāmāmāyaṇas: The Diversity of a Narrative Tradition in South Asia.* Berkeley: University of California Press, 1991.

Ramnami, Shivanandan Ram, Sur Sadhu Bharaduaj Ramnamu, and Śriram Lahare. *Ram Rasik Gītā.* Raipur: Śriram Lahare, 1979.

Rao, M. S. A. "Introduction." In *A Survey of Research in Sociology and Social Anthropology.* Vol. I. Bombay: Popular Prakashan, 1974.

Redfield, Robert. *The Little Community: Viewpoints for the Study of a Human Whole.* Chicago: University of Chicago Press, 1955.

Richman, Paula, ed. *Many Rāmāyaṇas: The Diversity of a Narrative Tradition in South Asia.* Berkeley: University of California Press, 1991.

Risley, Sir Herbert H. *The People of India.* 2d ed. Edited by W. Crooke. 1915. Reprint, Delhi: Oriental Books Reprint Corp., 1969.

Rizvi, Saiyid Athar Abbas. *A History of Sufism in India.* 2 Vols. Delhi: Minshiram Manoharlal, 1986.

Robinson, Richard. *The Buddhist Religion.* Belmont, CA: Dickenson Publishing Co., 1970.

Rocher, Ludo. *The Purāṇas.* Vol. II:3 of *A History of Indian Literature.* Edited by Jan Gonda. Wiesbaden: Otto Harrassowitz, 1986.

Russell, R. V. and R. B. Hira Llal. *Tribes and Castes of the Central Provinces of India.* 4 Vols. 1916, Reprint, Delhi: Cosmo Publications, 1975.

Sankalia, H.D. *The Ramayana in Historical Perspective.* Delhi: Macmillan India Ltd., 1982.

Śaraṇa, Gopāla. *Anthropological Method and Indian Anthropology.* Madras: University of Madras, 1972.

Sarkar, Amal. *A Study on the Rāmāyaṇas.* In "Vālm īki Rāmāyaṇa and other Rāmāyaṇas," 51–96. Calcutta: Ṛddhi India, 1987.

Sarkar, Sumit. "The Kalki-Avatar of Bikrampur: A Village Scandal in Early Twentieth Century Bengal." In *Subaltern Studies VI.* Edited by Ranajit Guha. Delhi: Oxford University Press, 1989.

Saunders, Kenneth J. *Epochs in Buddhist History*. Chicago: University of Chicago Press, 1924.

Sen, Sukumar. *Origin and Development of the Rama Legend*. Calcutta: Rupa and Co., 1977.

Sethi, V. K. *Kabir:The Weaver of God's Name*. Beas: Radha Soami Satsang Beas, 1984.

Schomer, Karine. "Introduction: The Sant Tradition in Perspective." In *The Sants: Studies in a Devotional Tradition of India*. Edited by Karine Shomer and W. H. McLeod. Delhi: Motilal Banarsidass, 1987.

Shah, Ahmad. *The Bijak of Kabir*. Delhi: Asian Publication Service, 1977.

Shah, Priyabala. *Tilaka: Hindu Marks on the Forehead*. Ahmedabad: The New Order Book Co., 1985.

Sharma, Chandradhar. *A Critical Survey in Indian Philosophy*. Delhi: Motilal Banarsidass, 1973.

Sharma, Krishna. *Bhakti and the Bhakti Movement: A New Perspective*. Delhi: Munshiram Manoharlal Publishers, 1987.

Sharma, Rajendra Nath, *Ancient India According to Manu*. Delhi: Nag Publishers, 1980.

Sharma, Ram Sharan. *Śūdras in Ancient India*. Delhi: Motilal Banrasidass, 1958.

Sharma, Surendra. *Sociology in India: A Perspective From Sociology of Knowledge*. Jaipur: Rawat Publications, 1985.

Sharma, T. R. *Studies in the Sectarian Upanisads*. Delhi: Indological Book House, 1972.

Shastri, Hari Prasad, trans. *The Ramayana of Valniki*. Vol. III. London: Shantisadan, 1962.

———. *Vālmīki Rāmāyaṇa*. 3 Vols. London: Shanti Sadan, 1959.

Sherring, Reverend. M. A. *Hindu Tribes and Castes*. 3 Vols. 1878–1881. Reprint, Delhi: Cosmo Publications, 1974.

Shils, Edward. *Center and Periphery*. Chicago: University of Chicago Press, 1972.

———. *The Intellectual Between Tradition and Modernity: The Indian Situation*. Supplement I of *Comparative Studies in Society and History*. The Hague: Mouton and Co., 1961.

Shulka, H. L. *Chhattiśgaṛh Rediscovered: Vedantic Approaches to Folklore*. New Delhi: Aryan Books International, 1995.

———. *Social History of Chhattisgarh*. Delhi: Agam Kala Prakashan, 1985.

———. *Language, Ethnicity and History*. Delhi: B.R. Publishing Corp., 1985.

Singer, Milton, ed. *Krishna: Myths, Rites, and Attitudes*. Honolulu: East-West Center Press, 1966.

Singer, Milton and Bernard Cohn, eds. *Structure and Change in Indian Society*. New York: Wenner-Gren Foundation for Anthropological Research, 1968.

Singh, Sukhdeo and Linda Hess, trans. *Selections from the Bījak of Kabir.* Varansi: Bani Prakashan Kendra, 1977.

Smart, Ninian. "A Theory of Religious and Ideological Change: Illustrated From Modern South Asian and Other Religious Nationalisms." A lecture delivered at Arizona State University, Tempe, April 12, 1984.

Smith, Brian K. *Reflections on Resemblance, Ritual, and Religion*. New York: Oxford University Press, 1989.

Soothill, W. E. *The Lotus of the Wonderful Law*. Oxford: Clarendon Press, 1930.

Spear, Percival. *A History of India*. Vol.2. Middlesex: Penguin Books, Ltd., 1971.

Srinivas, M. N. *The Cohesive Role of Sansktirization and Other Essays*. Delhi: Oxford University Press, 1989.

———. *The Remembered Village*. Berkeley: University of California Press, 1976.

———. *Social Change in Modern India*. Berkeley: University of California Press, 1971.

Srinivas, M. N. and M. N. Panini. "The Development of Sociology and Social Anthropology in India." *Sociological Bulletin*. 22, No. 1 (1973): 179–215.

———. *Religion and Society Among the Coorgs of South India*. Berkeley: 1952.

Srivastava, S. K. "The Process of Desanskritization in Village India." In *Anthropology on the March*. Edited by Bala Ratnam, 263–67. Madras: The Book Center, 1963.

Staal, Frits. "Ritual, Mantras, and the Origin of Language." In *Amṛtadhārā, Professor R.N. Dandekar Relicitation Volume*. 403–425. Poona, 1984.

———. "Sanskritization and Sanskritization." *Journal of Asian Studies*. 22 (1963).

Stoller, Paul and Cheryl Olkes. *In Sorcery's Shadow*. Chicago: University of Chicago Press, 1987.

Subrahmanian, N. S., trans. *Encyclopedia of the Upanisads*. New Delhi: Sterling Publishers Pvt., Ltd, 1985.

Swahananda, Swami, trans. *Chāndogya Upaniṣad*. Madras: Sri Ramakrishna Math, 1956.

Tapasyananda, Swami, trans. *Adhyātma Rāmāyaṇa*. Mylapore: Sri Ramakrishna Math, 1985.

Tax, Sol. "Forward." In M. N. Srinivas. *The Remembered Village*. Berkeley: University of California Press, 1976.

Thapar, Romila. *Ancient Indian Social History: Some Interpretations*. Hyderabad: Orient Longman, 1978.

———. "Epic and History: Tradition, Dissent and Politics in India." *Past and Present* 125 (Nov. 1989): 3–26.

Thiel-Horstmann, Monika, ed. *Contemporary Ramayana Traditions: Oral, Written, Performed*. Wiesbaden: Otto Harassowitz, 1991.

Tripathi, Rebati Ballav. *Dalits: A Sub-Human Society*. New Delhi: Ashish Publishing House, 1994.

Tulsidas. *Kaultāvatī*. Translated by F. R. Allchin. New York: A. S. Barnes and Co., 1964.

Turabian, Kate L. *A Manual for Writers*. 3rd ed. Chicago: University of Chicago Press, 1967.

Turner, Victor. *The Ritual Process*. Ithaca: Cornell University Press, 1977.

Upadhyay, K. N. *Nām-bhakti: Goswāmī Tulsīdās*. Beas: Radhaswami Satsang, 1989.

van Buitenen, J. A. B. "Hindu Sacred Literature." *Encyclopedia Britannica III, Macropaedia*, 1970.

Vaudeville, Charlotte. *Kabīr*. Vol.I. Oxford: Oxford University Press, 1974.

———. "Rāmāyaṇa Studies I: The *Krauñca-vadha* Episode in the Vālmīki Rāmāyaṇa." *Journal of the American Oriental Society*. 83 (1963).

———. "*Sant Mat:* Santism as the Universal Path to Sanctity." In *The Sants: Studies in a Devotional Tradition of India*. Edited by Karine Shomer and W. H. McLeod. Delhi: Motilal Banarsidass, 1987.

Vidich, Arthur J. "Participant Observation and the Collection and Interpretation of Data." *Qualitative Methodology*. Edited by William J. Filstead. Chicago: Markham Publishing Co., 1970.

Vidyarthi, P. B. *Early Indian Religious Thought*. New Delhi: Oriental Publishers and Distributors, 1976.

Waghorne, Joanne P., and Norman Cutler, eds. *Gods of Flesh, Gods of Stone: The Embodiment of Divinity in India*. Chambersburg, PA: Anima Publications, 1984.

Wax, Rosalie. *Doing Fieldwork: Warnings and Advice*. Chicago: University of Chicago Press, 1971.

Wayman, Alex. *Manjuśrī-nāma-samgiti*. Translated by Alex Wayman. Boston: Shambala, 1985.

———. *The Buddhist Tantras: Light on Indo-Tibetan Esotericism*. New York: Samuel Weiser, 1973.

———. "The Significance of Mantra-s, From the Veda Down to Buddhist Tantric Practice." *Adyar Library Bulletin*. 39 (1975).

Weber, Albrecht. "On the Ramayana." In *Indian Antiquary*. 1872:120–24; 172–82; 239–53.

Westcott, G .H. *Kabir and the Kabir Panth*. 1907. Reprint, Delhi: Munshiram Manoharlal Publishers, rep. 1986.

Whaling, Frank. *The Rise on the Religious Significance of Rāma*. Delhi: Motilal Banarsidass, 1980.

Whyte, W. F. *Street Corner Society*. Chicago: University of Chicago Press, 1981.

Wilson, H. H., trans. *Viṣnu Purāṇa*. 1840. Reprint, Calcutta: Punthi Pustak, 1972.

Winternitz, Maurice. *A History of Indian Literature*. Vol. I. Translated by S. Ketkar. 1927. Reprint, New Delhi: Oriental Books Reprint Corp., 1972.

———. *A History of Indian Literature*. Vol. II, Pt.1. Translated by Subhadra Jha. Delhi: Motilal Banarsidass, 1963.

Woodroffe, Sir John. *Principles of Tantra*. Pt. II. Madras: Ganesh and Co., 1978.

Wolpert, Stanley. *A New History of India*. New York: Oxford University Press, 1979.

Zelliot, Eleanor. *From Untouchable to Dalit*. New Delhi: Manohar, 1992.

Index